cooking with a
BRAZILIAN TWIST

by Cynthia Presser

Dear Damon and Nancy,

I hope you enjoy the recipes in this book, especially the Brazilian ones!!

Com amor,
Cynthia

Cooking with a BRAZILIAN TWIST

by Cynthia Presser

Experience the flavorful, spicy culture of Brazil

& twists on other recipes from around the world

Text © 2013 by Cynthia Presser
Finished food photography © 2013 by Cynthia Presser
Food Styling by Cynthia Presser

Location photography on the cover and pages 2, 8, 11, 14-15, 18, 50, 76, 86, 98, 108, 148-149 © 2013 by Carol Sábio
Location photography on pages 4,140, 236 and food photography on pages 10, 28 © 2013 by Kelly Gayer
Location photography on pages 6, 44-45, 138-139 © 2013 by Steve Presser

Book design © 2013 by Steve Presser
Project editing by Helen Burkart Presser

All rights reserved. No part of this book may be reproduced in any form without written permission from the publisher.

Printed in the USA by Walsworth Publishing Company

ISBN-13: 978-1-62847-180-9

First Edition

To my loving family
in the United States and Brazil

Contents

Introduction 9
Brazilian Cuisine 13

Brazilian Recipes

Appetizers & Starters (Aperitivos e Entradas) 16
Seafood (Frutos-do-Mar) 46
Meat (Carnes) 74
Chicken (Aves) 84
Sides (Acompanhamentos) 96
Desserts (Sobremesas) 106
Drinks (Bebidas) 138

World Inspired Recipes

Fusion 152
Argentina 176
Asia 178
France 182
Italy 188
Mexico 210
Middle East 214
Paraguay 218
Spain 220
United States 222
Uruguay 234

Acknowledgements 237
Recipe Index 239

Introduction

Olá Amigos!

I would like to introduce myself. I am Cynthia Presser, a wife, mother, professional cook and big-time foodie. I was born with the name Ana Cynthia Ferreira in the Southern part of beautiful Brazil. I moved to the United States in March of 2000 when I was 24 years old. My English wasn't great; it was my first time leaving the comfort of my parent's home; I had only $1,200 in my pocket, and very little certainty of how my new venture would end. Many things have changed since I moved to the US. Fortunately, all those changes are for the better.

There are some things, though, that will never change. For example, I believe the true essence of a person never changes. Images, sounds, scents, faces, and flavors that we carry in our memory shape our souls and define who we are.

I grew up in a house where food was made from scratch every single day. The image of my mother cooking, the sound that the ingredients made when they touched hot oil, the scents that came out of the pan, the excitement on my father's face coming home for a nice meal and the flavors we would taste in that food, are events so fresh in my memory! I can close my eyes and recall all these sensational feelings, as though they were happening today.

I have to confess that cooking was not my first passion in life, but eating was! Food was great at my home, at my friends' homes, at the restaurants where we dined, and at the street fair down the block. Food was delicious! Ingredients were fresh and abundant! Eating was not done while standing up, or in a hurry, or while driving. Gathering around a table and eating was an everyday event where families would touch base and connect. Food was good and food was fun! My next challenge was to learn how to make it.

I loved to look at pictures of food. My mother, my aunt, and the mothers of my friends had some really cool cookbooks with some amazing pictures. My mouth would water as I flipped through the pages of those books. Many times I would catch myself drooling over images. Some pictures were so enticing that they would force me to read the actual recipe. That's when I realized that cooking was far from open-heart surgery. I could follow the directions in a recipe and make food that looked almost like those pictures! The first time I decided to give cooking a shot, I was alone. My only companion was one of my mother's cookbooks. I was around 15 or 16 years old, and while it definitely wasn't the meal of a lifetime, my first attempt at cooking was not bad!

I decided I loved cooking and was determined to teach myself. Looking back, it's strange that my mother, who cooks amazing meals from scratch, did not teach me the art of cooking. I never even considered going to culinary school after finishing high school. Though the opportunities are rare these days, my mother and I have a lot of fun cooking together.

The more people tried my food, the stronger my passion for cooking grew. The compliments I received were so fulfilling! I was only 19 when I was asked by family and friends to make birthday, engagement, and graduation dinners. I had so much fun planning the courses, shopping for the ingredients, and preparing the feast!

I graduated from an advertising college at 22, and worked for a couple of years in marketing and advertising. I soon discovered that work wasn't as fulfilling as cooking. Needing a change, I decided to travel abroad to San Diego. I packed my carefully crafted, homemade recipe book in the event I needed to make money cooking! As it turned out, I did not end up cooking professionally the first few years, but my friends and roommates in San Diego loved my food so much that they nicknamed my recipe book *The Bible*.

Originally planning 6 months, I ended up staying in the US and eventually married Steve Presser in 2009. As luck would have it, he is the perfect guinea pig and will try anything I create in the kitchen. I taught him the joy of cooking, and we look forward to dinner every night at our house. At the moment we have a beautiful son, Sebastian, and another boy on the way.

After Sebastian was born, I had the opportunity to spend more time at home. It was finally the perfect time to follow my culinary dreams. In 2011, I started a cooking blog, www.cynthiapresser.com, called Cooking with a Twist. The response was overwhelming! In less than two years I was getting more than 10,000 visitors from around the world each month! Being able to share my recipes, my passion for cooking and eating, my culinary point-of-view, and my cultural background with people has been a dream. I am grateful and blessed.

My path to cooking has been long and enriching. Over the years I have learned from my mistakes, and celebrated the many occasions I cooked something great.

Moving to the United States inspired me to incorporate new ingredients and flavors in my recipes. It also made me appreciate my cooking roots, as my childhood food is not widely available in the US. I have had the opportunity to travel a lot the last 12 years, learn about many different cultures through food, and expand my culinary knowledge through travel.

This book is a refined collection of my culinary journey. Cooking means the world to me, and sharing my recipes and twists in this book is a dream come true. I humbly open the doors of my kitchen to you. Turn on some blues, flamenco, bossa nova, or samba, and pour yourself a glass of wine. Relax and be my guest. I hope you enjoy the flavors as much as I do.

Bom apetite!

Cynthia

Brazilian Cuisine

Countless times I have been asked the same question: "What is Brazilian cuisine?" There is no easy answer because Brazil is a very large country with different climates, and influenced by many different backgrounds. Traditional Brazilian cuisine mixes techniques and ingredients from Indigenous, Portuguese, and African cuisines. Modern Brazilian cuisine is influenced by those who arrived in Brazil during the beginning of the twentieth century including people of European (mainly Italian), Middle-Eastern and Japanese decent.

Some of the ingredients that are common to all parts of Brazil are tropical fruits such as mango, pineapple, coconut, guava, passion fruit, papaya, cashew fruit, oranges, and bananas. Rice, beans, cassava or yuca, corn, hearts-of-palm, and squash fruits including pumpkin, butternut, acorn, and sugar pumpkin are also very popular. Herbs are widely used, and the combination called *cheiro-verde* (which translates to green smell) is the go-to herb pairing in Brazilian cuisine, consisting of either scallions and cilantro, or scallions and flat-leaf parsley. The preservation of meat and seafood, especially red meat, cod and shrimp, through a drying process is a very common method of conserving protein and adding flavor.

Red meat, pork, chicken and lamb are very common in the South, Southwest, Midwest and parts of the North and Northwest. The Brazilian coast is almost 5,000 miles long, making seafood readily available for consumption. River fish from the Amazon Basin, Araguaia-Tocantins Basin and Paraguay River Basin is available especially to the North and Midwest regions.

One of the most common mistakes people make about Brazilian food is assuming it is always spicy. While that's true toward the North and Northeast regions, food from the Midwest and South is mild, or just slightly spicy. Hot sauces are often served tableside so each person can season to taste.

Brazilian cuisine reflects the mood of its people: vibrant and exotic, yet simple and approachable. Explore the delicious recipes in this book and enjoy a little taste of Brazil!

Brazilian Recipes

Appetizers & Starters
(Aperitivos e Entradas)

Appetizers & Starters
(Aperitivos e Entradas)

Brazilian Cheese Bread (Pão-de-Queijo) 21

Traditional Brazilian Cheese Bread from Minas
(Pão-de-Queijo Mineiro) 23

Chicken and Asparagus Mini-Pies
(Empadinhas de Frango com Aspargo) 24

Cod Croquettes (Bolinho de Bacalhau Fresco) 27

Creamy Hearts-of-Palm Soup (Creme de Palmito) 29

Hearts-of-Palm, Mushrooms, and Fresh Mozzarella Salad
(Salada Verde com Palmito, Cogumelos e Queijo Branco) 31

Pastel 33

Pastel with Meat and Cheese Filling
(Pastelzinho de Carne com Queijo) 35

Brazilian Style Chicken Salad (Salpicão) 37

Shrimp and Yuca Bowl (Escondidinho de Camarão) 39

White Chili (Creme de Feijão Branco) 42

Brazilian Cheese Bread
(Pão-de-Queijo)

Cheese bread is a Brazilian staple! Cheesy and fluffy, this typical snack is a crowd pleaser: for children and adults alike! Many different versions are available, including the Traditional Brazilian Cheese Bread recipe (page 23). This one is easiest, since the batter is mixed in the blender. Serve warm, right off the oven. I dare you to have only one!

Yields 30 Units

3 cups tapioca starch
3 eggs
1 cup milk
¾ cup vegetable oil
1 teaspoon salt
1 cup mozzarella cheese, shredded
¼ cup Parmesan cheese, shredded

Grated Parmesan cheese, for sprinkling

Preheat oven to 375 degrees F. Add tapioca starch, eggs, milk, vegetable oil and salt to a blender. Blend 40 seconds, or until mixture is smooth. Transfer to a large mixing bowl and gently fold in shredded mozzarella and shredded Parmesan. Spray a large mini muffin pan (at least 30 cups) with vegetable oil. Divide cheese bread mixture into cups and sprinkle grated Parmesan on top. Bake 17 to 20 minutes, or until top turns golden brown. If using a convection oven, preheat to 350 degrees F and bake 13 to 15 minutes, or until top turns golden brown. Remove from oven and serve immediately.

Cook's Notes

Standard size for mini muffin pan is 24-cups. Divide mixture into two batches, if you have only one pan available. For larger cheese bread use a pan for regular muffins and bake for an extra 3 to 5 minutes.

Tapioca starch can be found in Latin markets or international grocery stores.

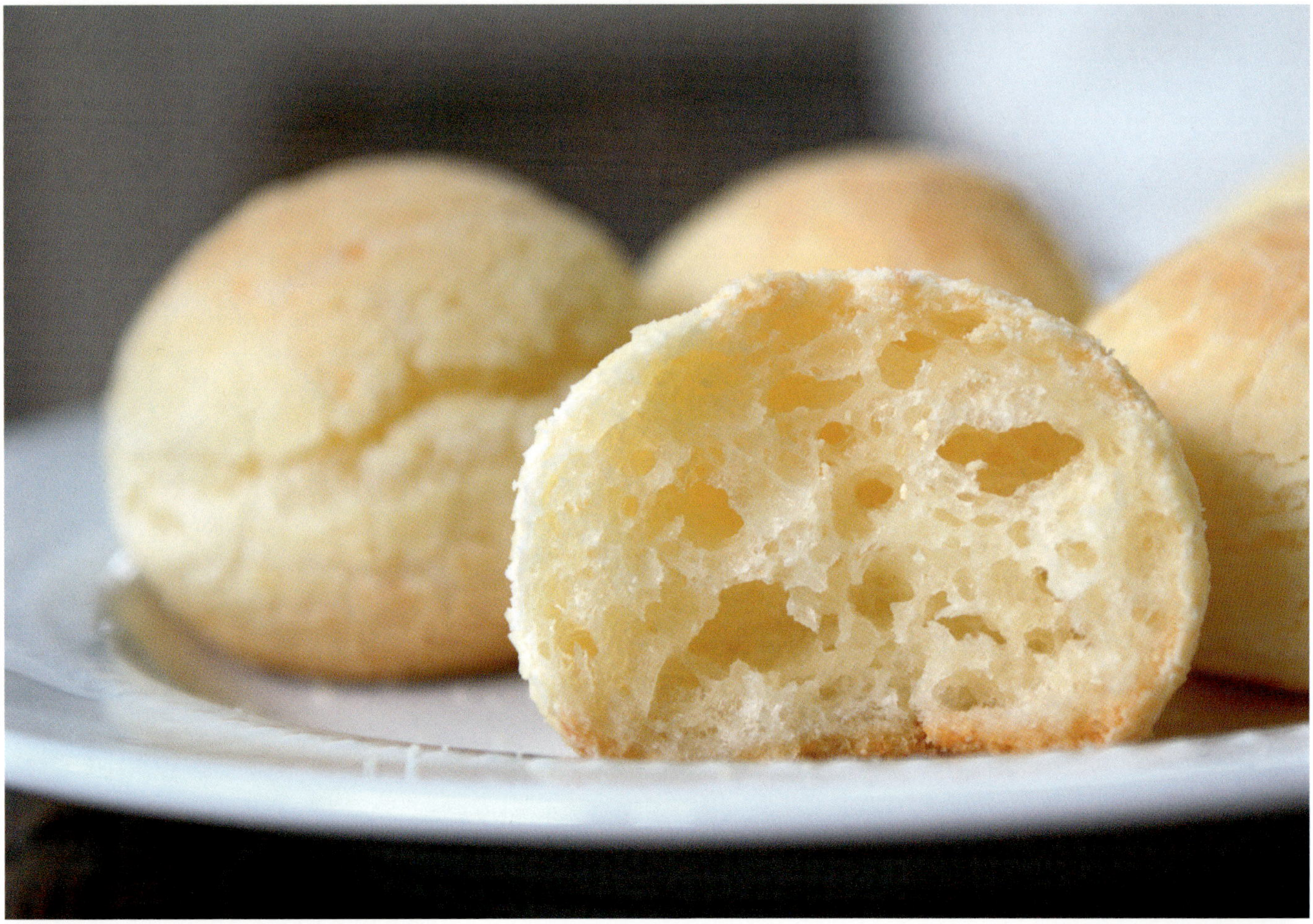
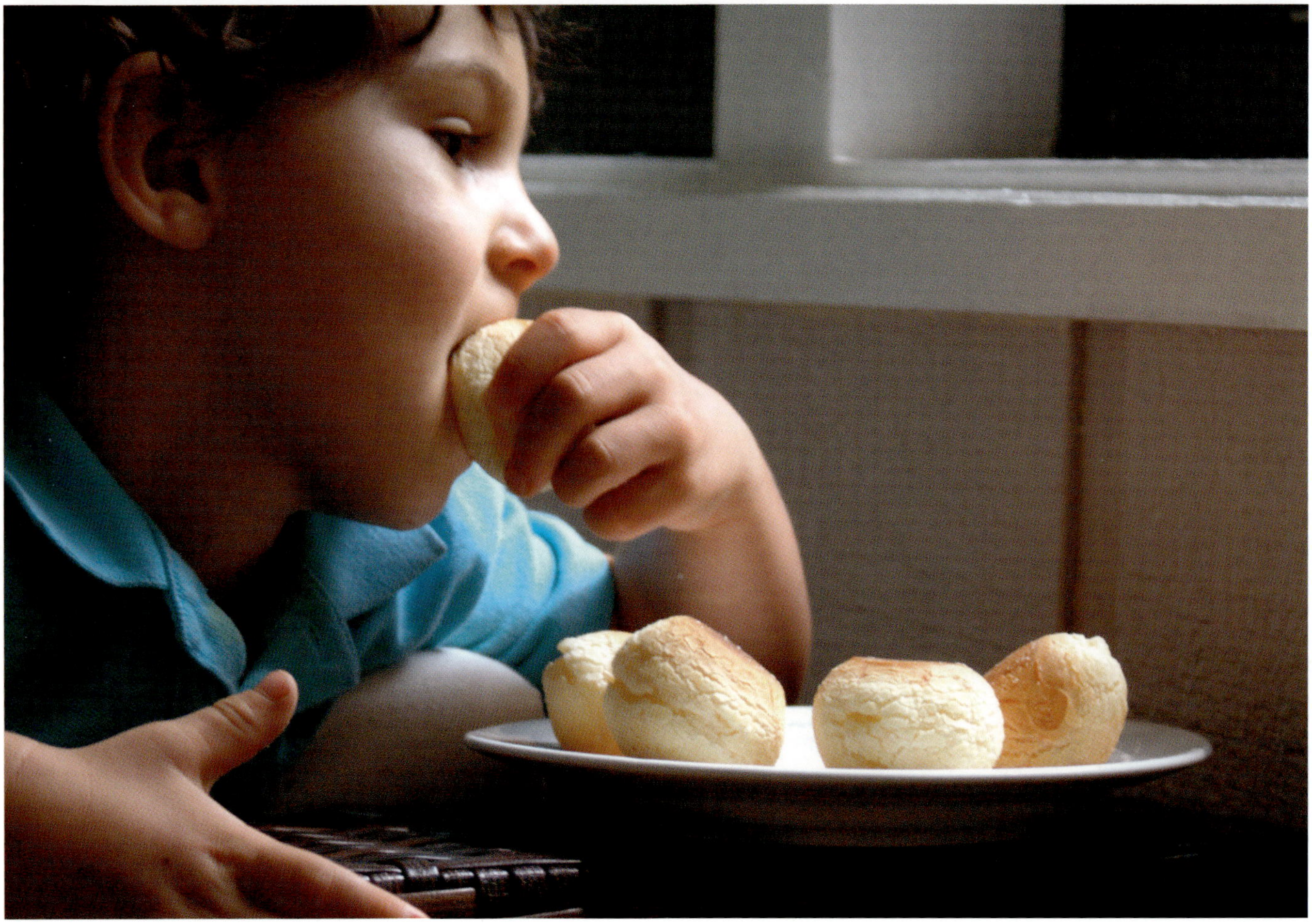

Traditional Brazilian Cheese Bread from Minas
(Pão-de-Queijo Mineiro)

This is the most traditional version of cheese bread, which originated in the state of Minas Gerais. The original recipe calls for Minas cheese. However, since that kind of cheese is difficult to find in the United States, I usually replace it with some variety of Farmer's cheese. The Mexicans Queso Fresco and Cotija work really well in this recipe. Fluffy and gooey, this delicious snack is always a crowd pleaser!

Yields 40 units

5 cups tapioca starch
½ cup vegetable oil
1½ cups milk
1 teaspoon salt
3 large eggs
3 cups Farmer's cheese (Minas, Queso Fresco, or Cotija), shredded

Preheat oven to 350 degrees F. Place tapioca starch in a large mixing bowl and set aside.

In a medium sauce pan, heat vegetable oil, milk and salt over moderate heat until it just starts boiling. Remove from heat and add to bowl, mixing with a wooden spatula. Add eggs, one at a time, still mixing with wooden spatula. Add cheese and knead dough for a few minutes, until smooth. Shape dough into small balls, approximately the size of ping-pong balls. Place cheese balls on a non-greased cookie sheet, leaving about ¾-inch space in between them. Bake until golden on top, about 25 to 30 minutes. Remove from oven and serve immediately.

If using a convection oven, pre-heat to 275 degrees F. Bake until golden on top, 18 to 23 minutes.

Cook's Notes

If using a stand mixer, follow directions above, setting the mixer at high speed.

Tapioca starch can be found at most Latin or international grocery stores.

Chicken and Asparagus Mini-Pies
(Empadinhas de Frango com Aspargo)

These mini-pies are great for large parties because they can be made in advance and reheated when your guests arrive. Creamy in the center, with a crumbly dough, these chicken and asparagus mini-pies are irresistible!

Serves about 20

Dough Ingredients:
3 sticks of butter at room temperature
3 ½ cups all-purpose flour, plus more for top
2 egg yolks
1 teaspoon baking powder
½ teaspoon salt

Filling Ingredients:
1 skinless chicken breast, bones attached
1 garlic clove, peeled
1 onion, peeled and quartered
1 bay leaf
3 cups water
2 tablespoons olive oil
1 cup asparagus, chopped into ½-inch rings, ends trimmed and discarded
2 tablespoons rosemary, finely chopped
1 cup leeks, finely chopped
Salt and freshly ground black pepper
3 tablespoons corn starch
1 cup Cynthia's Special White Sauce (page 233)
½ cup scallions, finely chopped

Dough Directions

Place butter, all-purpose flour, egg yolks, baking powder, and salt in a bowl and mix well. Do not knead the dough; it is not supposed to be really smooth. Cover and let rest for 30 minutes.

Spray standard-size muffin pan cups with butter. Press dough into cups: start pressing on bottom and slowly move up to the sides until really thin, about 1/8-inch thick. Remove excess and save. Prick tiny holes over surface with a fork.

Pre-heat oven to 375 degrees F. Add 1 to 1 ½ cups of all-purpose flour to the remaining dough and crumble it.

Spoon chicken and asparagus filling into cups, leaving 1/4-inch space on top. Cover with dough crumbles and bake 20 minutes, until golden brown. Remove from oven and let cool 10 minutes before serving. Serve warm.

For convection oven, bake at 350 degrees F 15 minutes, or until golden brown.

Filling Directions

In a large sauce pan, place chicken breast, garlic, onion, bay leaf, and water. Bring to a boil and reduce heat to medium-low. Cook 40 minutes, until chicken is fully cooked. Remove from heat and strain. Save broth and chicken. Set aside to cool. When chicken is cool to touch, shred into small pieces. Do not use food processor. Discard the bones.

In a large skillet, heat olive oil over medium-high heat until shimmering. Add asparagus, rosemary, leeks and shredded chicken. Season with salt and pepper. Cook 2 minutes, stirring occasionally, until vegetables are nearly tender, but still crispy. Dissolve corn starch into ½ cup broth. Turn heat to medium-low and slowly add corn starch slurry to skillet, whisking constantly. Add remaining broth, stirring constantly, until mixture thickens. Stir in Cynthia's Special White Sauce and cook for an additional minute, until blended. Remove from heat and fold in scallions.

Cook's Notes

This savory dough can also be pressed into a 10-inch mold pan and sliced.

Béchamel or store-bought white sauce can serve as a substitutes for Cynthia's Special Sauce (page 233).

Cod Croquettes
(Bolinho de Bacalhau Fresco)

Cod croquette is one of the most popular bar foods in Brazil, but this tasty fritter had its origins on the other side of the Atlantic, in Portugal. Traditionally made with salted cod, I use fresh cod in my recipe since I have a hard time finding salted cod where I live. The result is a more achievable recipe, less time consuming and equally delicious! Enjoy with a cold beer and hot sauce on the side, just like the Brazilians do.

Yields 25 units

1 pound fresh cod
2 tablespoons extra virgin olive oil
Salt and freshly ground black pepper
3 large potatoes, peeled, cooked and smashed
½ onion, finely chopped
½ cup Port wine
1 ½ cup Panko breadcrumbs
1 cup cilantro, finely chopped
1 teaspoon nutmeg, freshly ground
1 egg, lightly beaten
Vegetable oil for frying

Preheat oven to 400 degrees F. Place cod in an ovenproof dish and coat both sides with olive oil. Season generously with salt and pepper. Bake 10 to 13 minutes, or until fish flakes easily with a fork. Remove from oven and let cool. Using your hands, not food processor, shred fish into really small pieces.

Place smashed potatoes in large mixing bowl. Add fish, onion, wine, breadcrumbs, cilantro and nutmeg. Mix well. Add salt and pepper to taste. Add egg and mix. Shape croquettes into ping-pong size balls. You can form balls with an ice cream scoop.

Heat up the vegetable oil until shimmering. Immerse the croquettes into the oil and fry until golden brown. Serve hot or warm.

Cook's Notes

The dough is supposed to be fairly soft. If you are having a hard time shaping the croquettes, add more breadcrumbs until they hold their shape, probably ½ cup.

Creamy Hearts-of-Palm Soup
(Creme de Palmito)

Hearts-of-palm has a very delicate and distinctive flavor similar to the flavor of artichoke. Cream and Parmesan cheese add a velvety and nutty finish to this traditional Brazilian creamy soup.

Yields 6 cups, or 3 to 4 bowls

1 can (14 ounces) hearts-of-palm
4 tablespoons butter, divided
2 tablespoons olive oil
1 onion, finely chopped
2 garlic cloves, minced
2 tablespoons all-purpose flour
2 cups low-sodium chicken broth
¾ cup heavy cream
¼ teaspoon freshly grated nutmeg
Salt and freshly ground black pepper
½ cup Parmesan cheese, shredded
¼ cup scallions, finely chopped

Transfer hearts-of-palm to a working surface, and save the water from the can. Roughly cut hearts-of-palm into rings. Set aside.

In a large sauce pan, heat 2 tablespoons butter and olive oil over medium heat. Add onion and cook 4 minutes, stirring occasionally, until soft. Add garlic and cook an additional minute until fragrant. Sprinkle in flour and cook 2 minutes, stirring constantly. Slowly add chicken broth and hearts-of-palm water, whisking constantly, until thickened. Reduce heat to medium-low. Stir in hearts-of-palm, heavy cream and nutmeg. Season lightly with salt and pepper. Simmer 10 minutes, stirring occasionally.

Remove from heat and transfer to a food processor or blender. Process until smooth, 40 seconds. Return soup to pan. Stir in Parmesan cheese and remaining butter. Bring to a low simmer. Remove from heat and fold in scallions. Serve immediately. .

Hearts-of-Palm, Mushrooms, and Fresh Mozzarella Salad
(Salada Verde com Palmito, Cogumelos e Queijo Branco)

I make this salad often during summertime because it is perfect with grilled steak, and my husband loves to fire up the grill when it is warm outside! I like to use the traditional Minas cheese in this recipe, but since it is hard to find in the United States, fresh mozzarella serves as a great substitute.

Serves 4

½ cup extra-virgin olive oil
6 ounces white mushrooms, wiped and finely sliced
1 large garlic clove, minced
1 tablespoon Dijon mustard
1 tablespoon honey
1 tablespoon aged balsamic vinegar
12 ounces mixed greens
¼ cup cilantro, finely chopped
4 large slices fresh mozzarella
6 ounces canned hearts-of-palms, drained and sliced
Salt and freshly ground black pepper

Heat oil in a medium skillet over medium-high heat until smoking. Sauté mushrooms and garlic 2 minutes, or until tender. Remove mushrooms from skillet and set aside.

Strain remaining oil from skillet into a medium mixing bowl. Let cool. Add mustard, honey and balsamic vinegar to the bowl, stirring vigorously. Set aside.

Assemble mixed greens on a large platter and top with cilantro. Place fresh mozzarella, hearts-of-palm and mushrooms over the greens. Drizzle with dressing and season with salt and pepper. Serve it immediately.

Cook's Notes

A mixture of baby lettuce, spinach and arugula work well as a selection of greens for this recipe.

This salad may also be assembled on individual plates.

Pastel

Pastel is one of the most beloved bar foods in Brazil. This savory pastry is usually served inside small baskets and ordered by the dozen or half dozen at bars where friends gather around the table to munch on *pastelzinhos* (small pastels) while chatting, drinking a cold beer and having a good time. The variety of fillings is endless, but two of the most popular are hearts-of-palm and ground beef with cheese. Crunchy on the outside with a creamy filling, this typical Brazilian appetizer can also become a dessert if filled with dulce de leche, or guava paste and cheese. Get creative and experiment!

Yields about 15 pastels (4-inches each)

Dough

2 cups flour, plus additional for working surface
1 pinch sugar
1 teaspoon salt
2 tablespoons vegetable oil, plus more for deep-frying
2 tablespoons vodka, tequila, or cachaça
¾ cup warm water

In a large bowl, combine flour, sugar, salt, vegetable oil and liquor. Add water slowly, ¼ cup at a time, while mixing with hands.

Work the dough until it becomes a smooth ball without sticking to your hands. On a clean working surface, knead dough a few minutes, until smooth. Return to bowl. Cover with a damp cloth and let sit 30 minutes.

Sprinkle working surface with flour and spread dough as wide as possible. Sprinkle a little more flour and roll out as wide as possible, using a rolling pin, until really thin.

With the help of a cutter, create 4-inch circles. Place 1 to 1 ½ tablespoons filling in center and fold over tightly with your finger, creating a semicircle. Sprinkle a little bit of flour over the border of each pastel and press all around with a fork, making sure the filling is well sealed inside. Repeat process until all dough circles are filled. Place each pastel on a large plate sprinkled with flour.

Shape leftover dough into a ball again and knead until smooth. Roll out with a roller pin and repeat process until dough is gone. Recipe yields 12 to 18 pastels, depending on size.

Deep-fry two or three pastries at a time in hot vegetable oil (375 degrees F) turning once; or use an electric fryer. When the surface turns golden brown, they are ready. Carefully remove each pastel with a skimmer and arrange on a platter covered with paper towels. Serve immediately.

Hearts-of-Palm and Tomatoes Filling

2 tablespoons olive oil
1 small onion, finely chopped
4 garlic cloves, minced
2 medium tomatoes, peeled, seeded and chopped
Salt and freshly ground black pepper
2 cans (14 ounces each) hearts-of-palm, drained and coarsely chopped
2 tablespoons scallions, finely chopped
2 tablespoons parsley, finely chopped
1 cup mascarpone cheese

In a medium skillet, heat olive oil until shimmering. Add onions and cook over medium high heat for 3 minutes, stirring occasionally until soft. Add garlic and cook 1 minute, until fragrant. Add tomatoes and cook 2 minutes, until soft. Season with salt and pepper. Remove from heat and fold in the hearts-of-palm, scallions, and parsley.

Place one tablespoon of filling on the center of the dough and top with ½ tablespoon of mascarpone. Close tightly, following directions listed under dough.

Cook's Notes

Traditionally, this recipe calls for *requeijão*, which is the Brazilian cream cheese. Less acidic, milder and creamier than American cream cheese, *requeijão* can be hard to find in the United States. Italian mascarpone serves as a good substitute.

Pastel with Meat and Cheese Filling
(Pastelzinho de Carne com Queijo)

Yields 16 pastels

1 ½ tablespoons olive oil
1 medium onion, finely diced
2 garlic cloves, minced
12 ounces lean ground beef
1 large tomato, seeded and chopped
½ tablespoon sugar
½ tablespoon chili paste
Salt and freshly ground black pepper
3 tablespoons scallions, finely chopped
16 rounds of empanada dough, store-bought
4 ounces Gouda or sharp cheddar, cubed
Vegetable oil, for frying

Heat oil in a medium skillet over medium-high heat. Add onions and cook 3 minutes until soft, stirring occasionally. Add garlic and cook 40 seconds, until fragrant. Add ground beef and cook until browned, stirring occasionally. Add tomatoes, sugar and chili paste. Cook 5 minutes, stirring occasionally, until tomatoes are soft and incorporated into the sauce. Season with salt and pepper. Remove from heat, fold in scallions. Set aside and let cool.

Sprinkle a working surface with flour. Place one empanada dough round on surface and top with 1 tablespoon of ground beef. Place 1 cheese cube over ground beef and carefully fold the dough over, while securing the filling inside with hands. Press fingers around dough, then press a fork around the border of pastel to secure. Trim excess dough with a pastry cutter.

Deep fry the pastries in hot vegetable oil. When the outside is golden brown, remove from oil and transfer to a large plate lined with paper towel. Let stand 3 minutes before serving.

Cook's Notes

If you like spicy, add extra chili paste to filling. In this recipe, ½ tablespoon gives a mild-medium level of heat.

In Brazil, the most popular cheese variety for this recipe is Prato, which is hard to find in the US. Gouda and Cheddar serve as substitutes. I even like it better with Gouda!

Easy to work with, store-bought empanada dough is a good substitute for homemade pastel dough. Much quicker and less messy, empanada dough can be found in the frozen aisle of large grocery stores and at Latin markets. Widely available, frozen store-bought spring roll dough can also be used. I personally recommend the use of home-made dough because it is thinner, more crumbly, giving the pastel a more traditional taste.

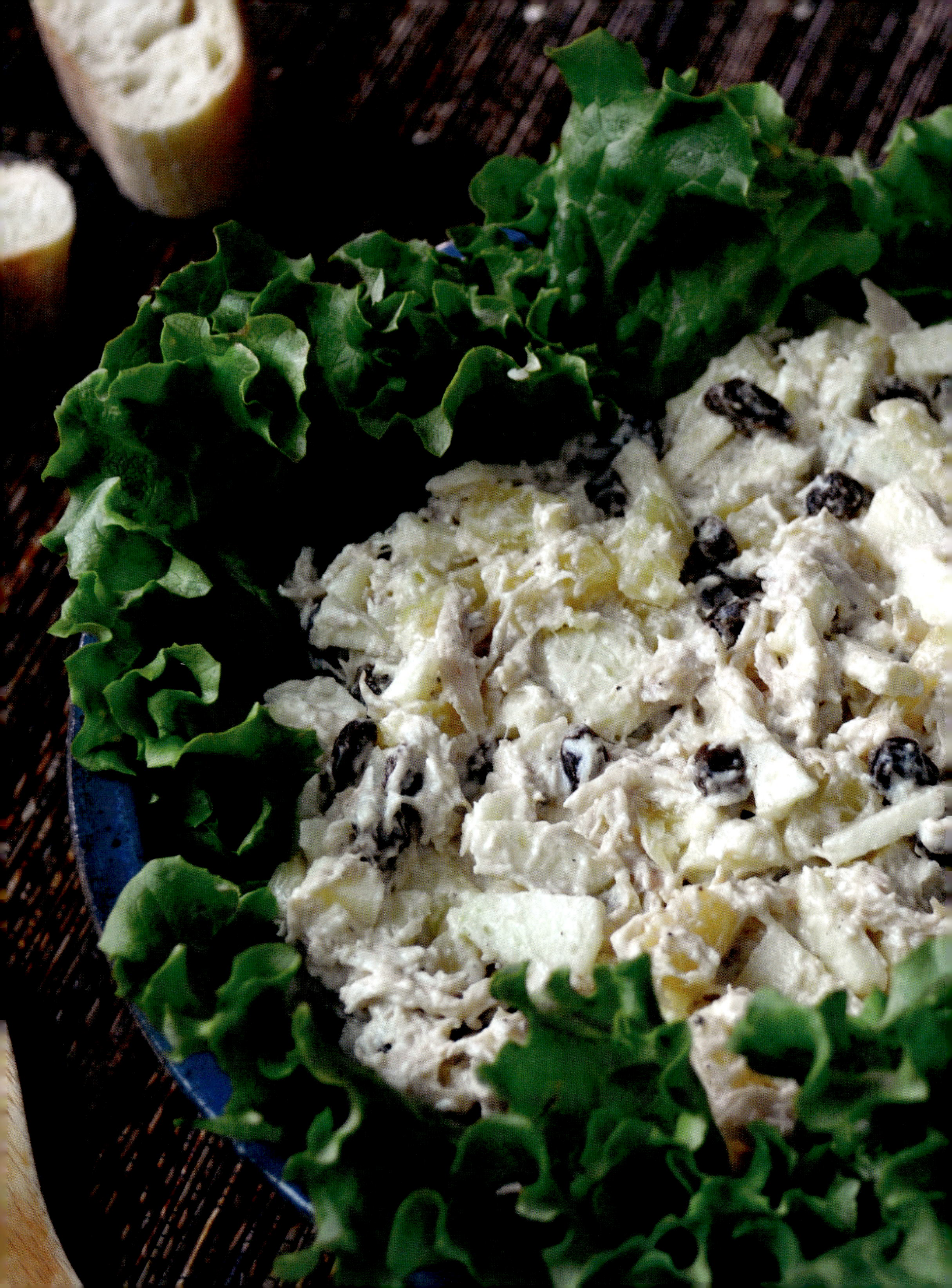

Brazilian Style Chicken Salad
(Salpicão)

Salpicão is what we call a Brazilian style chicken salad, and this recipe is my favorite! Since it is made with rotisserie chicken, it is extra moist and tasty. One of the secrets to achieving a good blend of flavors and great texture is to manually shred the chicken into really tiny pieces. This secret was passed on to me by two ladies who have been making this recipe for over 25 years: my mom, and one of her best friends, Leila. Crunchy, slightly sweet and creamy, this salad is often found on the large salad bars in Brazilian steak houses. Served on top of crusty bread or inside lettuce rolls, it serves as a great appetizer, or a light lunch.

Serves 6

1 medium rotisserie chicken, skin removed, finely shredded
1 cup raisins
1 cup canned pineapple, finely chopped
1 green apple, skin removed, finely diced
1 red apple, skin removed, finely diced
Juice of 1 large lime
1 can Media Crema (table cream)
½ cup light mayonnaise
Salt and freshly ground black pepper
Lettuce, for garnishing and serving

In a large bowl, mix chicken, raisins and pineapple. Set aside.

In a separate bowl, gently stir green apple, red apple and lime juice.

In a small bowl, whisk together table cream and light mayonnaise until incorporated. Set aside.

Gently fold apples and mayonnaise dressing into bowl of chicken. Season with salt and pepper and gently mix until combined.

Arrange a few lettuce leaves on the bottom of a large serving plate and cover with the chicken salad (Salpicão). Serve immediately with more lettuce leaves on the side (for chicken salad cups) and hard crust bread.

Cook's Notes

Media Crema (table cream) can be found in the Latin section or next to the condensed milk aisle of large grocery stores.

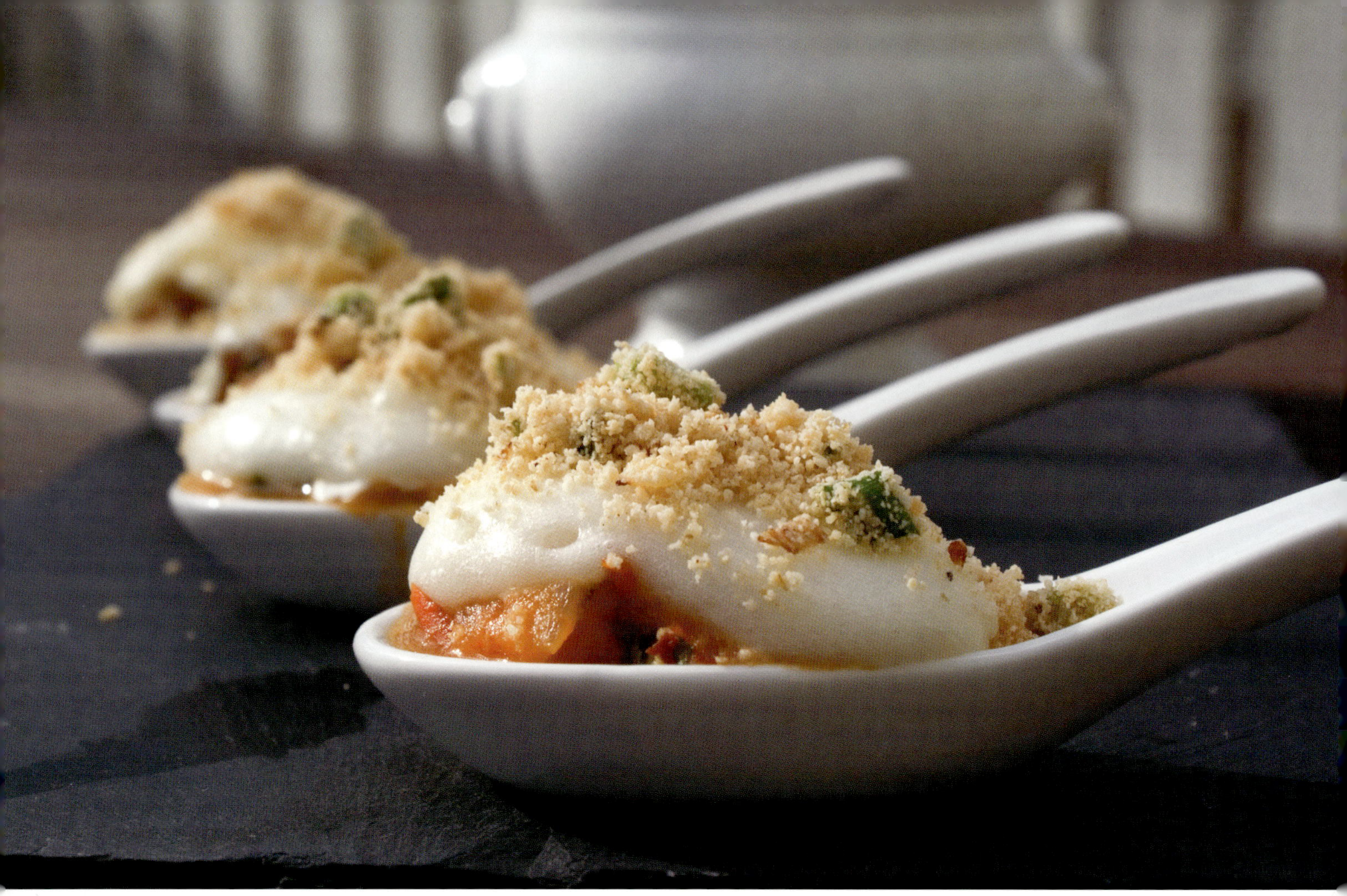

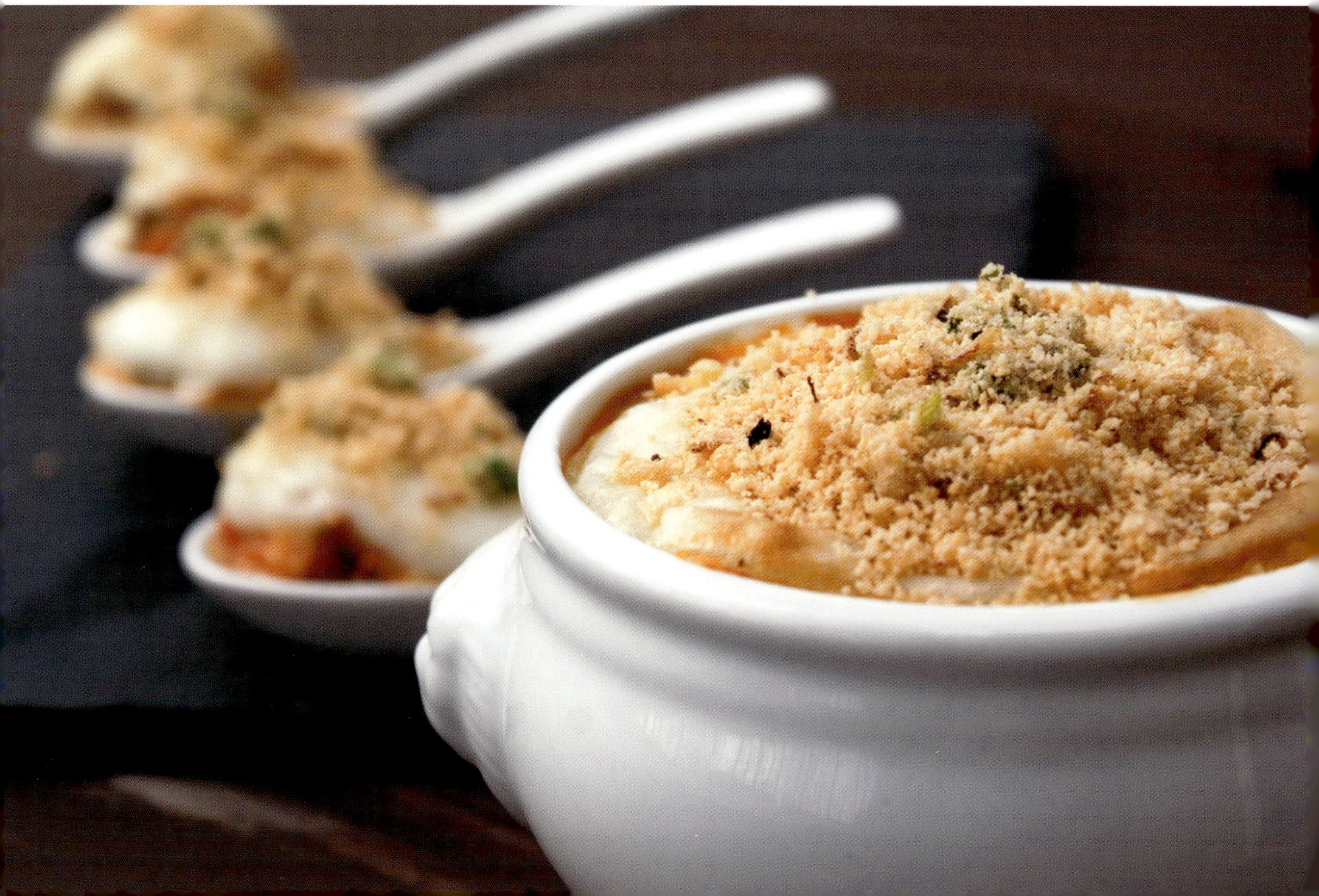

Shrimp and Yuca Bowl
(Escondidinho de Camarão)

The literal translation to the name of this dish is "Little Hidden Shrimp," because the shrimp is hiding underneath layers of creamy tomato sauce and yuca purée. You really need to dig into the creaminess to find the "real treasure." Very popular in Brazil, the shrimp and yuca bowl usually has *requeijão* (a Brazilian cream cheese that is milder and less aciditic than the American version). Since *requeijão* can be hard to find in the US, I recommend using mascarpone cheese as a substitute. The result is just as delicious!

Serves 4

1 ½ pounds yuca (cassava) peeled
½ cup milk
¼ cup butter, softened
Salt and freshly ground black pepper
2 tablespoons olive oil
½ medium onion, finely chopped
2 garlic cloves, minced
1 tablespoon fresh rosemary, finely chopped

12 ounces jumbo shrimp, cleaned and deveined, cut crosswise into 4 parts
2 tablespoons brandy or cognac
2 large tomatoes, chopped
½ tablespoon chili paste
4 tablespoons mascarpone cheese
2 tablespoons fresh scallions, finely chopped
2 tablespoons fresh flat-leaf parsley, finely chopped
4 tablespoons Farofa (page 105)

Place yuca in a large sauce pan, cutting the longest roots crosswise, to fit into pan. Cover with water and bring to a boil. Cover with lid and cook 40 to 60 minutes on medium heat until roots are tender. Remove from heat, strain, and let cool 10 minutes. Transfer to a large bowl. Cut in half lengthwise and remove any stems from center. Add milk and butter. Using a potato masher, mash until ingredients are blended and smooth. You can also use a food processor. Season with salt and set aside.

Preheat oven to 375 degrees F.

In a medium skillet, heat olive oil over medium-high heat until shimmering. Add onion, garlic and rosemary and cook 3 minutes, stirring occasionally. Add shrimp and cook 2 minutes until shrimp turns pink and starts to curl. Stir in cognac and season with salt and pepper. With a large skimmer, remove shrimp from sauce and set aside. Add tomatoes and chili paste to skillet and cook 7 minutes, stirring occasionally until tender. Remove from heat and return shrimp to skillet. Fold in mascarpone, scallions, and parsley.

Divide shrimp sauce into 4 individual ovenproof deep dishes. Top with the mashed yuca and sprinkle with farofa. Bake 5 to 10 minutes, or until heated through. Remove from oven and let stand 5 minutes before serving.

Cook's Notes

This appetizer can also be made with different kinds of meats, like chicken and ground beef. The most common version is made with *carne-seca*, a Brazilian-style beef jerky.

Yuca

Yuca

Yuca (or cassava) is a potato-like root. It can be found in major grocery stores or at international and Latin markets.

Appetizers & Starters (Aperitivos e Entradas)

White Chili
(Creme de Feijão Branco)

Velvety and rich, this White Chili recipe is topped with decadent shrimp and bay scallops (you can use one or the other depending on preference). Serve in cups as an appetizer, or in large bowls as an entrée.

Serves 6 to 8

1 pound great northern beans
3 tablespoons olive oil
4 ounces mild Italian sausage, casing removed, chopped
½ onion, finely chopped
1 jalapeno pepper, seeded and minced
6 garlic cloves, minced
8 cups low sodium vegetable broth
1 dried bay leaf
¾ cup *crème fraîche*
½ cup fresh cilantro, chopped
Salt and freshly ground black pepper
12 ounces medium shrimp, cleaned and deveined
12 ounces bay scallops
2 tablespoons dry white wine
White truffle oil (optional)

Rinse and sort beans in large pot. Add 6 cups cold water. Let stand overnight or at least 8 hours. Drain soaking water and rinse beans. Set aside.

In a large pot, heat 2 tablespoons olive oil and add sausage, onions and jalapeno. Cook, stirring and breaking apart sausage with spoon, until onions are soft, 5 minutes. Stir in 4 garlic cloves and cook for another minute. Add vegetable broth, bay leaf and rinsed beans. Simmer gently for 1 ½ to 2 hours with lid tilted until desired tenderness is reached.

Turn off heat and remove bay leaf. Add 3 cups cooked beans to food processor. Process until smooth, 30 seconds. Return cream of beans to pot and fold in *crème fraîche* and cilantro. Season with salt and pepper.

In a medium skillet over high heat, add remaining olive oil and heat until smoking. Add shrimp, bay scallops and remaining garlic. Sauté 1 minute, or until the shrimp turns pinks and starts to curl. Add wine and cook an additional minute.

Remove from heat, season with salt and pepper.

Place chili in bowls or cups and top with seafood. Serve immediately with a drizzle of white truffle oil.

Cook's Notes

Crème fraîche adds an extra velvety texture, and a slightly sour bite. Media Crema (table cream) can serve as a substitute.

If you are not a fan of shrimp and bay scallops, just leave them out. This white chili recipe has plenty of flavors, even without the seafood.

Brazilian Market

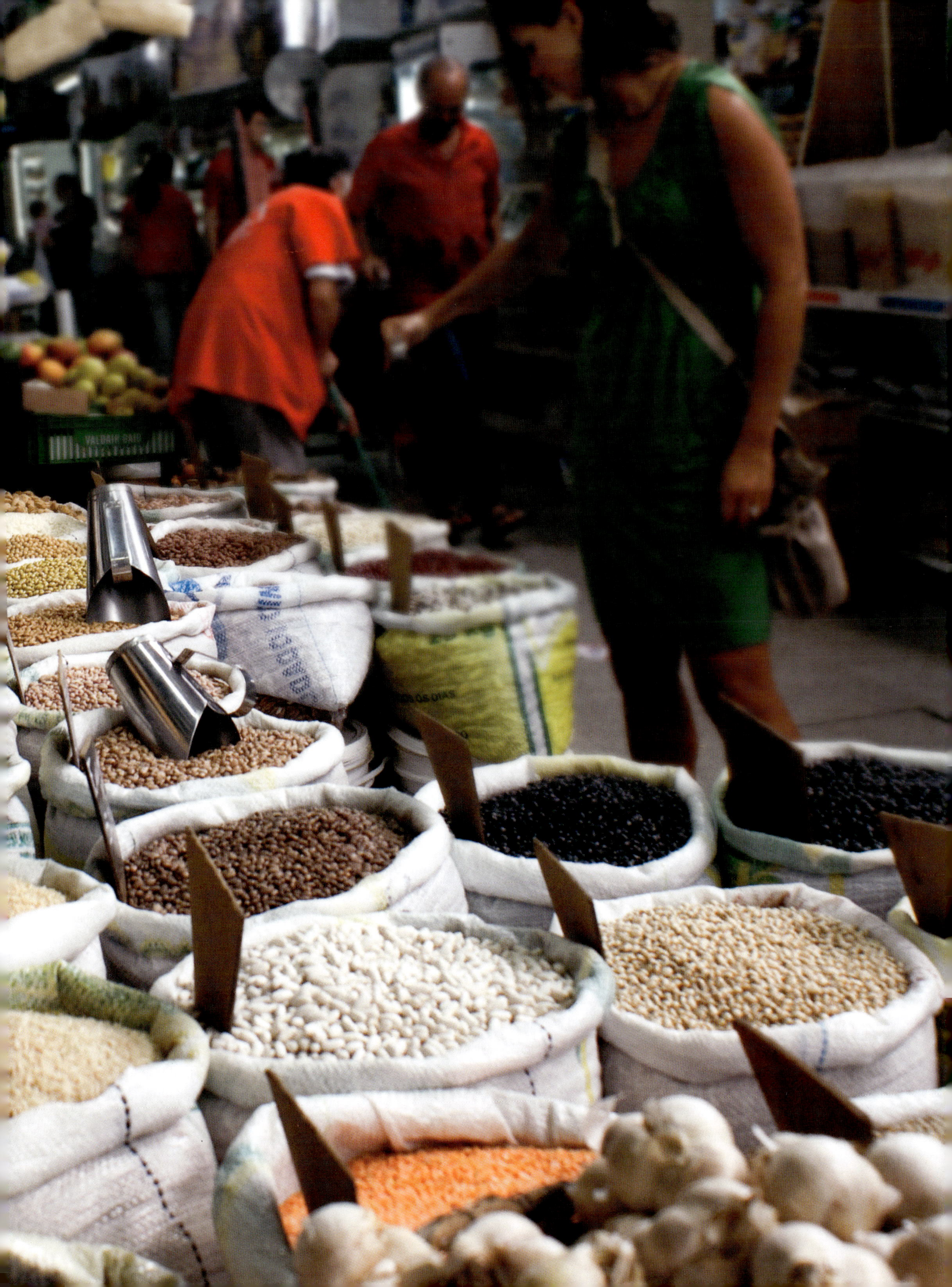

Seafood
(Frutos-do-Mar)

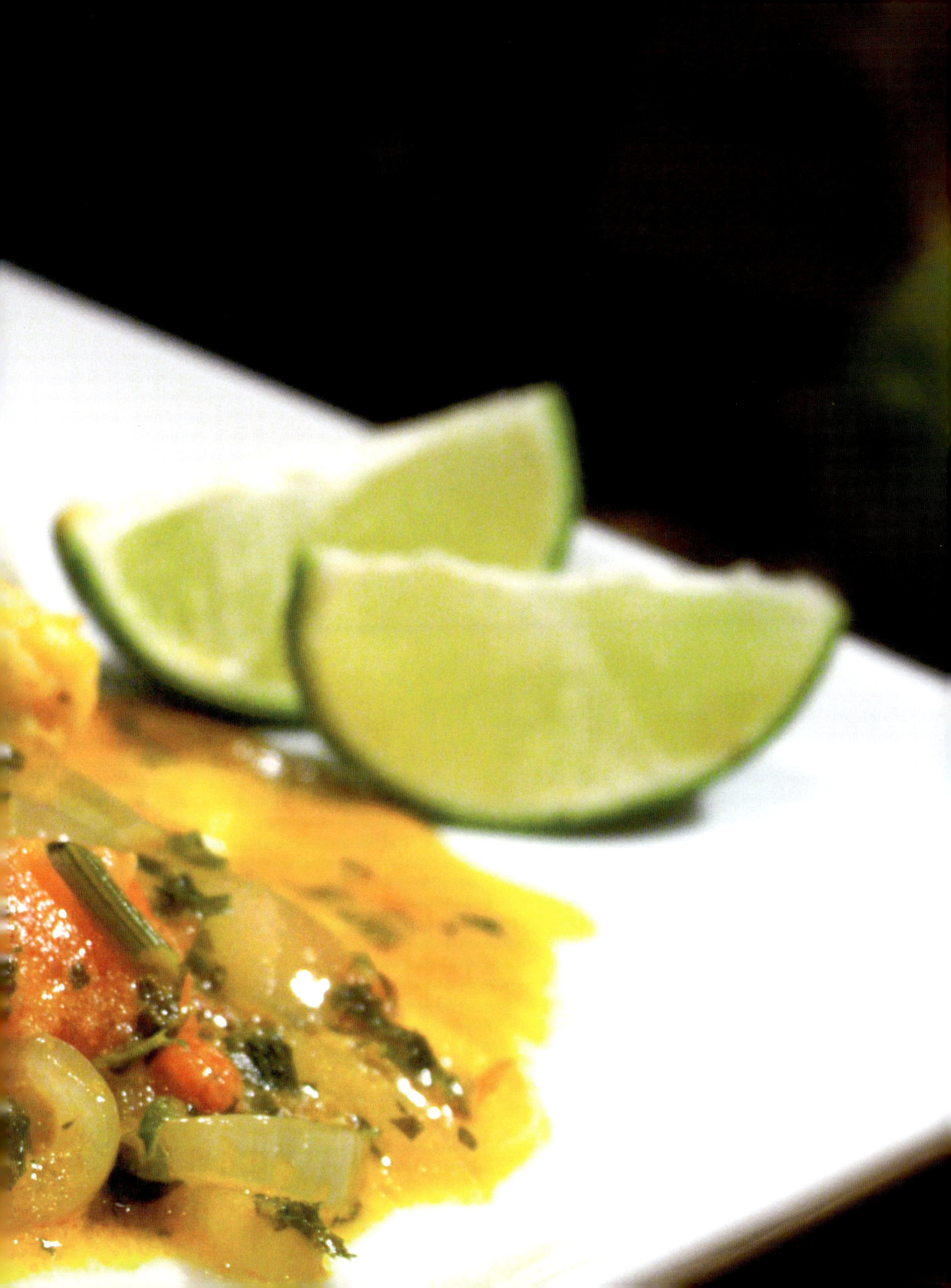

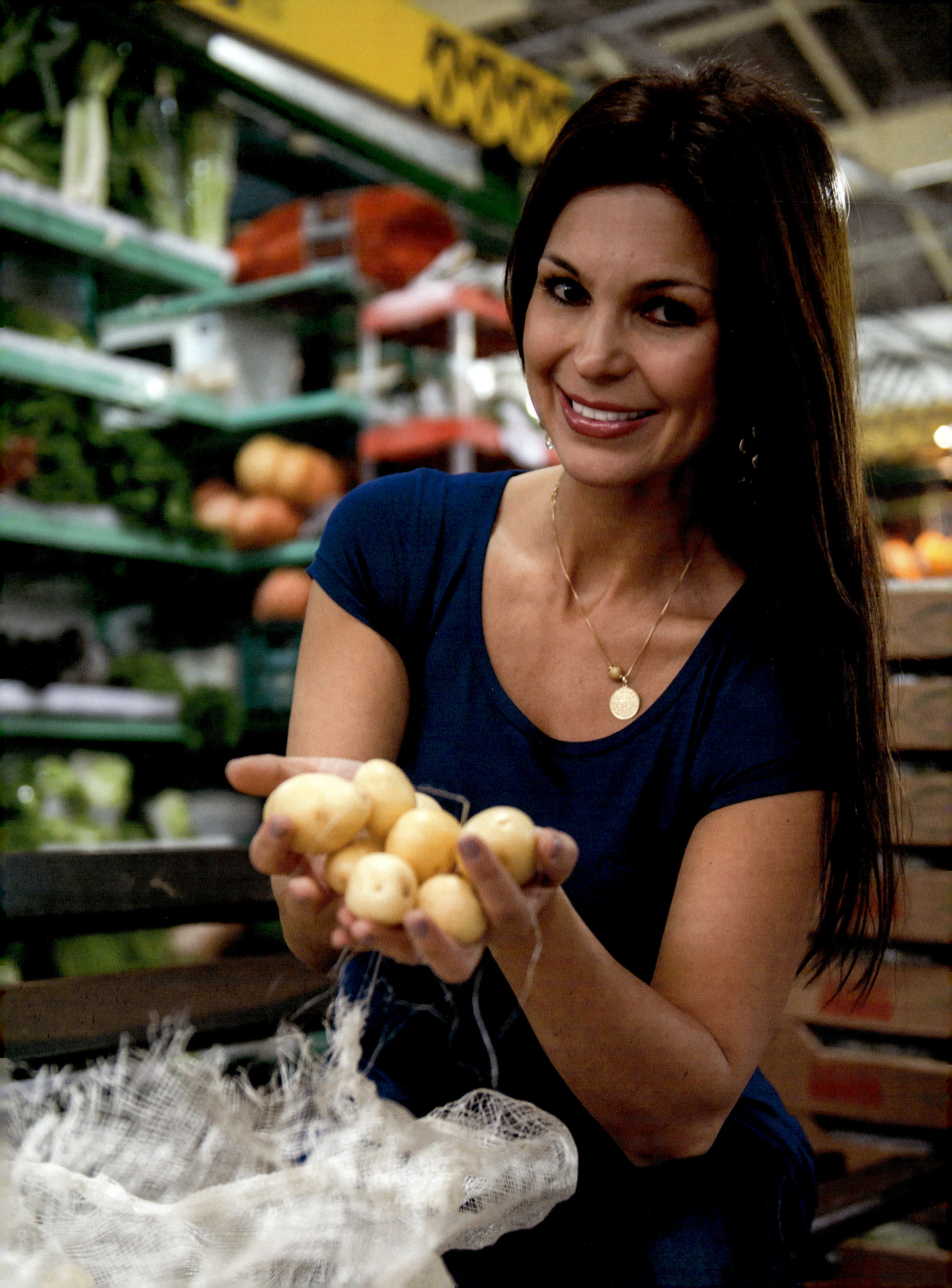

Seafood
(Frutos-do-Mar)

Shrimp Bobó (Bobó de Camarão) 50

Black-Eyed Pea Fritters (Acarajé) 52

Coconut Milk and Dried Shrimp Stew (Vatapá) 54

Fish Casserole (Peixada) 57

Fish Moqueca (Moqueca de Peixe) 59

Shrimp Moqueca (Moqueca de Camarão) 61

Layered Shrimp with Toast and Savory Meringue
(Camarão à Marta Rocha) 62

Pumpkin with Shrimp (Camarão na Moranga) 65

Salmon with Coconut Milk and Cashews
(Salmão ao Leite de Coco e Castanhas de Caju) 66

Salmon with Mango Sauce and Coconut Rice
(Salmão ao Molho de Manga com Arroz de Coco) 68

Salmon with Passion Fruit Sauce (Salmão ao Molho de Maracujá) 71

Shrimp and Hearts-of-Palm Pie (Empadão de Camarão e Palmito) 72

Shrimp Bobó
(Bobó de Camarão)

Shrimp Bobó is a traditional recipe from one of the richest culinary states of Brazil: the state of Bahia. Yuca, coconut milk and red palm oil give this delicious stew its rich color and flavor. When I throw a dinner party where I want to showcase some of the best authentic flavors from my country, I include this recipe. Fairly simple to make, it is perfect over a bed of jasmine rice (some like to serve with Farofa (page 105) on the side). This dish will awaken your palate and transport you to Bahia, Brazil.

Serves 4 to 6

1 ½ pounds large shrimp, cleaned and devained, shells and heads saved
Juice of 1 lime
Salt and freshly ground black pepper
1 pound yuca, peeled and cut into 4 sections (crosswise)
2 tablespoons olive oil
1 medium chili pepper, seeded and minced
1 medium green bell pepper, seeded and chopped
1 medium red bell pepper, seeded and chopped
2 medium onion, chopped
2 garlic cloves, minced
3 large tomatoes, seeded, peeled and chopped
¼ cup red palm oil (dendê oil)
¾ cup unsweetened coconut milk
¼ cup cilantro, chopped

Place cleaned shrimp in a large sealable container and season with lime juice, salt and pepper. Refrigerate 30 minutes.

Add shrimp shells and heads to a large sauce pan and cover with 5 cups water. Bring to a boil and reduce heat to medium. Simmer 20 minutes. Remove from heat and strain. Discard shells and heads.

Return shimp broth to sauce pan and add yuca pieces. Bring to a light boil and reduce heat to medium-low. Simmer, covered, until yuca is soft, 40 to 60 minutes. Remove from heat and allow to cool. Remove stem from the center of yuca pieces. Tranfer yuca and simmering liquid to a blender, or food processor, and blend until smooth. Set aside.

Heat olive oil in a large skillet over high heat until shimering. Cook shrimp 1 minute per side, until it turns pink and starts to curl. Remove from skillet and set aside.

Add chili peper, green pepper, red pepper and onions to same skillet, reducing heat to moderate. Cook 4 minutes stirring occasionally, until vegetables are soft. Add garlic and cook an additional minute until fragrant. Add tomatoes and cook 5 minutes until blended, stirring occasionally. Add blended yuca to skillet and simmer, covered, 5 minutes. Stir in shrimp, red palm oil and coconut milk. Simmer for an additional minute. Remove from heat and fold in cilantro. Serve immediatelly over a bed of jasmine rice.

Cook's Notes

To easily remove the skin of tomatoes, place them into a pot with boiling water for 1 minute. Remove and transfer immediately to a bowl of ice water. As soon as tomatoes are chilled, transfer to a cutting board. Remove top and peel off skin.

Red palm oil can be found in international markets, and Latin or African grocery stores.

Black-Eyed Pea Fritters
(Acarajé)

Acarajé is a traditional street food in Brazil, especially popular in the state of Bahia. This fritter is light in texture and bold in flavor: the red palm oil (where it is deep-fried) and the unique ingredients in the filling make the acarajé extremely distinctive. This is one of the best things Brazil has to offer! If you have been to Bahia, you know exactly what I am talking about.

Yields 10 to 15 cakes

1 pound black-eyed peas
1 pound white onions (3 medium onions), roughly chopped
Salt
1 ½ cups red palm oil
1 ½ cups vegetable oil
1 small onion, skin-on, whole

In a large bowl, cover peas with 2 quarts water and let soak overnight or up to 24 hours.

While still soaking, rub beans between the palm of your hands to free outer skins, which should float to the surface. Scoop off skins and discard. Drain. Refill bowl with water so more skins float to surface (repeat as many times as necessary to remove as many skins as possible). Rubbing handfuls of beans vigorously between the hands assists in this process. After several changes of water, drain, and individually remove any skins that are left. This process takes awhile, but it is very important.

Process peas and onion in a food processor. If they do not all fit, process them in batches, transferring to a large mixing bowl. Once peas and onions have been processed, season with salt. Beat batter for a few minutes with a wooden spoon, until light and fluffy.

In a large pan, heat red palm oil and vegetable oil. Place the whole onion in the pan. Form balls of batter using a large wooden spoon and gently drop into hot oil. Fry small batches of batter for 3 to 4 minutes on each side. The cakes are done once they turn bright orange and crispy on the outside. Remove from oil, and transfer to a plate lined with paper towels.

Carefully carve a slit on the cake across the longest side and fill with Vatapá (page 54), hot pepper sauce, finely chopped tomatoes, onions or cilantro, or a mixture of everything. Serve immediately.

Cook's Notes

This recipe is a typical street food from the Brazilian state of Bahia. There, the *baianas*, beautiful ladies wearing traditional white garments and turbans, prepare and sell these cakes in stations filled with traditional recipes and ingredients from that part of Brazil. It is a wonderful tradition and everyone who visits Bahia falls in love with the food prepared by the *baianas*.

This fritter has some little tricks that are critical to the success of the recipe. For example, peeling the peas thoroughly takes a long time but this process is necessary for the cakes to become light and fluffy. Also, the red palm oil used for frying gives unique color and adds a very distinctive flavor that cannot be replaced by any other oil. The onion that is dropped whole in the frying pan prevents the oil from burning.

Red palm oil can be found in Latin or African markets, or at international grocery stores.

Seafood (Frutos do Mar)

Coconut Milk and Dried Shrimp Stew
(Vatapá)

Typical from the Northern region of Brazil, and especially popular in the state of Bahia, the unique flavors in this stew come from coconut milk, red palm oil, dried and fresh shrimp, cashews, peanuts, herbs and ginger. In the North, Vatapá is usually served over rice; In Bahia it is usually one of the fillings for the exotic and delicious Acarajé recipe (page 52).

Serves 8 to 10

8 ounces dried shrimp (or 2 ½ cups pre-processed dried shrimp)
½ cup unsalted cashews
½ cup unsalted peanuts
3 cups day-old French or Italian bread, torn
3 ½ cups unsweetened coconut milk, divided
1 large tomato, roughly chopped
1 medium onion, roughly chopped
2 tablespoons fresh ginger, peeled and roughly chopped
1 cup cilantro, roughly chopped
1 cup scallions, roughly chopped
1 large jalapeno pepper, cored
1 ½ cups red palm oil
Salt and freshly ground black pepper
1 tablespoon canola oil
1 pound large shrimp, cleaned and deveined

Clean dried shrimp by removing head and tails with a sharp knife. Place dried shrimp in food processor and pulse a few times until it turns into powder (skip this step if using pre-processed dried shrimp). Add cashews and peanuts to food processor and process 2 minutes, until blended. Remove from food processor and set aside.

Place bread in bowl and cover with 1 ½ cups unsweetened coconut milk. Mix and soak a few minutes. Place bread in food processor and process 40 seconds, until a paste forms. Remove from food processor and set aside.

Place tomato, onion, ginger, cilantro, scallions and jalapeno in food processor. Process 40 seconds. Remove from food processor and set aside.

In a large sauce pan over medium-high heat, add remaining coconut milk, tomato and spices mixture, and dried shrimp mixture. Bring to a light boil and reduce heat to medium. Add red palm oil and bread mixture, stirring constantly until sauce thickens. Cook over medium-low heat 30 minutes, stirring constantly. Serve over rice, or as a filling for Acarajé.

Cook's Notes

Dried shrimp is available in Latin Markets or international grocery stores.

Red palm oil can be found in Latin or African markets. Many international grocery stores also carry red palm oil.

Seafood (Frutos do Mar)

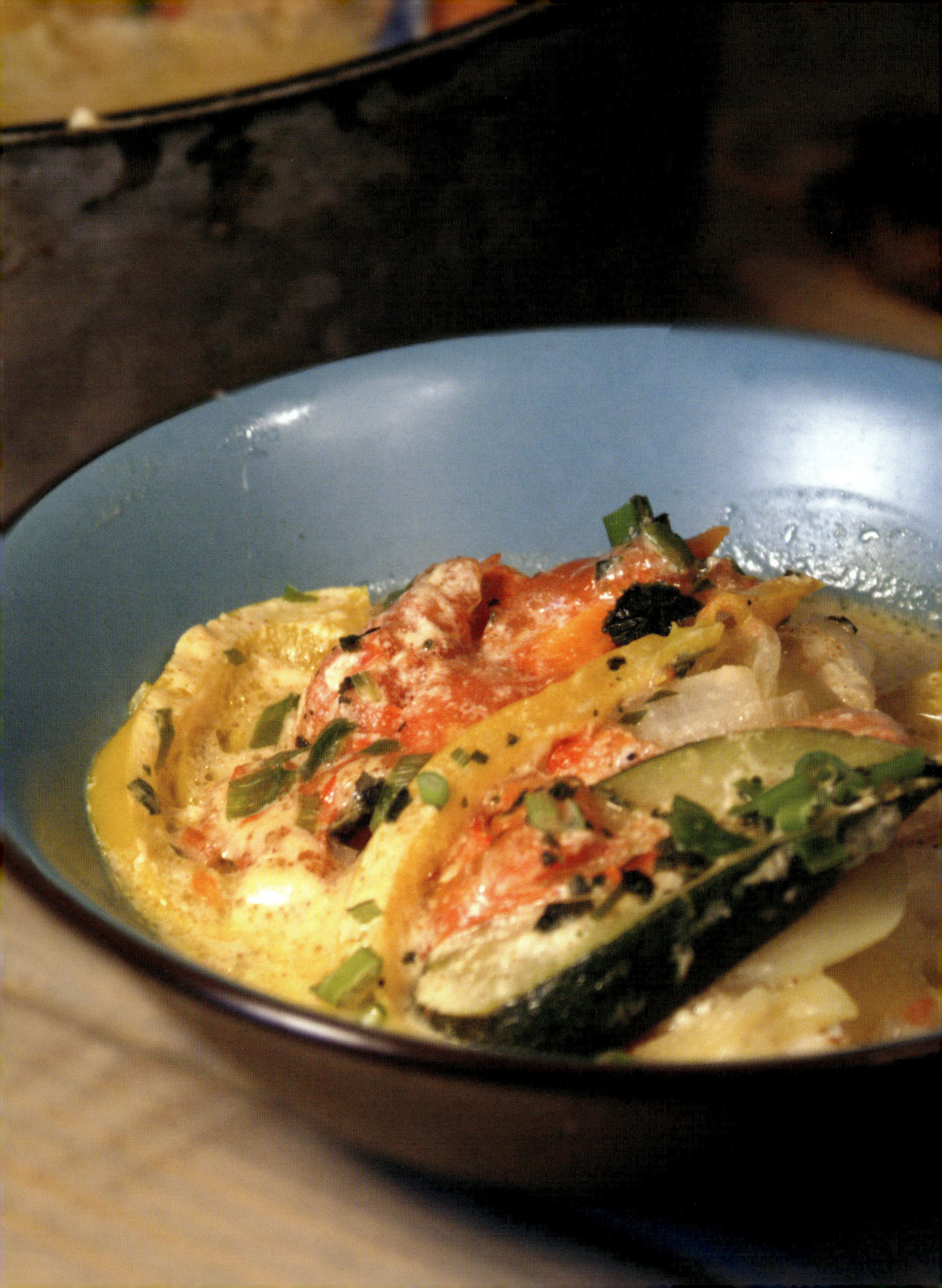

Fish Casserole
(Peixada)

Layered fish and vegetables are slow cooked, smothered in coconut milk then finished with fresh herbs; the result is a delicious and healthy casserole full of delicate flavors and textures, perfect served over rice. Easy to make, this dish is a great weeknight meal.

Serves 6

- 2 tablespoons olive oil
- 12 ounces skinless fish, cut into 1-inch thick fillets (tilapia, cod, or halibut)
- Salt and freshly ground black pepper
- 2 medium potatoes, peeled and finely sliced
- 1 medium onion, finely sliced
- 1 medium carrot, peeled and finely sliced crosswise
- 1 medium zucchini, finely sliced crosswise
- 1 medium yellow squash, finely sliced crosswise
- 2 large tomatoes, finely sliced crosswise
- 1 yellow bell pepper, cored and finely sliced crosswise
- 2 cups unsweetened coconut milk
- ½ cup low-sodium chicken broth
- 1 teaspoon smoked paprika
- 2 tablespoons scallions, finely chopped
- 2 tablespoons cilantro, finely chopped

Coat a large casserole pan with olive oil and layer fish on the bottom. Sprinkle with salt and pepper. Spread potato slices evenly over fish and sprinkle with salt and pepper. Layer onions and then carrots. Sprinkle with salt and pepper. Layer zucchini and then yellow squash. Sprinkle with salt and pepper. Layer tomatoes and top with yellow bell peppers. Sprinkle with salt and pepper. Set aside.

In a medium bowl, mix coconut milk, chicken broth, and smoked paprika. Season with salt and pepper. Whisk until blended.

Pour coconut sauce over casserole. Cover with lid and place over high heat. Bring to a boil and turn heat down to medium-low. Tilt lid and cook 20 to 25 minutes, or until vegetables are soft but still holding their shape.

Remove from heat and top with scallions and cilantro.

Serve over a bed of brown or white rice.

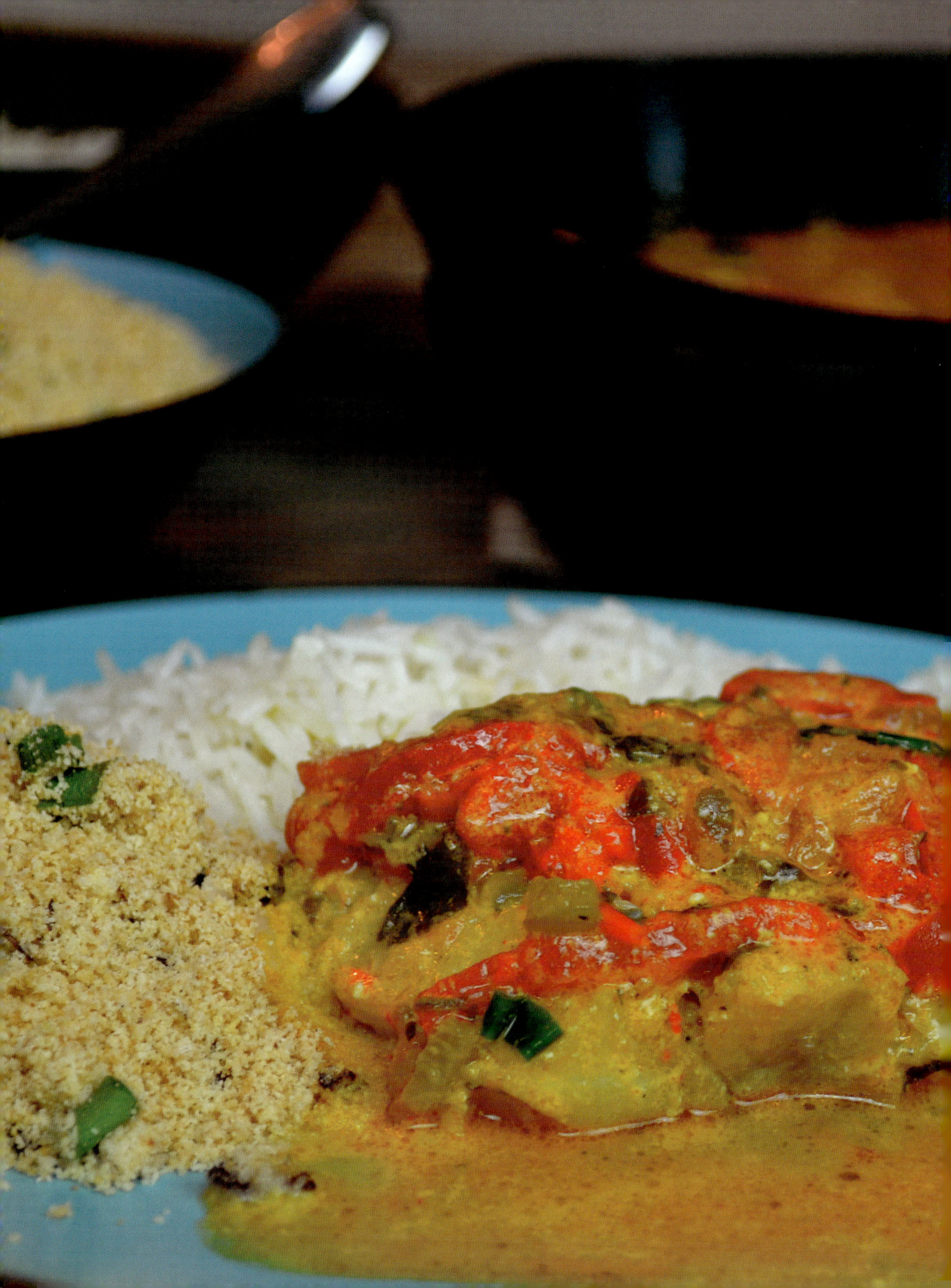

Fish Moqueca
(Moqueca de Peixe)

Light and earthy, the only hard thing about this dish is to pronounce its name: Moqueca. This quick and easy dish has a beautiful orange color due to the use of red palm oil as one of the ingredients. Originated in the beautiful state of Bahia, this recipe can also be made with different kinds of seafood, and sometimes more than one variety is used in the same stew.

Serves 6

1 ¾ pounds deboned, skinless fish (cod, swordfish, halibut) cut into filets
Juice of 1 lime
3 cloves of garlic, minced
Salt and freshly ground black pepper
4 tablespoons red palm oil
1 small chili pepper, seeded and minced
1 large onion, finely sliced
1 large tomato, seeded and finely sliced
1 green bell pepper, cored and finely sliced
1 red bell pepper, cored and finely sliced
1 ½ cups unsweetened coconut milk
¼ cup cilantro, roughly chopped

Place fish in a large sealable container. Drizzle with lime juice and sprinkle garlic on top. Season with salt and pepper. Cover and transfer to refrigerator 30 to 60 minutes.

Coat the bottom of a large heavy-duty sauce pan with 2 tablespoons red palm oil. Spread the chili pepper and half of the onion slices over the red palm oil. Place fish fillets over onions, and cover with tomatoes. Season with salt and pepper. Spread remaining onions, green pepper and red pepper. Season with salt and pepper.

Set uncovered pan on stove top over medium high heat and cook 5 minutes. Turn heat to medium and drizzle with coconut milk and remaining red palm oil. Cover and cook until vegetables are tender and fish flakes easily with a fork, 15 to 20 minutes.

Spread cilantro on top, cover and cook 2 more minutes. Remove from heat and serve immediately over a bed of rice and Farofa (page 105) on the side.

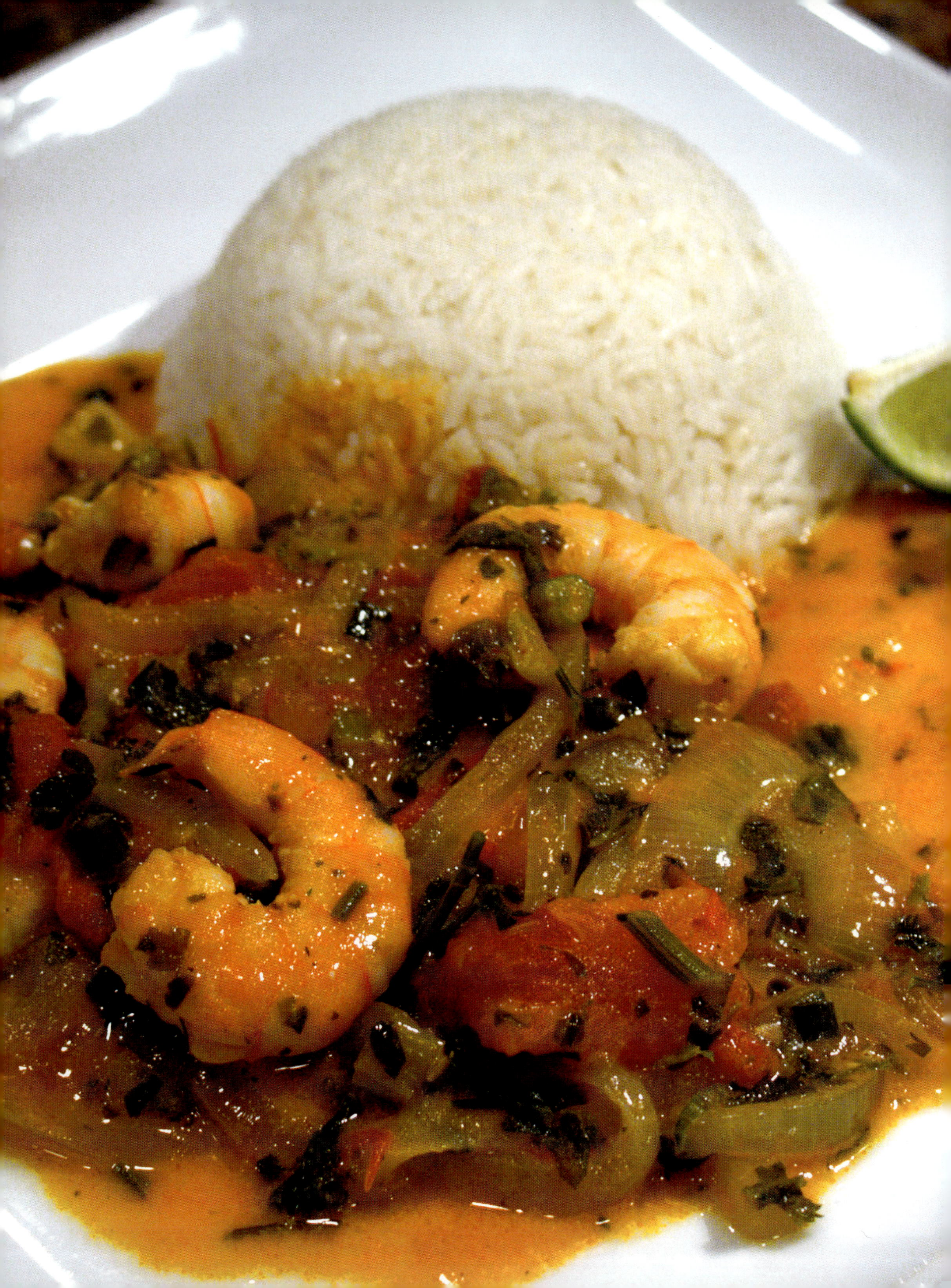

Shrimp Moqueca
(Moqueca de Camarão)

Serves 4

½ lime
1 pound large shrimp, shelled and deveined
Salt and freshly ground black pepper
¼ cup red palm oil (dendê oil)
1 large onion, sliced crosswise
3 garlic cloves, minced
2 large tomatoes, sliced crosswise
½ cup cilantro, roughly chopped
3 tablespoons scallions, chopped
2 tablespoons flat-leaf parsley, chopped
1 cup unsweetened coconut milk

Squeeze lime over shrimp and season with salt and pepper. Set aside.

Heat up red palm oil in a large skillet over medium-high heat. Add onions, garlic and tomatoes. Cook, stirring occasionally, 5 to 7 minutes until onions and tomatoes are tender.

Add shrimp and cook 2 minutes, or until they turn pink and start to curl. Turn off heat and fold in cilantro, scallions, parsley and coconut milk. Season with salt and pepper. Serve immediately over a bed of jasmine rice and Farofa (page 105) on the side.

Cook's Notes

Red palm oil is the ingredient that gives this dish its unique flavor and color. It can be found in Latin or African markets.

Layered Shrimp with Toast and Savory Meringue
(Camarão à Marta Rocha)

Developed by Brazilian chefs to honor Marta Rocha, Brazilian Miss Universe runner-up, this creamy and decadent layered shrimp entrée reminds me of some of the happiest days of my life growing up in Brazil. Since this was my mom's favorite shrimp dish, on her birthdays my dad would take us to his good friend's restaurant (Restaurante Iguaçu) where they served the best version of this layered shrimp.

Serves 6

- 3 tablespoons olive oil, divided, plus more for drizzling
- 1 pound large shrimp, cleaned and deveined
- ¼ cup cognac
- Salt and freshly ground black pepper
- 1 medium onion, finely chopped
- 3 garlic cloves, minced
- 1 tablespoon fresh rosemary, minced
- ¾ cup dry white wine
- 1 ½ cup heavy cream
- 1 14-ounce can hearts-of-palm, drained and sliced
- 8 ounces mascarpone cheese or requeijão
- 2 tablespoons flat-leaf parsley, chopped
- 6 egg whites
- 5 slices white bread, toasted and cut into cubes
- Bread crumbs, for topping

In a medium size skillet over high heat, add 2 tablespoons olive oil and heat until shimmering. Sauté shrimp 2 minutes or until they turn pink and start to curl. Add cognac and flame, stirring carefully until flames die. Season with salt and pepper. Remove from skillet and set aside.

In the same skillet, heat up remaining olive oil over medium heat, and sauté onions until soft, about 3 minutes. Add garlic and rosemary. Cook stirring constantly until fragrant, 40 seconds. Add wine and deglaze the skillet. Add heavy cream and bring to a light boil, stirring. Remove from heat. Fold in hearts-of-palm, mascarpone (or *requeijão*) and parsley. Set aside.

Using a hand mixer, beat egg whites 4 minutes until soft peaks form. Set aside.

Preheat oven to 350 degrees F. In an ovenproof deep-dish, assemble in layers:

1. Toasted bread on bottom
2. Drizzle of olive oil over bread
3. Shrimp sauce
4. Spread egg whites
5. Sprinkle top with bread crumbs

Bake 10 to 15 minutes or until top is golden brown. Serve immediately.

Cook's Notes

Requeijão is a mild, less acidic version of the American cream cheese. It is hard to find in the US, and the Italian mascarpone is a good substitute.

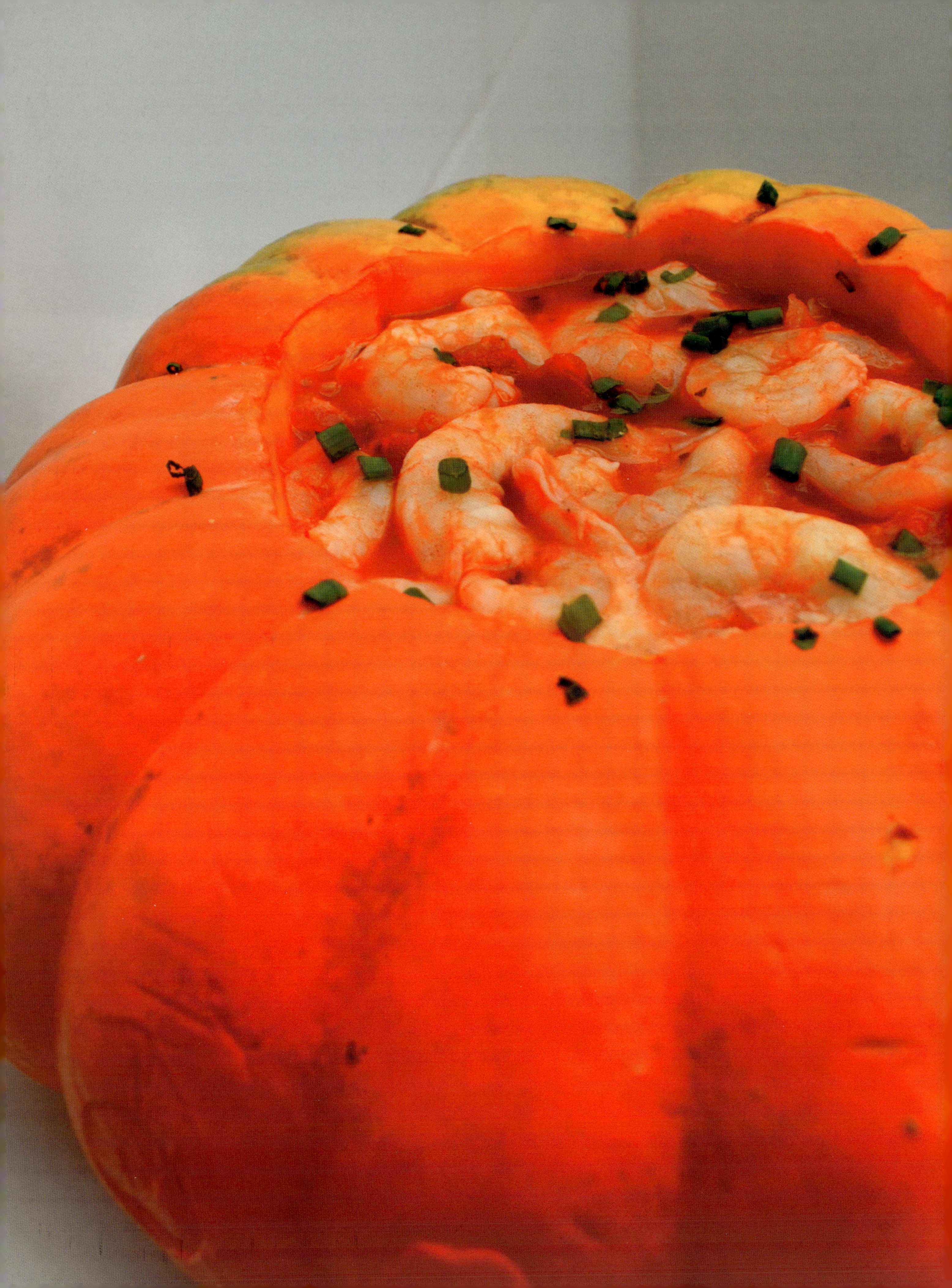

Pumpkin with Shrimp
(Camarão na Moranga)

In Brazil we have a large variety of pumpkins year round so this recipe can be served the entire year. In the United States, I look forward to fall when I can buy pumpkins and prepare this dish. My guests are always delighted by the presentation, and even more so by the great flavors. Scoop the inside of the pumpkin, along with the shrimp sauce, when serving this traditional Brazilian entrée.

Serves 12

- 1 medium pumpkin
- 2 pounds large shrimp, cleaned and deveined, shells saved
- 3 cups water
- 1 medium onion, peeled and divided
- 3 large garlic cloves, peeled
- 1 bay leaf
- Salt and freshly ground black pepper
- 2 tablespoons all-purpose flour
- 2 tablespoons olive oil
- 3 sprigs rosemary, chopped
- 10 large Roma tomatoes, chopped
- 1 cup cilantro, roughly chopped
- 8 ounces cream cheese or requeijão

Preheat oven to 350 degrees F.

Cut the top of the pumpkin and remove all seeds. Wrap in aluminum foil and place in large, shallow, ovenproof pan, cut-off side down. Bake 45 to 60 minutes, until soft. Remove from oven and carefully remove foil. Set aside.

In a medium sauce pan, add the shrimp shells, water, half the onion, 2 garlic cloves and bay leaf. Season with salt and pepper. Cook over medium heat about 25 minutes until the liquid is reduced to half. Remove from heat and strain. Discard shells and vegetables. Whisk flour into liquid and set aside.

Finely chop remaining onion and garlic. In a large pan, heat olive oil over medium high heat and cook onion until soft, 4 minutes. Add garlic and rosemary and cook until fragrant, about 40 seconds. Stir in tomatoes, cover, and cook 5 minutes. Remove lid and break apart tomatoes with a potato masher. Cover, reduce heat to medium low, and cook 20 minutes. Constantly stirring, add broth and cook until thickened. Add shrimp and cook 3 minutes, or until shrimp turns pink and start to curl. Remove from heat and fold in cilantro. Set aside.

Using a large spoon, spread cream cheese (or requeijão) along the pumpkin's inside walls. Pour shrimp sauce into pumpkin and return to oven. Bake at 350 degrees F for 15 to 20 minutes, or until cheese starts to melt.

Carefully place pumpkin on serving dish. To serve, scoop shrimp mixture with chunks of pumpkin and cream cheese. Serve over a bed of jasmine rice.

Salmon with Coconut Milk and Cashews
(Salmão ao Leite de Coco e Castanhas de Caju)

Served over creamy yuca purée, this rich salmon recipe has some bold flavors. First seared, then smothered in coconut milk and baked, this salmon melts in your month! This recipe has some of the most authentic ingredients found in Brazilian cuisine.

Serves 4

- 4 salmon fillets (5 to 6 ounces each)
- 4 tablespoons lime juice
- Salt and freshly ground pepper
- 4 tablespoons canola oil, divided
- ½ large onion, chopped
- 1 tablespoon brown sugar
- ½ fennel bulb, chopped
- 2 tablespoons fresh ginger, minced
- 2 garlic cloves, minced
- 1 red bell pepper, cored, seeded and chopped
- 2 cups unsweetened coconut milk
- 1 cup unsalted cashews, roasted
- 1 cup cilantro, chopped

Season salmon fillets with lime juice, salt and pepper. Cover and refrigerate 30 to 60 minutes.

Remove salmon from refrigerator and pat dry with paper towel. Heat 2 tablespoons canola oil in a large ovenproof skillet over high heat until shimmering. Sear salmon fillets, about 1 minute per side. Remove from skillet and set aside.

In the same skillet, heat remaining canola oil and cook onions on medium-high heat 3 to 4 minutes, stirring occasionally. Add brown sugar, stirring another minute. Add fennel, ginger, garlic and bell pepper. Cook 10 minutes, or until vegetables are tender, stirring occasionally. Add coconut milk and remove from stove. Fold in cashews. Season lightly with salt and pepper.

Preheat oven to 350 degrees F for 10 minutes. Return salmon fillets to skillet with the coconut milk sauce. If using a regular oven, bake 12 to 14 minutes, or until salmon flakes easily with a fork. If using a convection oven, bake 8 to 10 minutes.

Remove from oven and place salmon fillets on individual plates. Top each fillet with ¼ cup cilantro. Serve immediately over a bed of yuca purée.

Yuca Purée
(Purê de Mandioca)

Serves 4

1 ¼ pounds yuca (cassava)
¼ cup milk
¼ cup butter, at room temperature
Salt

Using a potato peeler, remove skin of yuca. Transfer to a large sauce pan and cover completely with water. Bring to a boil. Cook over medium heat until yuca is cooked through, 40 to 60 minutes. Drain and let cool, 10 minutes.

While still warm, cut yuca in half lengthwise. Remove the stem. Chop and transfer to a medium bowl. Add butter, milk and salt and smash until all ingredients are blended and the purée looks fairly smooth. Serve immediately or warm in microwave before serving.

Cook's Notes

A food processor can be used to make a smoother purée.

Yuca root (also called cassava or manioc) may be found in major grocery stores or at South American and African markets.

Salmon with Mango Sauce and Coconut Rice
(Salmão ao Molho de Manga com Arroz de Coco)

Mango, limes and coconut are some of the most traditional ingredients used in Brazilian cuisine. In this recipe, all three were used in a harmonic combination of flavors. Greek yogurt adds a creamy texture to this fresh, healthy and flavorful meal.

Serves 4 to 5

Sauce Ingredients:
1 tablespoon butter
½ medium onion, shredded
2 tablespoons dark brown sugar
¾ cup mango pulp (or 1 medium ripe mango processed in a blender or food processor)
Juice of 1 large lime
½ cup full-fat Greek yogurt
¼ cup cilantro, finely chopped
Freshly ground black pepper

Salmon Ingredients:
2 tablespoons extra-virgin olive oil
1 ½ pounds Sockeye salmon, cut into 4 or 5 fillets
Sea salt, medium grind
Freshly ground black pepper
½ cup cilantro, roughly chopped

Rice:
1 tablespoon butter
2 tablespoons grated coconut, preferably fresh
1 ½ cups Jasmine rice
2 cups unsweetened coconut milk
½ teaspoon salt

Sauce Directions

In a large skillet, melt butter over medium-high heat. Add onion and cook 3 to 4 minutes, until soft, stirring occasionally. Add brown sugar and stir an additional minute until completely dissolved. Reduce heat to medium and add mango pulp. When it comes to a light boil, remove from heat and fold in lime juice, Greek yogurt and cilantro. Season with black pepper and set aside.

Salmon Directions

Preheat oven to 400 degrees F for 10 minutes.

Coat the bottom of a large oven-proof dish with olive oil. Season salmon with salt and pepper and transfer to prepared oven-proof dish, skin side-down. Bake until salmon flakes easily with a fork, 10 minutes for medium-rare or up to 15 minutes for medium. Remove from oven and cover with foil; rest for 5 minutes.

Transfer salmon to individual plates. Drizzle mango sauce over the top and garnish with cilantro. Serve immediately with coconut rice on the side.

Coconut Rice Directions

In a medium sauce pan over medium-high heat, melt butter. Add coconut flakes. Cook 2 to 3 minutes until golden, stirring constantly. Add rice and stir until all grains are well coated with butter. Add coconut milk and salt and stir. Bring to a light boil and reduce heat to medium-low. Cover and cook 10 to 12 minutes until liquid has been absorbed. Remove from heat and let stand, covered, for 10 minutes. Fluff with fork and serve.

Cook's Notes

Frozen mango pulp, available in Latin markets and international grocery stores, can be used as a substitute for fresh pulp.

When making the sauce, add ½ minced Habanero pepper to the skillet with onions. If you like it spicy, Habaneros add a great kick!

Passion Fruit

70   Cooking with a Brazilian Twist

Salmon with Passion Fruit Sauce
(Salmão ao Molho de Maracujá)

Fresh and healthy, the combination of salmon and passion fruit might sound unusual for some, but it is very well known and loved in Brazil. In this recipe, I use brown sugar to break the acidity of the passion fruit, and table cream (or *crème fraîche*) to add a velvety texture to the sauce. Top with fresh herbs and serve over rice.

Serves 4

4 skinless salmon fillets (5 to 6 ounces each)
Salt and freshly ground pepper
2 tablespoons canola oil
1 tablespoon butter
1 small onion, shredded
3 tablespoons brown sugar

1 cup frozen passion fruit pulp
½ cup Media Crema (table cream) or *crème fraîche*
½ cup fresh mint, coarsely chopped
½ cup scallions, chopped
½ cup cilantro, coarsely chopped

Preheat oven to 375 degrees F. Season salmon fillets with salt, pepper and 1 tablespoon canola oil, rubbing fillets on both sides. If using a regular oven, bake 17 minutes, or until salmon flakes easily with a fork. For a convection oven, bake salmon fillets at 350 degrees F for 13 minutes, or until it flakes easily with a fork.

Meanwhile, heat butter and remaining canola oil in a medium skillet. Add onion and cook over medium-high heat about 3 minutes, until translucent. Stir in brown sugar and passion fruit pulp, cooking for an additional minute. Fold in *crème fraîche* and remove from heat.

Add mint, scallions, and cilantro to a bowl and mix gently.

Place salmon fillets on individual plates and top with 2 to 3 tablespoons of passion fruit sauce. Sprinkle on fresh herbs mix and serve immediately with a side of rice.

Cook's Notes

Passion fruit pulp may be found in the frozen section of main grocery stores, or international or Latin grocery stores. To make passion fruit pulp from scratch, place the pulp of 3 small passion fruits and ¼ cup water in blender and blend for 20 seconds. Strain and add to sauce.

Nedia Crema (table cream) can be found in the latin section of large grocery stores.

Shrimp and Hearts-of-Palm Pie
(Empadão de Camarão e Palmito)

Creamy on the inside, with delicious chunks of shrimp and hearts-of-palm in the filling, this pie has a buttery and crumbly dough that melts in your mouth! For something that tastes so good, this dough recipe has a curious name, "rotten dough" (*massa podre*). This savory Shrimp and Hearts-of-Palm Pie is a really popular dish in Brazil.

Serves 8 to 10

Filling Ingredients:
2 tablespoons olive oil
1 large onion, finely chopped
3 large garlic cloves, minced
7 large tomatoes, finely chopped
2 cans (27 ounces) hearts-of-palm
2 pounds large shrimp, cleaned and deveined
Salt and freshly ground black pepper
¼ teaspoon cayenne pepper
½ cup scallions, finally chopped
½ cup cilantro, finally chopped

Béchamel Sauce Ingredients:
2 tablespoons butter
2 tablespoons flour
2 cups milk
Salt and freshly ground black pepper
½ teaspoon freshly grated nutmeg

Dough Ingredients:
3 sticks butter at room temperature
3 ½ cups all-purpose flour, plus additional ½ cup for topping
2 egg yolks
1 teaspoon baking powder
½ teaspoon salt

Filling Directions

In a large sauce pan or deep-skillet, heat olive oil over medium-high heat. Add onion and cook 3 to 4 minutes until soft, stirring occasionally. Add garlic and cook until fragrant, 40 seconds. Stir in tomatoes and hearts-of-palm. Reduce heat to medium and cover partially with lid. Simmer 8 minutes, stirring occasionally, until tomatoes are soft. Stir in shrimp and cook 3 minutes, stirring occasionally until shrimp starts to curl. Season with salt, pepper and cayenne. Remove from heat and fold in scallions and cilantro. Set aside.

Béchamel Sauce Directions

In a medium sauce pan over medium heat, melt the butter until foamy. Add flour and whisk vigorously for one minute, forming a roux. Slowly whisk in milk and cook 2 to 3 minutes until Béchamel thickens. Remove from heat. Season with salt, pepper and nutmeg. Set aside.

Dough Directions

Place butter, all-purpose flour, egg yolks, baking powder and salt in a large bowl and mix well. Do not knead the dough; it is not supposed to be really smooth. Cover and let rest 30 minutes. Save ½ cup dough. Use remaining dough to cover the bottom and sides of a 13x9 inches baking deep dish. Start pressing the dough on the bottom, slowly moving it up and to the sides. Press dough until really thin, about 1/8-inch thick. Using a fork, prick tiny holes over surface. If there is any excess dough, add to the ½ cup of saved dough.

Pre-heat oven to 375 degrees F. Add ½ cup flour to remaining dough and crumble it.

Place shrimp and hearts-of-palm filling in pan. Cover with Béchamel sauce, leaving about ¼ -inch room on top. Cover with dough crumbles and bake 35 to 40 minutes, or until the top is golden brown. Remove from oven and let cool 10 minutes before serving. Serve warm or at room temperature.

For a convection oven, bake at 350 degrees F for 20 to 25 minutes, or until the top is golden brown.

Cook's Notes

If you are not crazy about shrimp or hearts-of-palm, try my Brazilian Chicken Pot Pie (Empadão de Frango) recipe (page 94). It's a delicious family recipe that uses the same dough, but a different filling.

Meat
(Carnes)

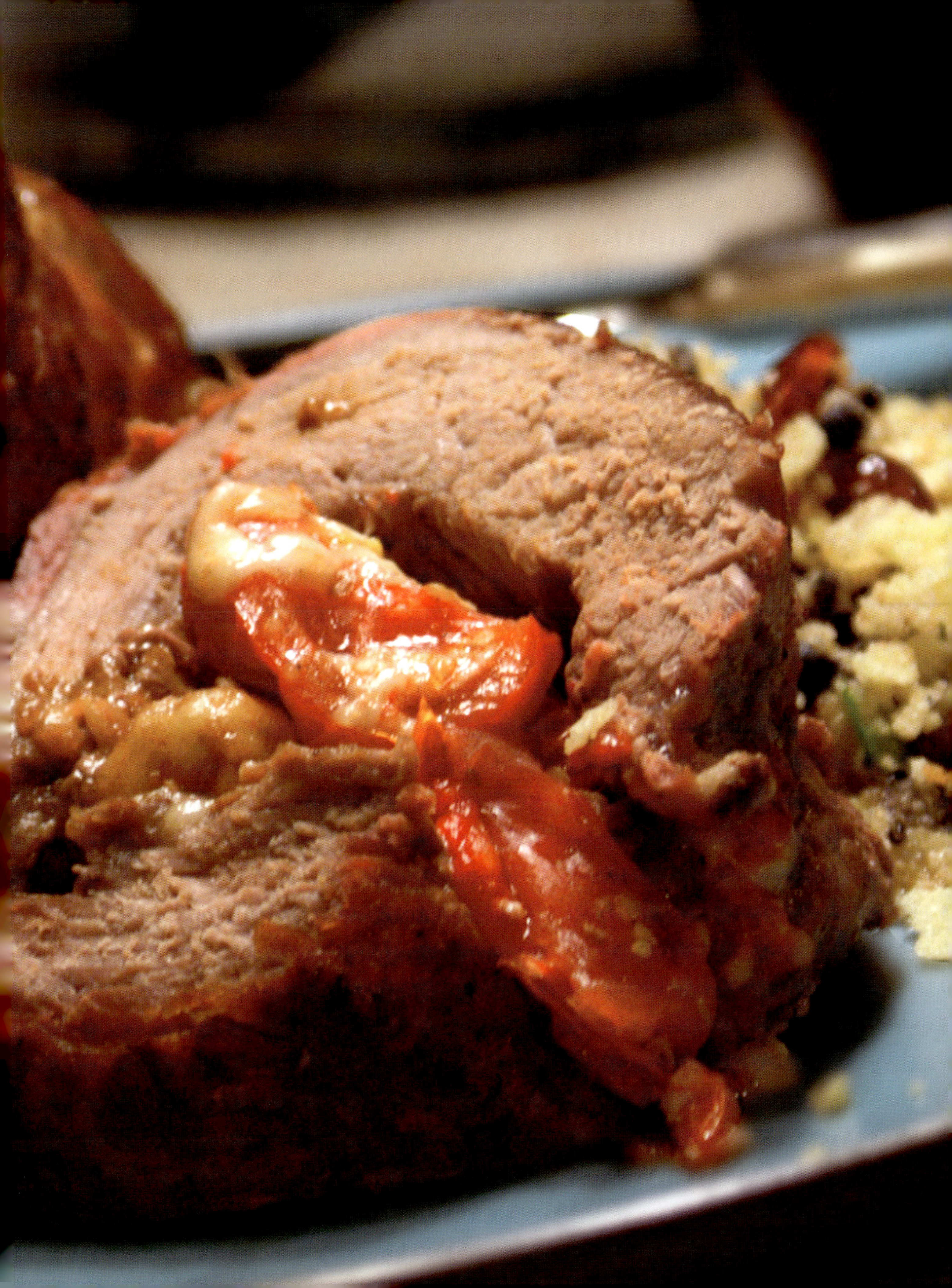

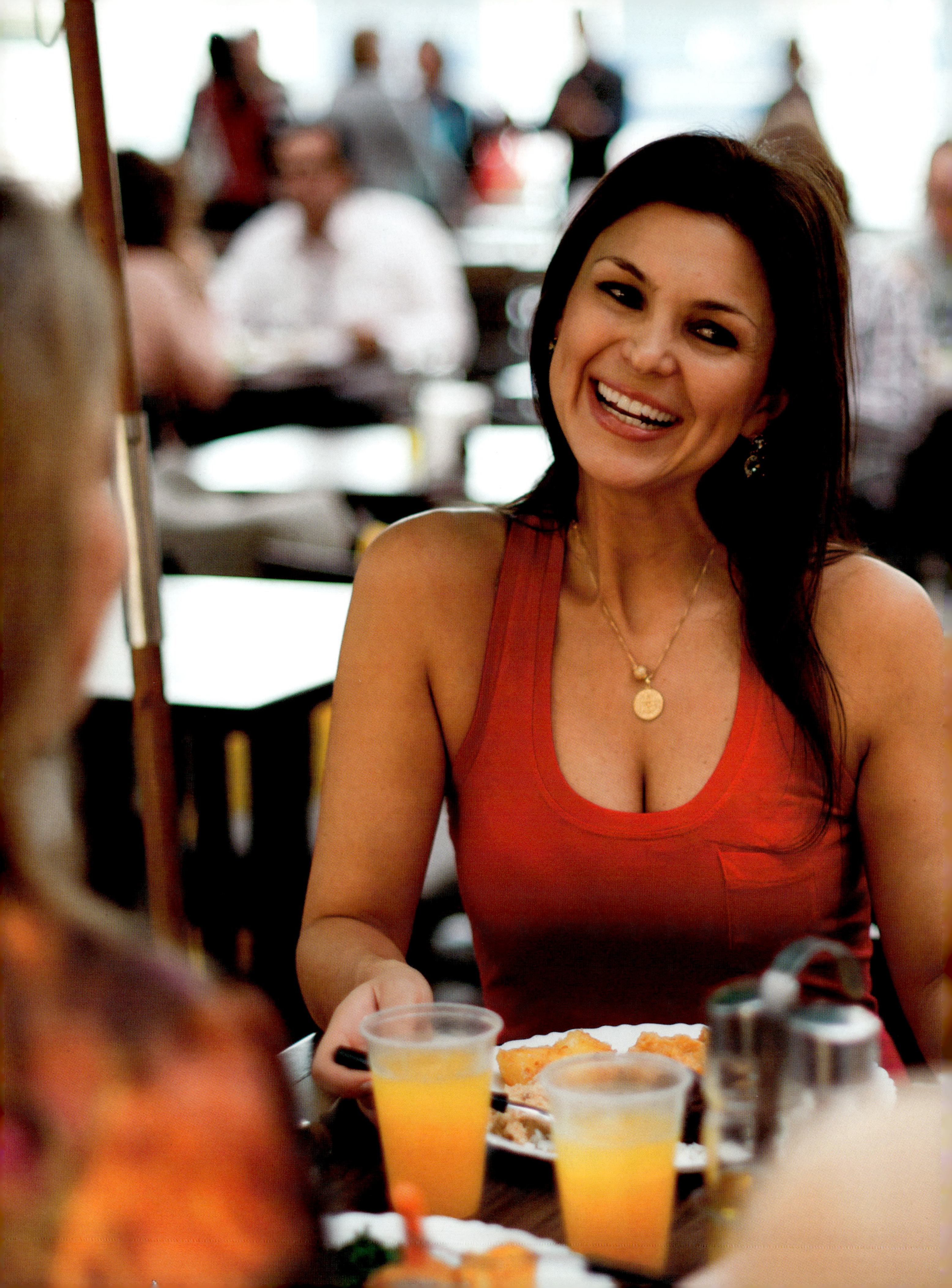

Meat
(Carnes)

Brazilian Style Stroganoff (Estrogonofe) 79

Lamb Roulade with Tomatoes and Gouda, Mint Pesto, and Farofa
(Carneiro Recheado com Tomate e Queijo, ao Molho de Menta e Farofa) 80

Pork Tenderloin with Dried Apricots, Gouda, and Mascarpone
(Lombo Recheado com Damascos Secos, Queijo Gouda e Mascarpone) 82

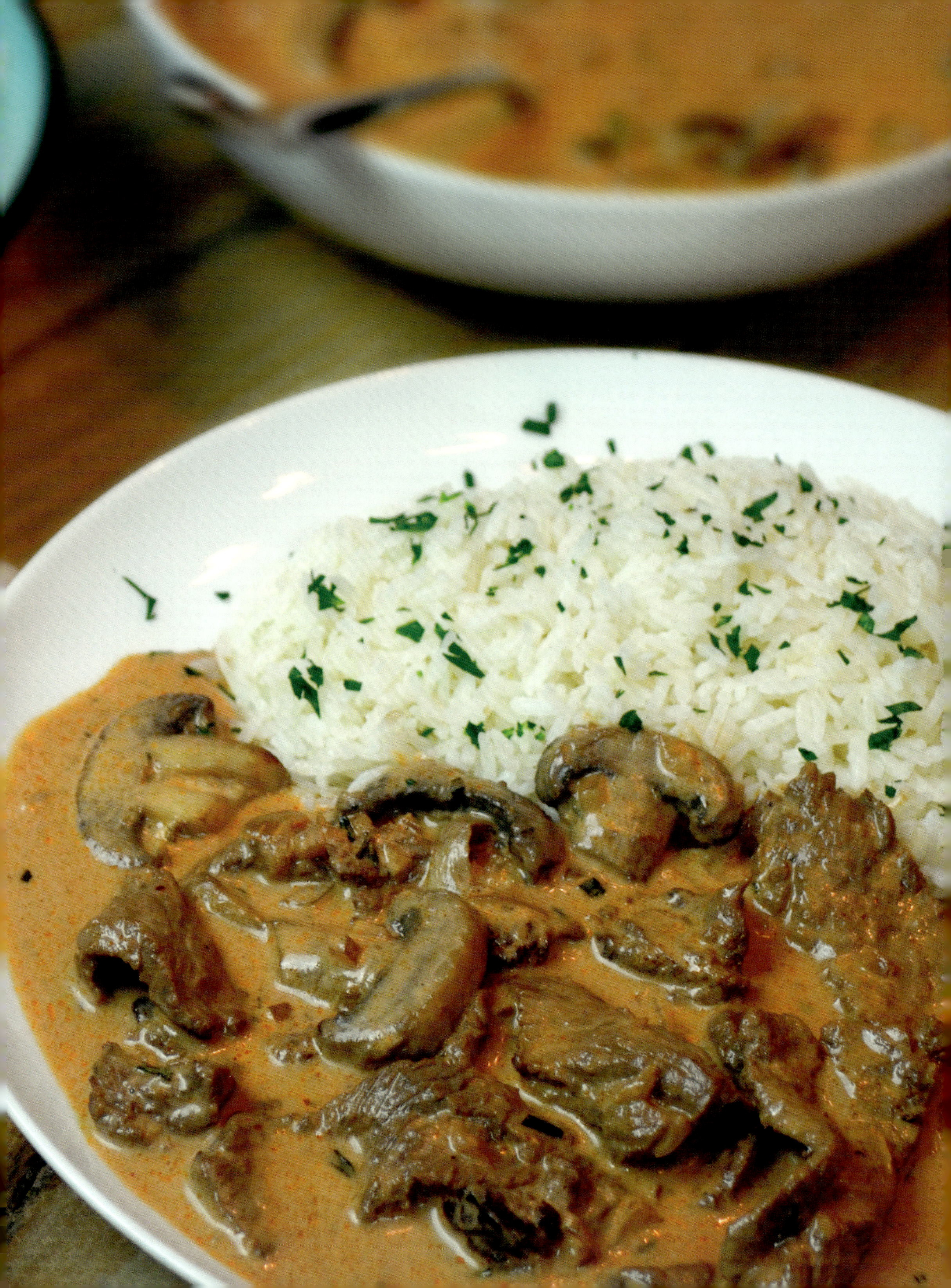

Brazilian Style Stroganoff
(Estrogonofe)

Today, this version of beef stroganoff is considered comfort food in Brazil, but as a child I remember it being an elegant dish. My mom would prepare such a meal only on very special occasions. Served over rice, *estrogonofe* is now featured on the menu of popular restaurants, and still a favorite among Brazilians!

Serves 6

4 tablespoons olive oil
1 ½ pounds tenderloin or other tender cut of steak, cut into small cubes
Salt and freshly ground black pepper
½ cup brandy or cognac, equally divided into two ¼ cup portions
3 ounces tomato paste
1 ½ cups low-sodium beef broth
2 tablespoons brown sugar
¼ cup ketchup
6 ounces white mushrooms, sliced
2 tablespoons fresh rosemary, finely chopped
1 cup *crème fraîche*

In a large sauce pan, heat 2 tablespoons olive oil on high heat until shimmering. Season steak cubes with salt and pepper and sear one minute. Add onions and garlic, cooking 3 minutes. Add ¼ cup cognac and stir until evaporated. Reduce heat to medium and add tomato paste, beef broth, brown sugar, and ketchup. Season lightly with salt and pepper. Cook 5 minutes, stirring occasionally. Remove from heat.

Heat remaining olive oil in a medium skillet over high heat until shimmering. Sauté mushrooms and rosemary 2 minutes until soft. Add remaining cognac, being careful as the alcohol might flame. Stir another minute. Remove from heat.

Add mushrooms to the steak sauce. Fold in *crème fraîche* and serve immediately over a bed of white rice.

Cook's Notes

This dish is widely served in Brazil and fairly common at big parties. The traditional side dish served with Brazilian Stroganoff is white rice, but you can also serve it over sautéed potatoes or noodles.

Crème fraîche may be replaced with Media Crema (table cream). Media Crema may be found in the Latin or international section of most large grocery stores.

Lamb Roulade with Tomatoes and Gouda, Mint Pesto, and Farofa

(Carneiro Recheado com Tomate e Queijo, ao Molho de Menta e Farofa)

Ever since I was a little girl, one of my favorite meats has been my dad's slow-cooked, grilled leg of lamb. One of my dad's tricks to add flavor was to insert chunks of cheese into small slits all around it, so the cheese would melt and blend with the meat. Inspired by my dad's recipe, I roast a butterflied leg of lamb filled with Gouda and tomatoes. I serve it topped with a mint, basil and scallion pesto, and Farofa (page 105) on the side. This is a typical meal from the South of Brazil, where I was born and raised.

Serves 8

- 3 ½ pounds leg of lamb, boneless and butterflied
- Salt and freshly ground black pepper
- 2 cups Campari tomatoes, quartered
- 2 cups Gouda cheese, shredded
- 2 tablespoons extra virgin olive oil
- ¾ cup scallions, chopped
- 1 cup mint, chopped
- ¾ cup basil, chopped
- 1 large garlic clove, chopped
- ½ cup raw almonds, roughly chopped
- 1 ½ tablespoon sugar
- 3 tablespoons aged balsamic vinegar
- ¾ cup extra-virgin olive oil

On a work surface, generously season lamb with salt and pepper on both sides. Lay it open on the work surface and spread the tomatoes, cut side down, over meat. Cover with cheese. Press the filling down with your hands, so it stays in place. Carefully roll meat, until tomatoes and cheese are secured inside the roll and both ends of lamb overlap. Secure with toothpicks or kitchen twine.

Preheat oven to 375 degrees F. In a large ovenproof skillet, heat olive oil until shimmering. Sear lamb 2 minutes per side until browned. Remove from heat. Cover skillet tightly with foil and transfer to oven. If using a regular oven, bake 25 minutes. Then remove foil and bake an additional 10 to 13 minutes, or until meat is fully cooked and cheese is melted. If using a convection oven, bake 20 minutes. Then remove foil and bake an additional 7 to 10 minutes. Remove from oven. Place foil back on top and let stand 5 minutes. Remove foil and transfer to a cutting board. Remove toothpicks or kitchen twine and carve into 3-inch slices. Drizzle with juices from the skillet.

While lamb is roasting, mix scallions, mint, basil, garlic, almonds, sugar, and balsamic vinegar in a food processor. Pulse until well blended. With food processor turned on, slowly add ¾ cup olive oil. Season with salt and pepper.

Serve lamb with a scoop of mint pesto and a side of Farofa (page 105).

Cook's Notes

Butterflying is a cutting technique used to transform a thick, compact piece of meat into a thinner, larger one. The piece of meat is laid out flat on a cutting board and cut in half parallel to the board from one side almost all the way to the other. A small "hinge" is left at the one side, which is used to fold the meat out like a book. The resemblance of this unfolding motion to the wings of a butterfly is what gives this cut its name.

Pork Tenderloin with Dried Apricots, Gouda, and Mascarpone
(Lombo Recheado com Damascos Secos, Queijo Gouda e Mascarpone)

This pork tenderloin recipe is traditionally served for Christmas supper in Brazil, but there is no reason for this moist, creamy and well-seasoned dish not to be served year-round. With a slightly sweet filling, the pork tenderloin is perfectly complemented by the richness of the cashew rice and crunchiness of the farofa. This family recipe was passed down to me by a friend, whose mother makes this meal every Christmas.

Serves 6

1 pork tenderloin (weighting approximately 1.8 pounds)
Salt and freshly ground black pepper
4 garlic cloves, minced
½ cup aged balsamic vinegar
½ cup extra virgin olive oil
½ cup scallions, chopped

¼ cup rosemary leaves, roughly chopped
1 ½ cup dried apricots, finely sliced
5 ounces Gouda cheese, freshly shredded
½ cup mascarpone
½ cup dry white wine

Butterfly tenderloin by slicing it lengthwise, cutting to other side without cutting through it. Open halves, laying tenderloin flat. Place between 2 sheets of plastic wrap. Using a meat mallet, pound tenderloin to ½-inch thickness. Transfer to a large cutting board and season both sides with salt and pepper. Set aside.

In a medium bowl, mix garlic, aged balsamic vinegar, olive oil, scallions and rosemary until blended. Transfer marinade and pork tenderloin to a sealable plastic bag. Remove as much air as possible from inside the bag. Place in the refrigerator for 12 to 36 hours.

Preheat oven to 400 degrees F.

In a medium bowl, mix dried apricots, Gouda and mascarpone. Set aside.

Remove tenderloin from marinade and lay flat on a large working surface. Add wine to marinade and refrigerate. Spread apricot and cheeses mixture over tenderloin. Roll up using kitchen twine or toothpicks at 1-inch intervals to secure. Transfer to a baking dish and cover with aluminum foil. Bake 25 minutes. Remove foil and cover with marinade. Bake uncovered an additional 15 minutes, basting two or three times throughout the process with the juices that accumulate on baking dish. Remove from oven and cover loosely with foil. Let rest 7 minutes. Remove foil and transfer to cutting board. Carve, drizzle with juices, and serve with Cashew Rice Pilaf (page 83) and Farofa (page 105).

Cashew Rice Pilaf
(Arroz de Castanha de Caju)

Serves 6

1 tablespoon olive oil
1 tablespoon unsalted butter
1 small onion, finely chopped
1 ½ cups Jasmine rice
2 cups low-sodium vegetable broth
Salt
1 cup unsalted cashew pieces or halves, roasted

In a medium sauce pan over medium-high heat, add olive oil and butter. When butter is foamy, add onion and cook 3 minutes until soft, stirring occasionally. Add rice and mix well to coat. Add broth and bring to a boil. Season with salt and reduce heat to medium. Cover and simmer 10 to 13 minutes until water is absorbed. Remove from heat. Cover and let stand 10 minutes. Fluff with fork and fold in cashews. Serve immediately.

Chicken
(Aves)

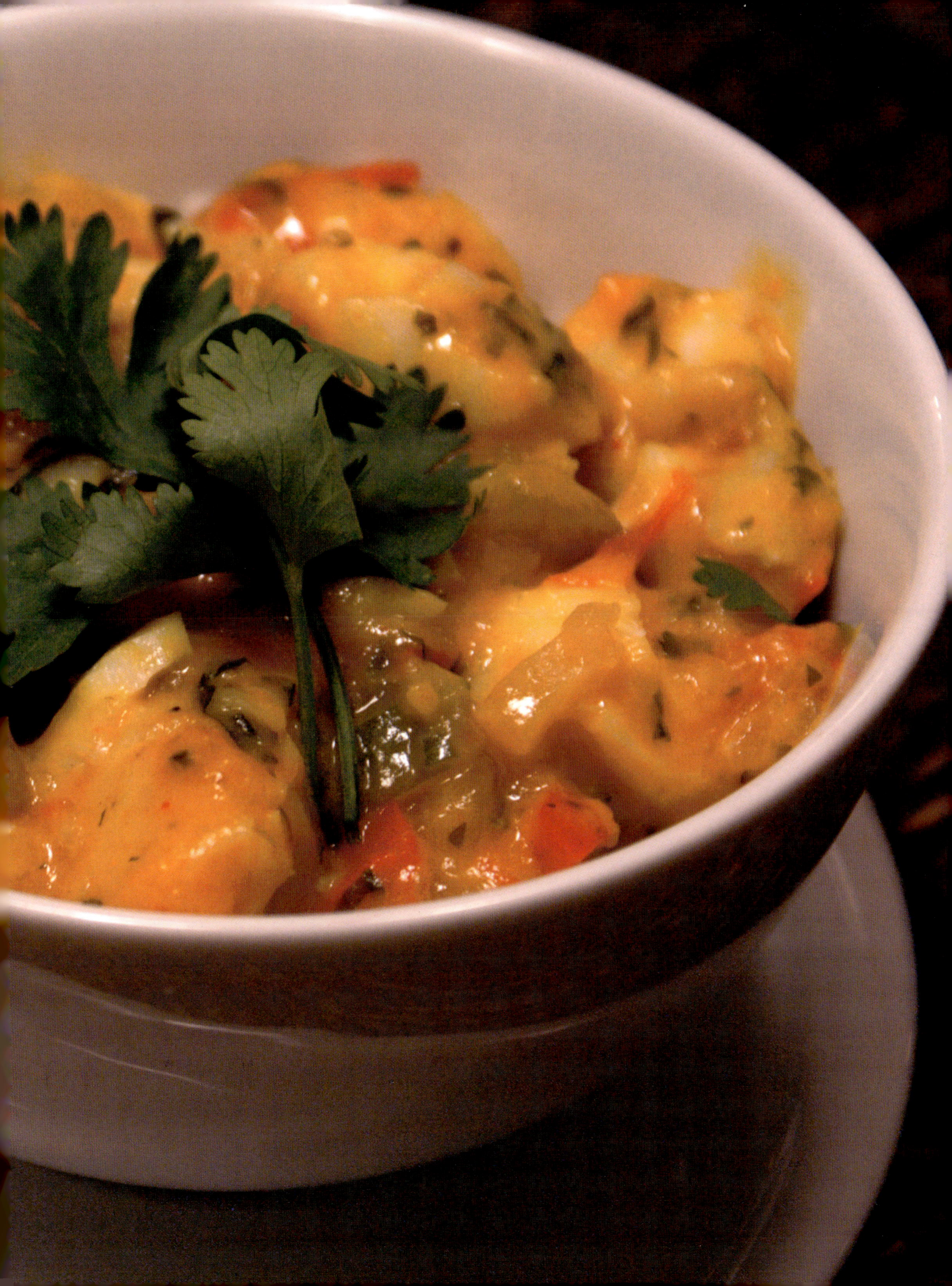

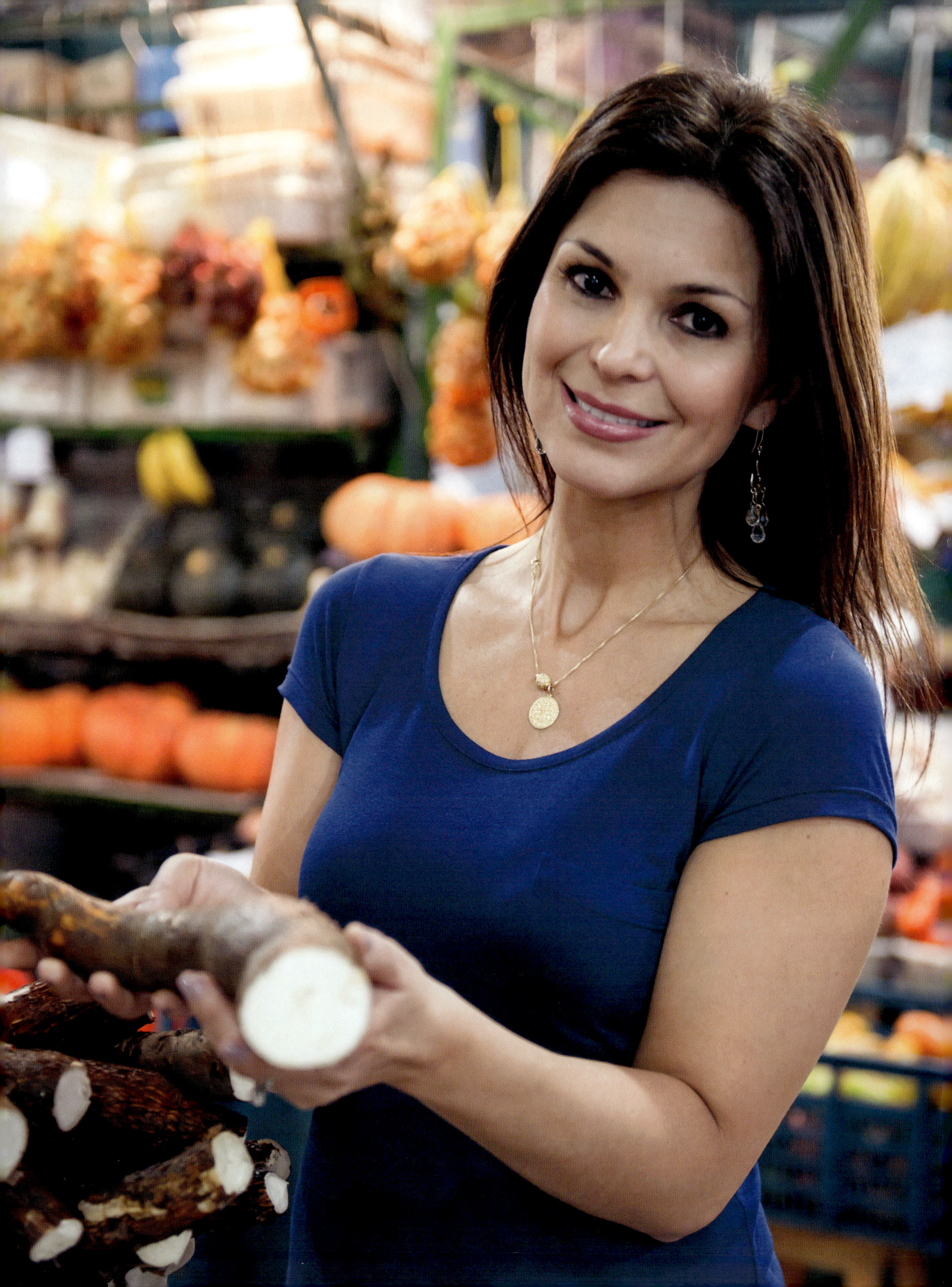

Chicken
(Aves)

Brazilian Chicken Stew (Chicken Bobó) 88

Chicken Fricassee (Fricassé de Frango) 90

Chicken in a Pumpkin with Coconut Milk

(Frango na Abóbora com Leite de Coco) 93

Chicken Pot Pie, Brazilian Style (Empadão de Frango) 94

Brazilian Chicken Stew
(Chicken Bobó)

Chicken Bobó is a traditional stew especially popular in Northeast Brazil. This delightful recipe might have an exotic name, but the method is quite simple. The secret to making this recipe so flavorful and creamy is to cook the yuca in chicken broth, then process it in blender or food processor to use as the thickening agent. Coconut milk and red palm oil add richness and a beautiful color to this gluten-free recipe. Serve over a bed of rice, and Farofa (page 105) on the side.

Serves 6

- 1 pound yuca (cassava)
- 3 to 4 cups low-sodium chicken broth
- 2 tablespoons vegetable oil
- 2 pounds mixed chicken thighs and breast, bones and skin removed, diced
- 1 large onion, finely sliced
- 1 red bell pepper, seeded and finely sliced
- 1 green bell pepper, seeded and finely sliced
- 2 large garlic cloves, minced
- 3 medium tomatoes, chopped
- 1 cup unsweetened coconut milk
- ½ cup red palm oil (dendê oil)
- 2 tablespoons red chili paste
- 1 cup cilantro, chopped
- 1 cup scallions, chopped
- Salt and freshly ground pepper

Peel yuca using a vegetable peeler. Transfer to a large pan and add chicken broth, covering all pieces. If yuca is too long to fit in pan, cut in half crosswise. Cover and cook on medium heat 40 to 60 minutes until yuca is soft.

Carefully remove yuca from pan and transfer to a plate, reserving liquid. Cool 10 minutes then remove the stem from the center. While still warm, smash the yuca with a fork.

Transfer yuca and cooking liquid to a blender. Blend until smooth. Set aside.

In a large sauce pan, heat oil on high until shimmering. Add chicken and sear 2 minutes. Add onions, red bell pepper, green bell pepper, and garlic. Cook 5 minutes, stirring occasionally. Add tomatoes, stir well and cover. Cook until all vegetables are soft and chicken is cooked through, 8 to 10 minutes. Add the yuca, coconut milk, red palm oil, and red chili paste. Cook another 2 minutes. Remove from heat and fold in cilantro and scallions. Season with salt and pepper. Serve over a bed of rice, or as a soup.

Cook's Notes

Red Palm Oil (also known as dendê oil) can be found in international grocery stores. It is also available online. This specialty oil adds an interesting earthy flavor and a beautiful bright orange color to this dish.

Yuca (or cassava) is a potato-like root. It can be found in major grocery stores or at international and Latin markets.

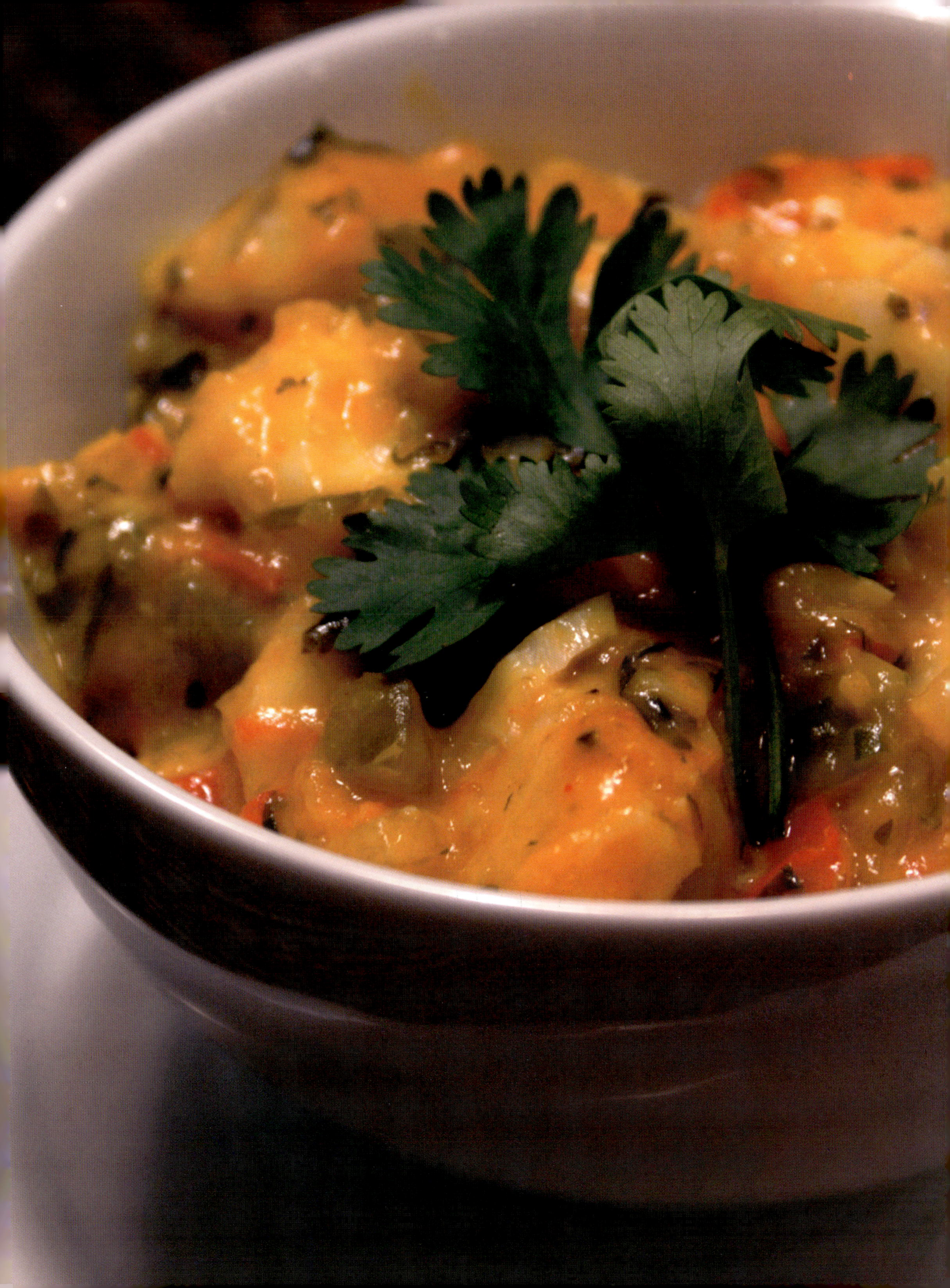

Chicken Fricassee
(Fricassé de Frango)

Originally from France, this recipe has been adopted by many different countries with slight variations. The Brazilian version is creamy with lots of herbs for extra flavor. Super easy to make, it is one of my go-to recipes when throwing large parties because it can be made in advance and stored in the refrigerator until it is time to top with cheese and bake.

Serves 6

3 cups low-sodium chicken stock
2 medium skinless chicken breasts, with bones attached
4 garlic cloves, peeled and sliced
2 sprigs thyme
2 tablespoons butter
1 medium onion, finely chopped
1 tablespoon flour
Salt and freshly ground black pepper
1 cup *crème fraîche* or Media Crema (table cream)
2 tablespoons scallions, finely chopped
2 tablespoons flat-leaf parsley, finely chopped
1 cup mozzarella cheese, shredded

Directions

In a medium sauce pan, combine chicken stock, chicken breasts, garlic, thyme and bring to a boil. Cover, reduce heat to medium and cook 40 minutes until meat is fully cooked. Remove chicken from broth and set aside to cool.

Strain broth and set aside (there should be about 1 ½ cups left). Discard thyme stems, saving small strained pieces (garlic, thyme leaves, and small pieces of chicken).

Shred chicken breasts into very small pieces, discarding any bones. Do not use a food processor.

Turn on oven broiler.

Heat butter in a large skillet until foamy. Add onions and cook 4 minutes until soft, stirring often. Stir in chicken. Dissolve flour in the broth. Stirring constantly, slowly add broth to the chicken until it thickens. Remove from heat and season with salt and pepper. Fold in *crème fraîche* (or Media Crema), scallions, and parsley.

Transfer chicken to a medium ovenproof deep dish. Top with mozzarella cheese and broil until cheese is melted. Remove from oven and serve immediately with a side of jasmine rice or sautéed potatoes.

Cook's Notes

Media Crema (table cream) can be found in the Latin section of large grocery stores. It is more affordable than *crème fraîche*.

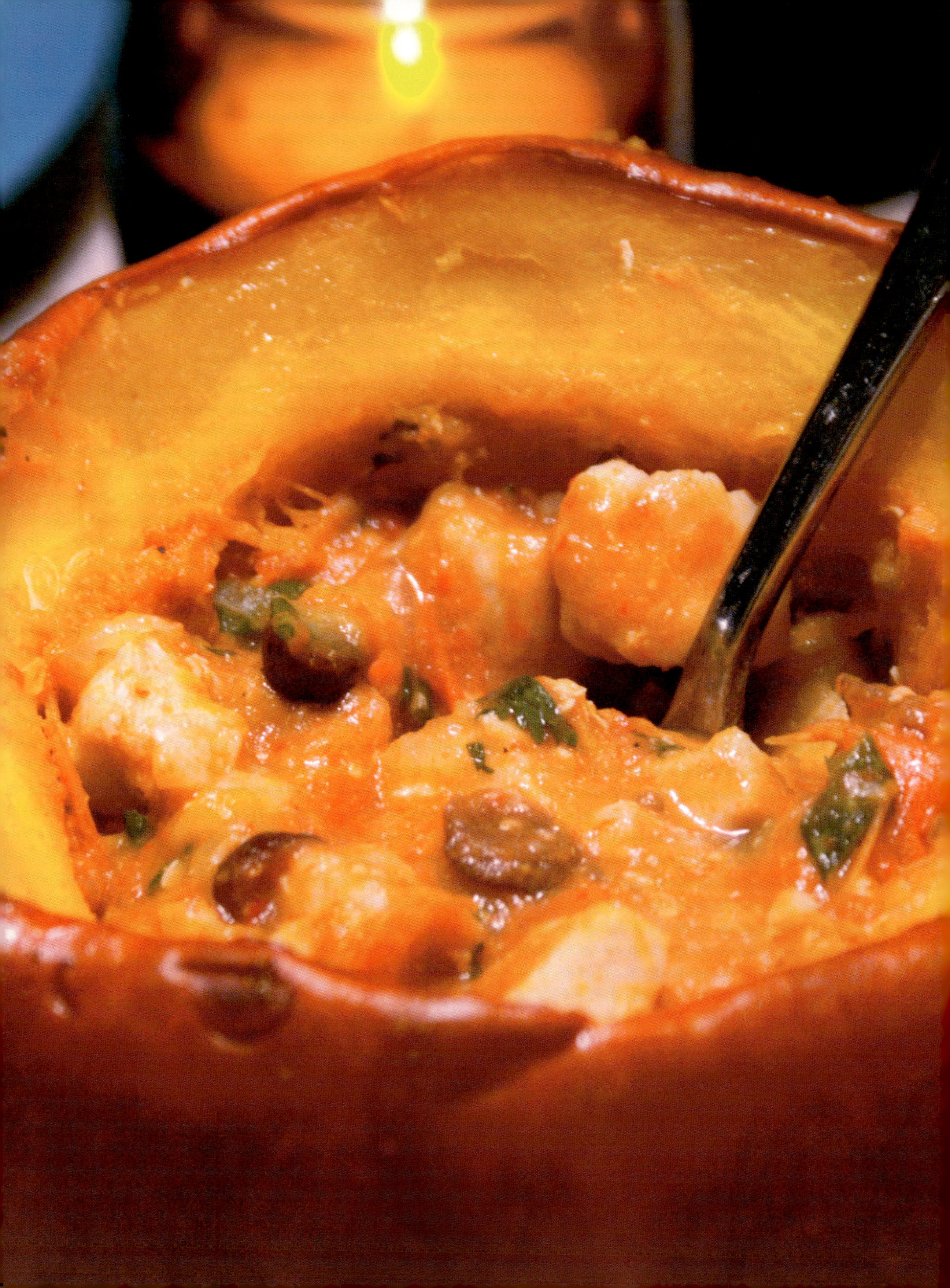

Chicken in a Pumpkin with Coconut Milk
(Frango na Abóbora com Leite de Coco)

Brazilians mix pumpkin and coconut in both sweet and savory dishes. This creamy and aromatic entrée features chicken smothered in coconut milk. When serving, scoop the flesh of the pumpkin along with the chicken sauce. Serve over rice.

Serves 6 to 8

2 tablespoons canola oil
2 ½ pounds chicken breast, diced
Salt and freshly ground black pepper
1 medium onion, chopped
1 red bell pepper, seeded and chopped
1 yellow bell pepper, seeded and chopped
4 garlic cloves, minced
1 tablespoon fresh ginger, peeled and minced
4 large tomatoes, chopped
1 tablespoon chicken base

1 tablespoon chili paste
½ cup raisins
2 tablespoons brown sugar
1 cup coconut milk
3 tablespoons cilantro, chopped
3 tablespoons scallions, chopped
2 medium size pumpkins

In a large skillet, heat canola oil on high heat until shimmering. Season chicken with salt and pepper and sear 2 minutes. Reduce heat to medium and stir in onion, red bell pepper, yellow bell pepper, garlic and ginger. Cook 5 minutes, stirring occasionally, until vegetables are soft. Add tomatoes and cook 7 minutes. Add chicken base, chili paste, raisins, brown sugar, and coconut milk. Cook 2 minutes. Season lightly with salt and pepper. Remove from heat and fold in cilantro and scallions. Set aside.

Preheat oven to 325 degrees F. With a sharp knife, carefully remove top of pumpkins and save. Remove seeds. Divide chicken sauce evenly and add to pumpkins. Replace tops and bake 45 to 60 minutes, until pumpkin is fully cooked.

Carefully remove from oven and let stand 10 minutes before serving. To serve, scoop out some pumpkin and sauce and place in individual bowls.

Cook's Notes

Baby Pam and Small Sugar are the best pumpkin varieties for this recipe.

Chicken Pot Pie, Brazilian Style
(Empadão de Frango)

This savory chicken pie is a staple in Brazil. Many different versions are available, but I really like this one because the dough is simple to make and it turns out amazingly crumbly, the kind of dough that melts in your mouth! The filling is really moist. You can add or remove vegetables to preference. This is my mom's recipe and it is one my favorite comfort foods!

Serves 10

Dough Ingredients:
3 sticks butter, room temperature
3 ½ cups all-purpose flour, plus additional for topping
2 egg yolks
1 teaspoon baking powder
½ teaspoon salt

Filling Ingredients:
1 ½ pounds bone-in chicken breast
1 pound bone-in chicken thighs
5 to 6 cups water
1 large garlic clove, roughly chopped
2 bay leaves
Salt
2 tablespoons canola oil
1 medium onion, finely chopped
3 rosemary sprigs, chopped
3 tablespoons cornstarch
4 tablespoons tomato paste
Freshly ground black pepper
1 cup frozen sweet corn (optional)
1 cup frozen sweet peas (optional)
½ cup black olives, chopped (optional)
1 cup hearts- of-palm, chopped (optional)
½ cup scallions, finely chopped
½ cup flat-leaf parsley, finely chopped

Dough Directions

Place butter, all-purpose flour, egg yolks, baking powder and salt in bowl and mix well. Do not knead the dough; it is not supposed to be really smooth. Cover and let rest 30 minutes. Cover the bottom and sides of a 10-inch cheesecake pan. Start pressing the dough on the bottom, slowly moving it up the sides. Press dough until really thin, about 1/8-inch thick.

Remove and save excess. Prick tiny holes over surface with a fork.

Add 1 cup all-purpose flour to remaining dough and crumble it.

Pre-heat oven to 375 degrees F.

Place chicken filling in the pan, leaving about 3/4-inch room on top. Cover with dough crumbles and bake 25 to 30 minutes, until the top is golden brown. Remove from oven and let cool 10 minutes before serving. Serve warm or at room temperature.

For a convection oven, bake 17 to 20 minutes at 350 degrees F, or until top is golden brown.

Filling Directions

Add chicken breast and thighs to a large pan; cover with water and add garlic and bay leaves. Season with salt and bring to a boil. Reduce heat to medium and cook 50 to 60 minutes partially covered until chicken is cooked through.

Remove chicken from pan and let cool. Strain and reserve broth.

Discard skin and bones and shred chicken into small pieces. Do not use a food processor.

Heat canola oil in a large sauce pan over medium-high heat until shimmering. Add onion and cook 3 minutes, stirring occasionally, until soft. Add rosemary and chicken and cook 1 minute, stirring. Add ¾ of the reserved broth to the pan. Dissolve corn starch in remaining broth. Reduce heat to medium and slowly add the corn starch broth to the pan, stirring constantly. Add tomato paste and cook 3 minutes, stirring constantly. Season with black pepper. Turn off heat and fold in corn, peas, olives, and hearts-of-palm. Fold in scallions and parsley, adding additional salt if necessary.

Cook's Notes

If making this pie without the corn, peas, olives and hearts-of-palm, add 2 more cups of shredded chicken to filling.

Sides
(Acompanhamentos)

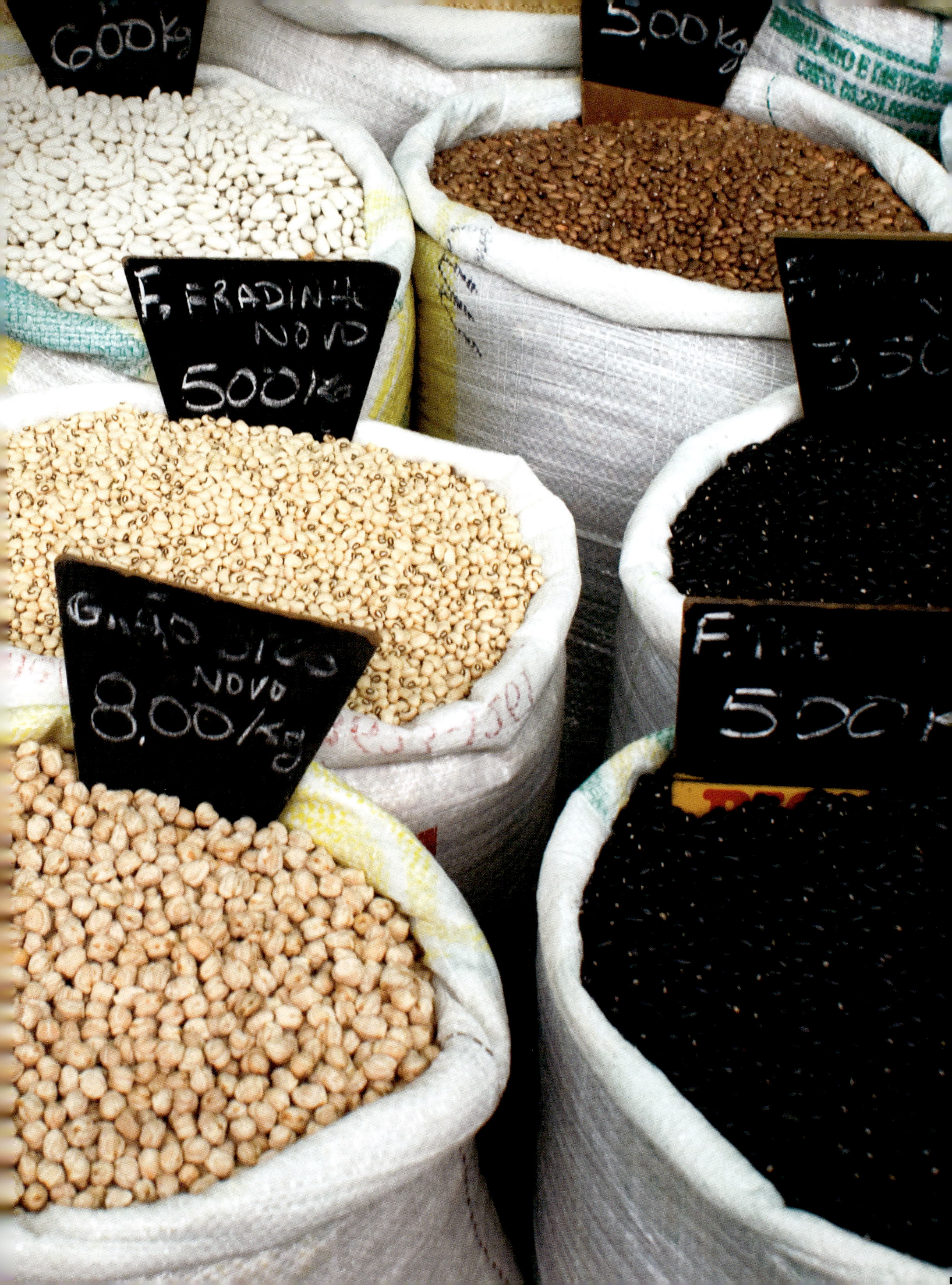
6,00Kg
5,00Kg
F. FRADINH
NOVO
500Kg
NOVO
8,00/Kg

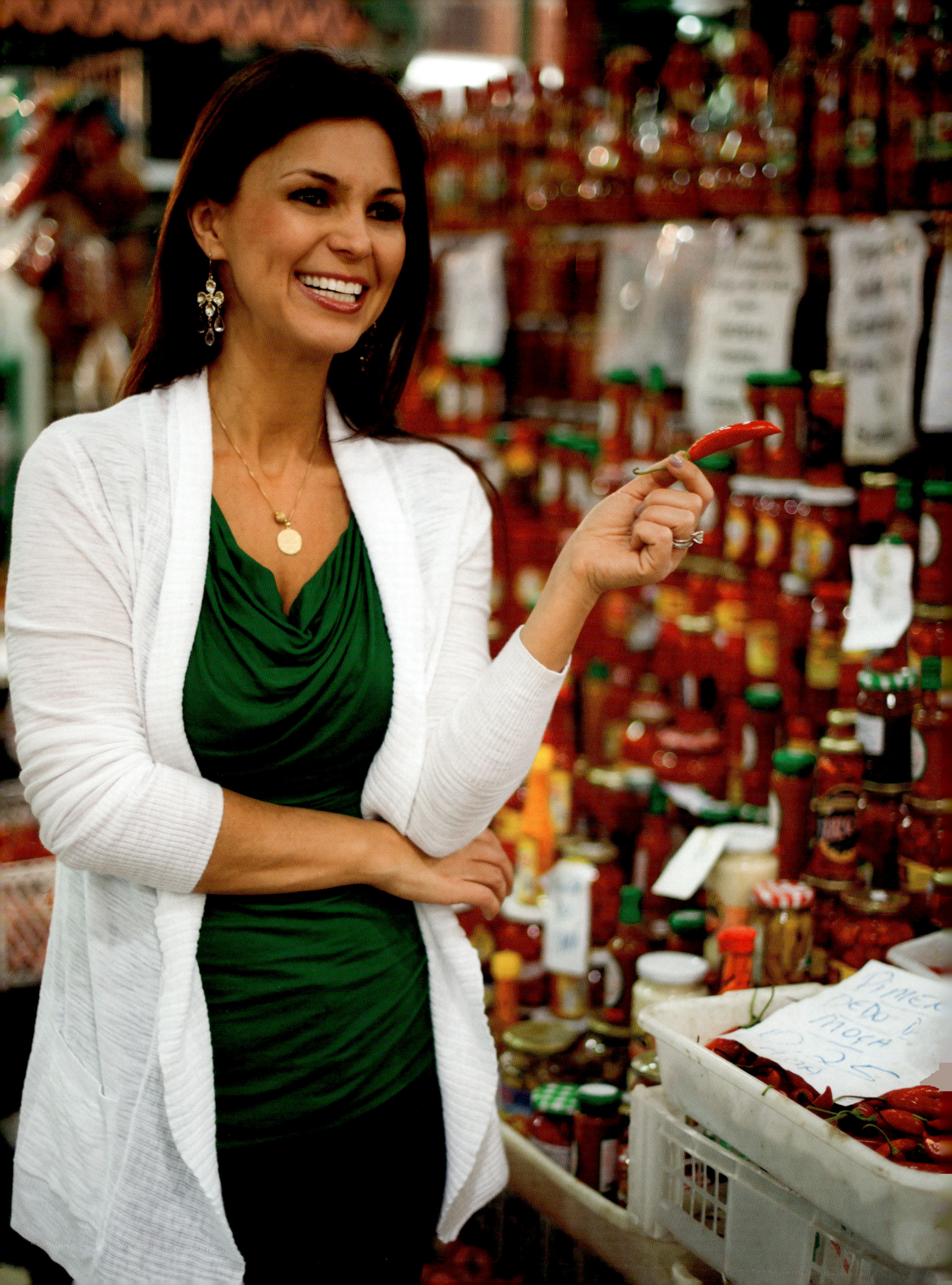

Sides
(Acompanhamentos)

Black Beans (Feijão Preto) 101
Rice (Arroz Branco) 103
Farofa 105

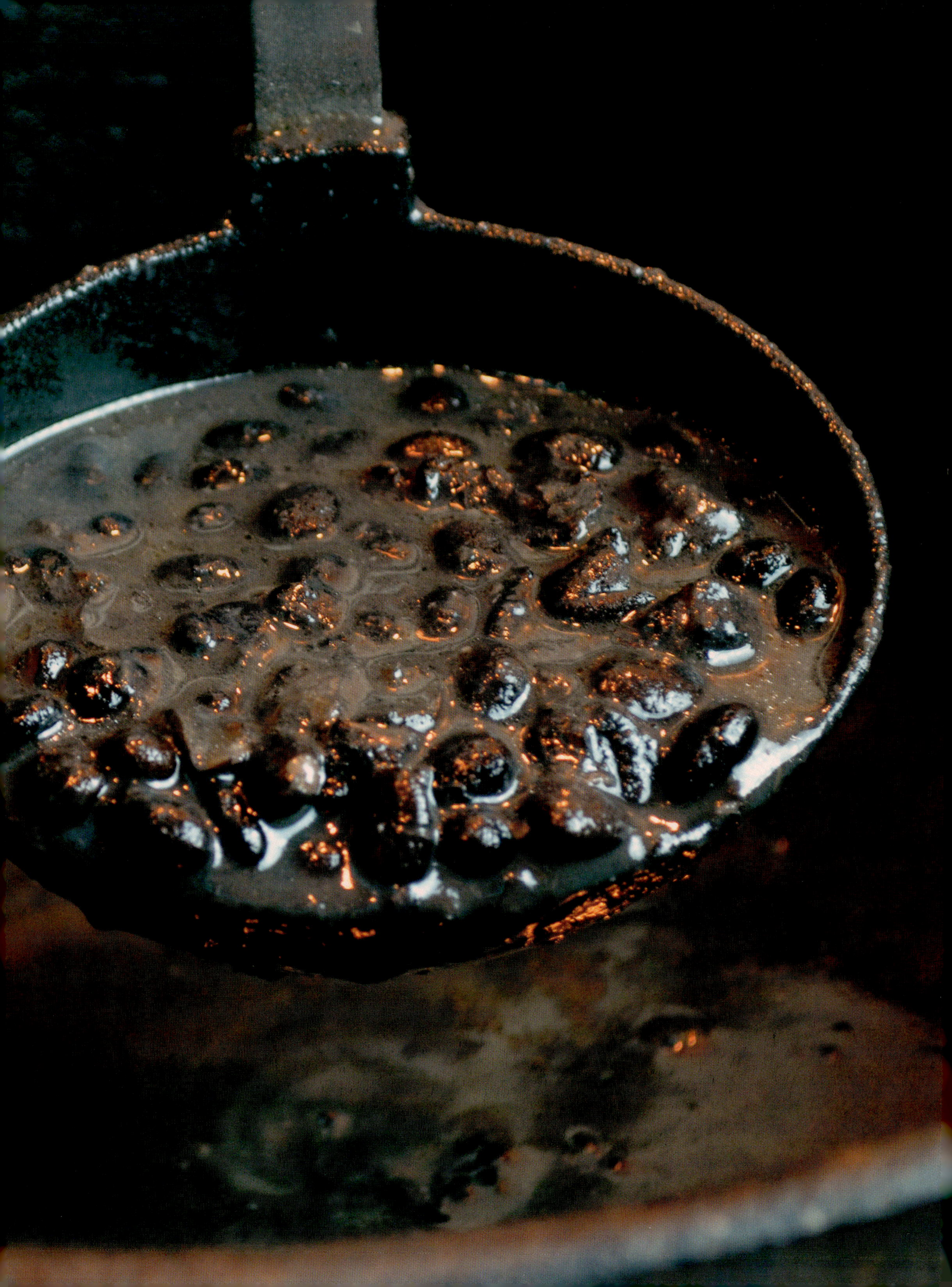

Black Beans
(Feijão Preto)

I grew up eating a combination of black beans, rice, meat and a simple salad five times a week. Only on weekends would we eat something more special. Sodas were also only allowed on Sundays. For me, beans are part of the simplest and most comforting of all meals. When prepared with the added flavors of onions, garlic, bay leaves and bacon, black beans are delicious and often become more than a side dish, shadowing the main dish, usually meat, chicken or fish. They are also nutritious and filling, especially when cooked from scratch. If I close my eyes I can still hear the loud sound of the pressure cooker, and smell the scents coming from the large pot of beans being prepared. Through this recipe, I am sharing a little piece of mom's everyday kitchen.

Yields 6 cups

16 ounces black beans
6 cups water
2 tablespoons olive oil
1 medium onion, finely diced

4 ounces bacon, diced (optional)
5 garlic cloves, minced
2 dried bay leaves
Salt

In a large colander, rinse beans thoroughly. Transfer to a large bowl. Sort and cover with water. Allow to soak overnight, or at least 6 to 8 hours.

In a large pot over medium high heat, add olive oil, onions and bacon. Cook 4 to 5 minutes stirring occasionally until onions are soft and bacon is cooked. Stir in garlic and bay leaves, and cook an additional minute. Add beans and soaking water. Bring to a boil and reduce heat to medium-low. Cover partially and simmer 1 ½ to 2 hours until beans are tender. Turn off heat and remove bay leaves. Serve over jasmine rice.

Cook's Notes

To achieve a thicker broth, place one cup of cooked beans in a food processor and pulse 4 to 5 times, until a thick paste forms. Add to bean pot and serve.

If you have a pressure cooker, you can use it to cook the beans and reduce both soaking and cooking times. Soaking time can be reduced 2 hours; and the cooking time can be reduced 45 to 50 minutes.

Sometimes, bacon can be left out of this traditional Brazilian recipe. I highly recommend the use of bacon because it adds a delicious smoky flavor to the beans.

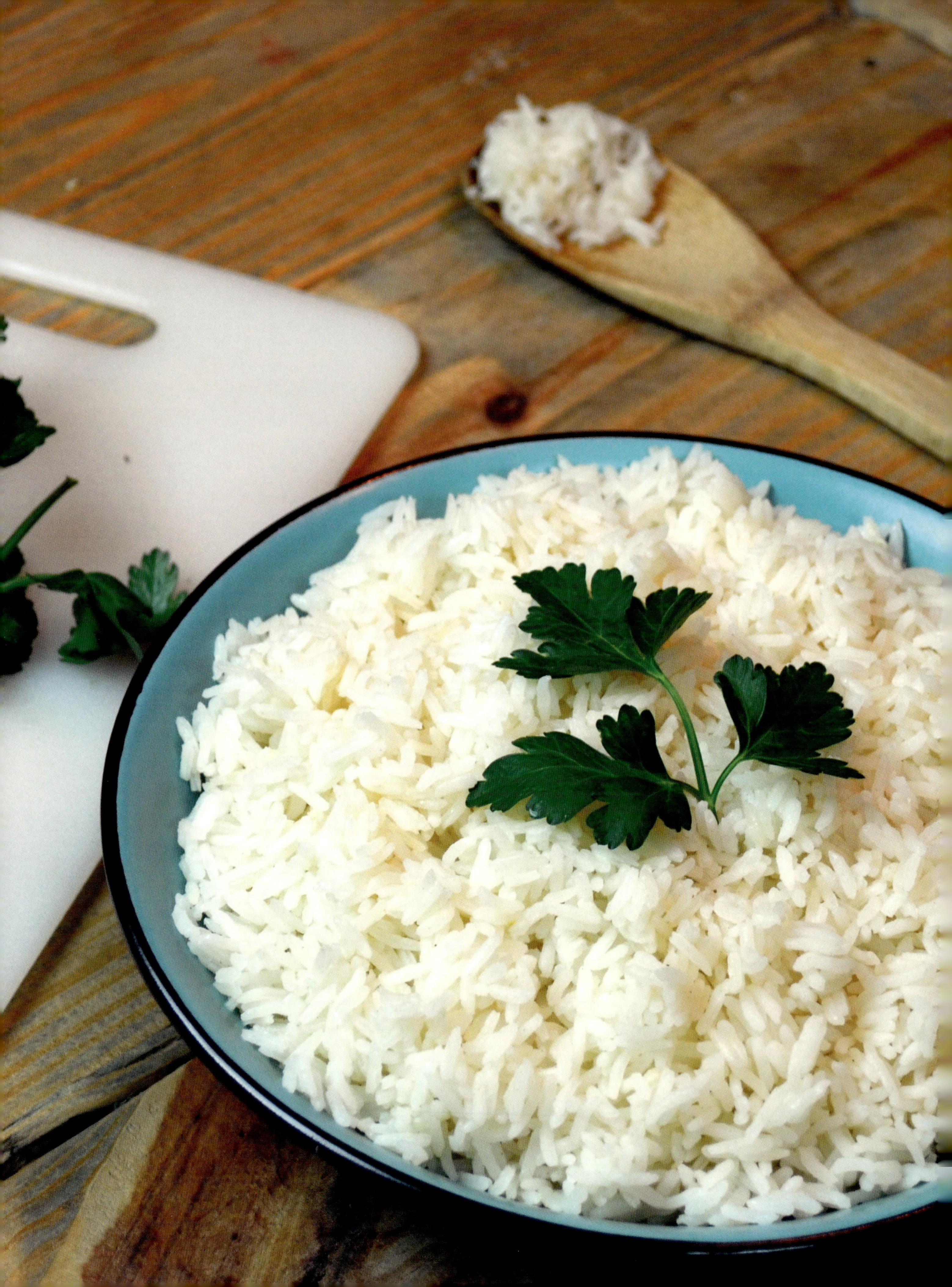

Rice
(Arroz Branco)

The ever-popular combination of rice paired with black beans, "Arroz com Feijão", is featured daily in Brazilian households. Since rice makers are not popular in Brazil, I decided to share the traditional, and easy, method. It only takes 15 to 20 minutes and the rice turns out fluffy, with a perfect texture and delicious flavor.

Yields 2 Cups

2 tablespoons butter
2 medium garlic cloves, minced
1 cup jasmine rice
1 ¼ cups boiling water
Salt

In a medium sauce pan over medium high heat, melt butter. Add garlic and rice; stir well to coat grains. Cook one minute. Add water, season with salt and stir once. Allow to come to a rapid boil. Cover and reduce heat to medium-low. Cook 10 to 13 minutes until water has been absorbed. Remove from heat and let sit, covered, 10 minutes. Fluff with a fork and serve immediately.

Cook's Notes

If using white rice instead of jasmine rice, increase water to 1 ¾ cups. Follow directions above, increasing the cooking time to 15 to 18 minutes.

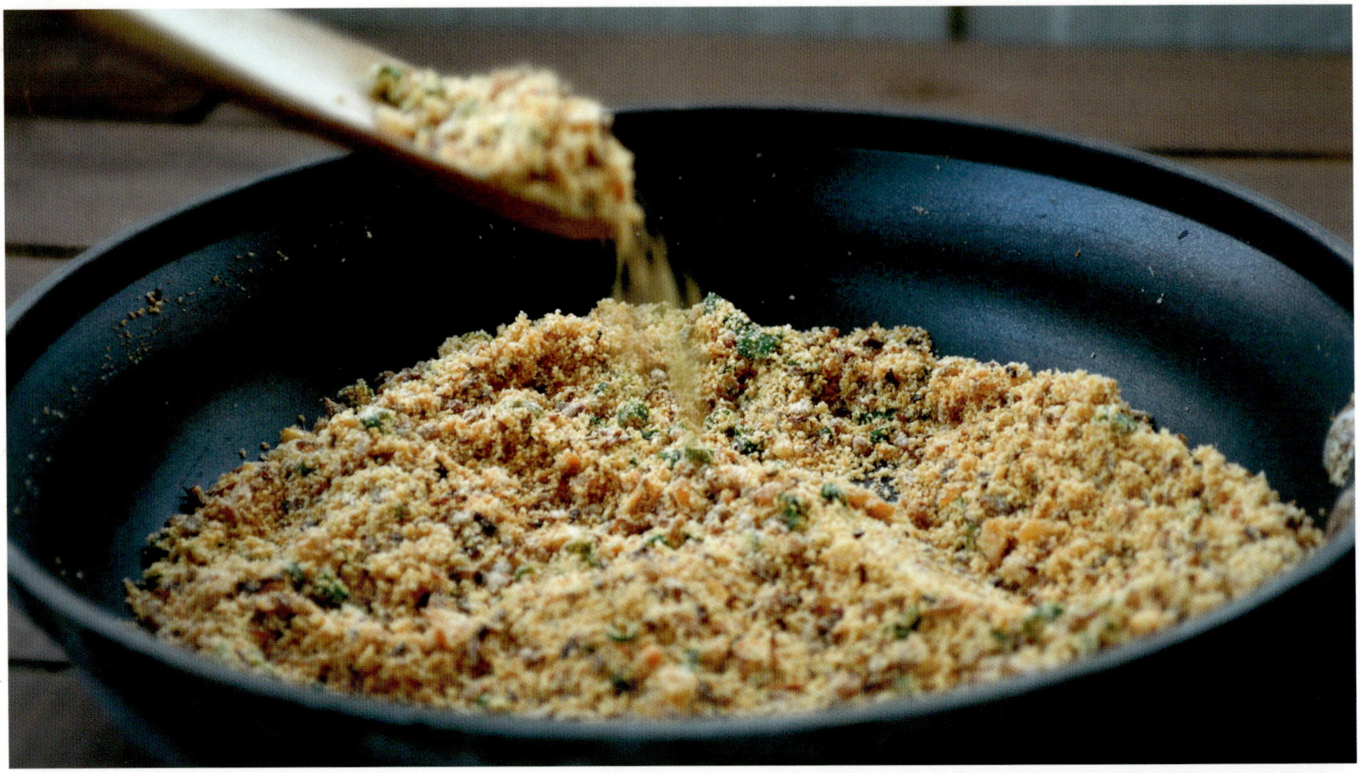

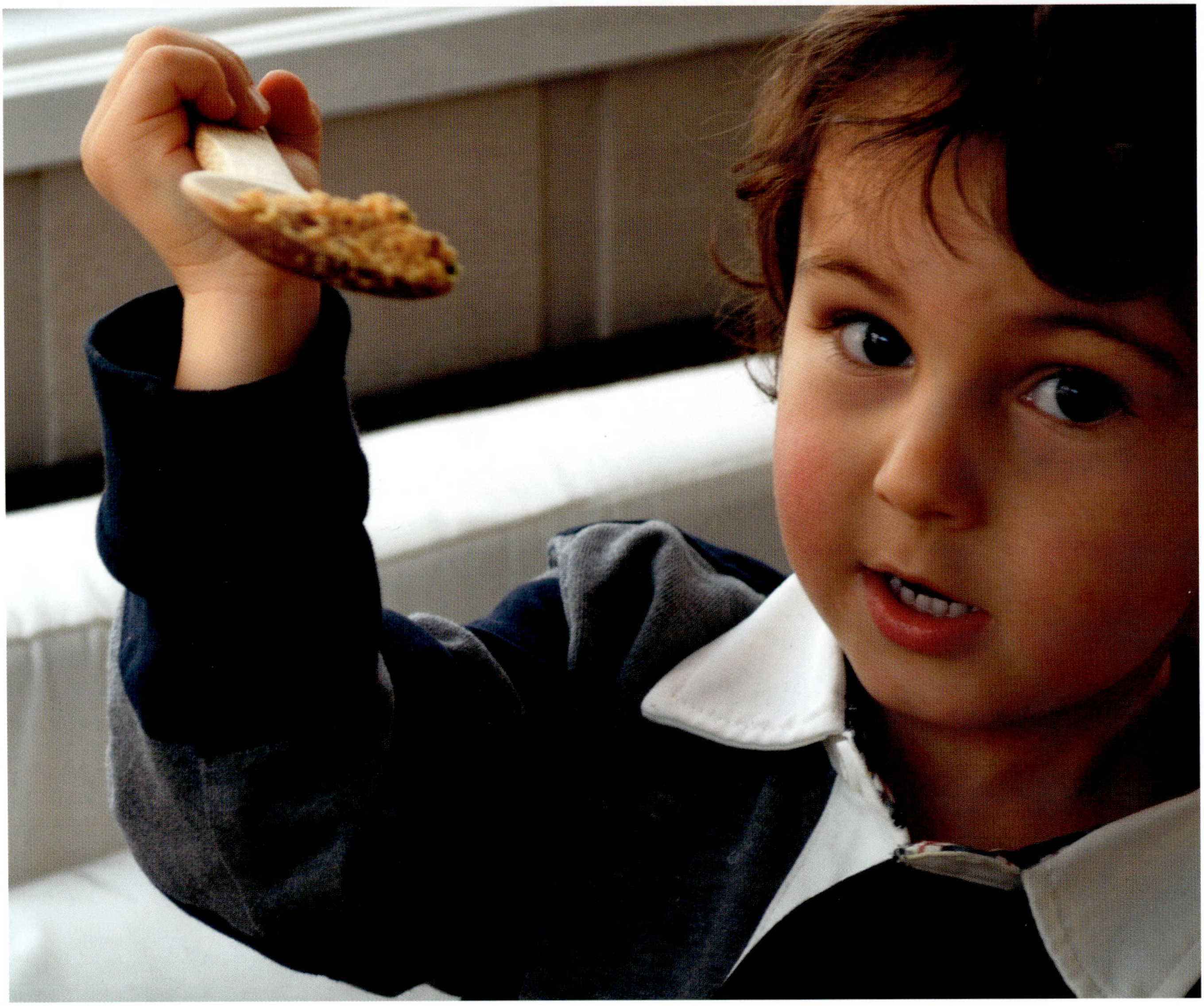

Farofa

Don't be fooled by the "dirty sand" look of this typical Brazilian side dish! Farofa is a delicious, crunchy side dish (or stuffing) that is eaten on a daily basis all over Brazil. Given the fact that Brazil is a huge country with a large variety of dishes from region to region, achieving that level of popularity is pretty impressive. It certainly does not taste like dirty sand. Farofa is crunchy and full of intense flavors that enhance the texture and add an interesting taste to the main course. It is almost like a crunchy hot sauce, but without the heat. It is extremely simple to make, but exotic at the same time.

Makes 2 Cups

3 tablespoons butter
2 tablespoons extra virgin olive oil
1 medium onion, finely diced
3 garlic cloves, minced
1 ½ cups yuca flour (manioc flour)
¼ teaspoon dried coriander
½ teaspoon smoked paprika
Salt and freshly ground black pepper
½ cup scallions, finely chopped

In a medium skillet melt butter and olive oil over medium-high heat until shimmering. Add onions and cook, stirring often, until translucent, 3 minutes. Add garlic and cook 40 seconds. Add yuca flour, dried coriander, and smoked paprika. Cook 7 to 9 minutes, stirring often, until golden brown. Remove from heat. Season with salt and pepper. Fold in scallions and serve.

Cook's Notes

Other ingredients can be added to farofa. Among the most common are: bacon, smoked meat, raisins, black olives, nuts and bananas. Farofa may be sprinkled over meats, used as stuffing for poultry, or served as a side dish.

Desserts
(Sobremesas)

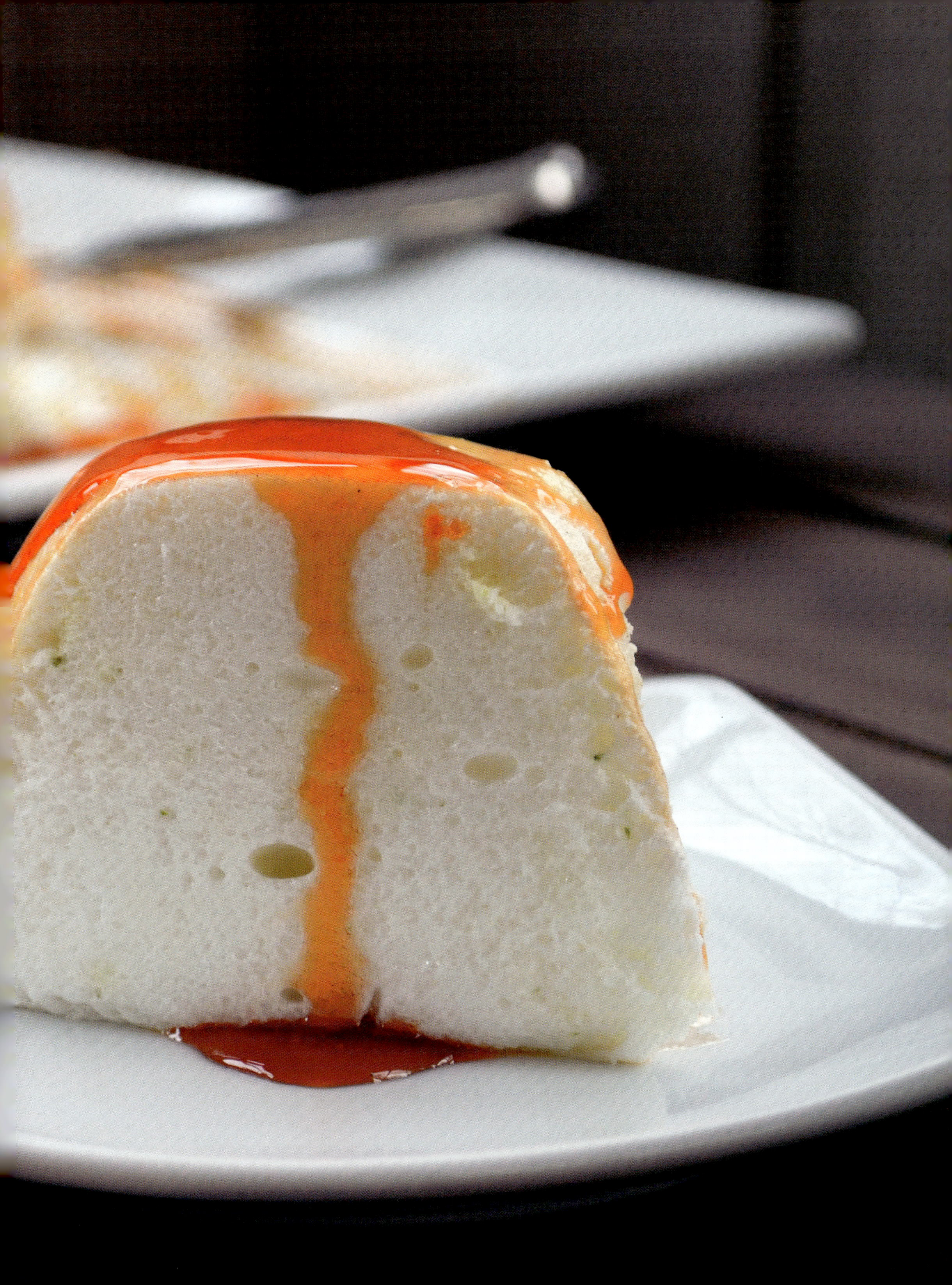

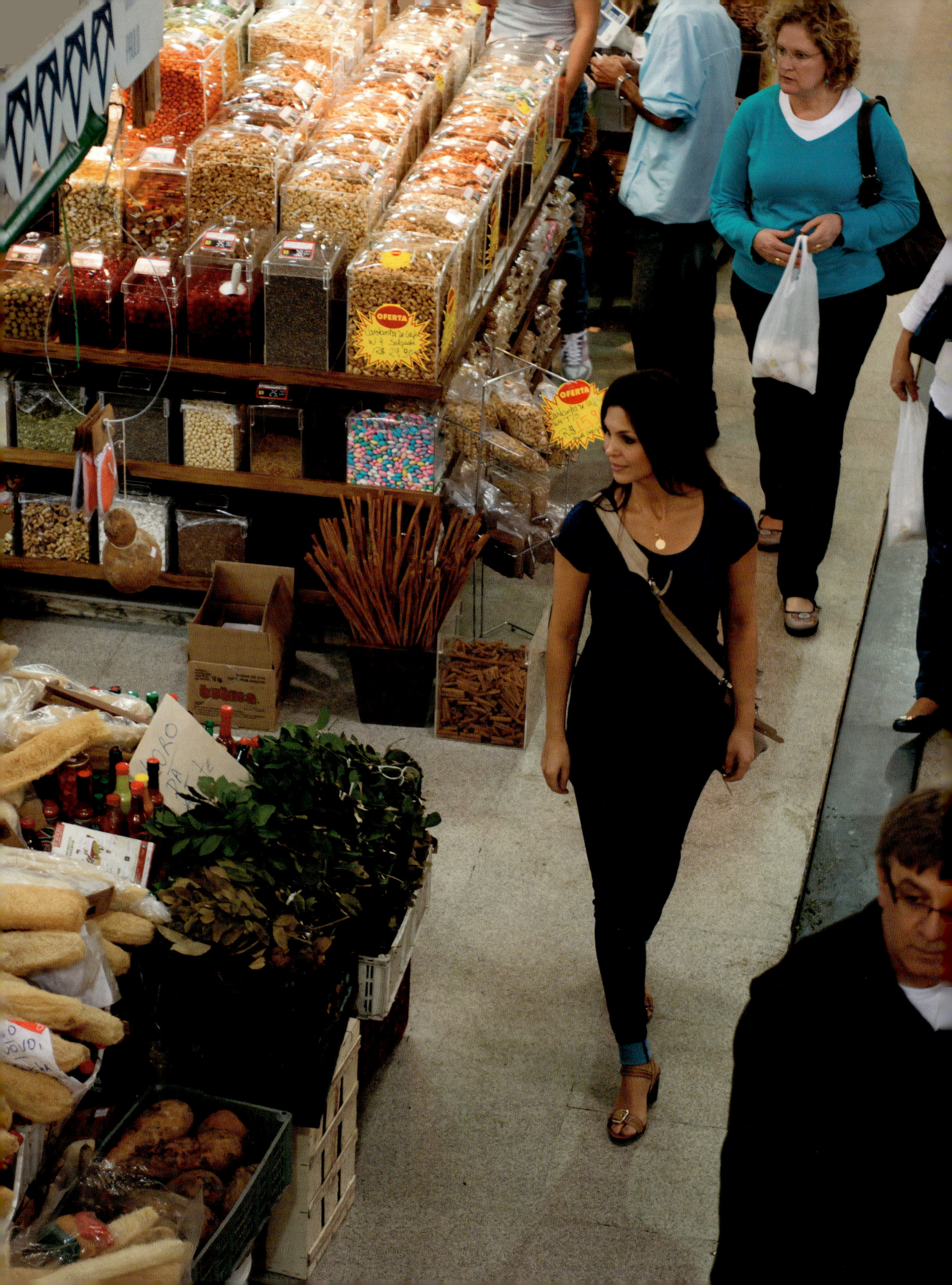
OFERTA
W4 Salgada
OFERTA

Desserts
(Sobremesas)

Avocado and Candied Cashews Pie
(Torta de Abacate com Castanhas de Caju) 110

Brigadeiro: The Famous Brazilian Chocolate Bonbon 113

Cheese Flan with Guava Sauce (Pudim Romeu e Julieta) 114

Coconut Balls (Beijinho de Coco) 117

Coconut Flan (Pudim de Coco) 119

Dulce de Leche and Coconut Layer Cake
(Torta Recheada com Doce de Leite e Coco) 120

Dulce de Monkey (Gelado de Doce de Leite e Banana) 125

Classic Brazilian Flan (Pudim de Leite Condensado) 127

Guava and Cheese Mousse (Mousse Romeu e Julieta) 129

Lime Meringue Flan (Pudim de Claras) 131

Passion Fruit Pie (Torta Mousse de Maracujá) 132

Salted Caramel and Guava Pie (Torta de Goiabada com Doce de Leite) 135

Brazilian Strawberry Shortcake (Torta Gelada de Morangos) 136

Avocado and Candied Cashews Pie
(Torta de Abacate com Castanhas de Caju)

I grew up having avocado in desserts. In fact, the first time I had avocado in a savory dish was in 2000 after I moved to the US. Avocado mousses, ice cream, and shakes are common Brazilian desserts, and my Avocado and Candied Cashew Pie is a unique and delicious combination.

Crust Serves 10

Crust Ingredients:
3 ½ cups Graham crackers, roughly crushed
8 tablespoons butter, softened
½ cup unsalted cashews, coarsely chopped
½ cup sugar

Filling Ingredients:
2 large avocados, coarsely chopped
1 can (14 ounces) sweetened condensed milk
2 teaspoons unflavored gelatin
¼ cup hot water
4 egg whites
½ cup unsalted cashews, coarsely chopped
4 tablespoons sugar

Pre-heat oven to 350 degrees.

Add Graham crackers, butter, cashews, and sugar to a food processor. Process 2 minutes, until incorporated. Press mixture into 9 inch pie dish. Using a fork, prick small holes all over crust surface.

Bake for 8 minutes, until golden brown. For a convection oven, bake at 300 degrees F for 6 minutes.

Filling Directions

In a food processor, add avocados and sweetened condensed milk. Process until smooth, about 1 ½ minutes.

Whisk gelatin and hot water until smooth. Carefully fold into avocado mixture. Set aside.

Using a hand mixer, beat egg whites at high speed 4 minutes until soft peaks form. They should be done when they don't fall if you turn the bowl upside down. Gently fold egg whites into avocado mixture.

Place avocado filling in pie crust. Refrigerate 4 hours.

In a medium skillet, combine cashews and sugar. Cook over medium heat, stirring constantly, until the sugar caramelizes and covers cashews evenly. Set aside and cool completely. Remove from skillet and crumble.

Sprinkle candied cashews on top of pie. Slice and serve.

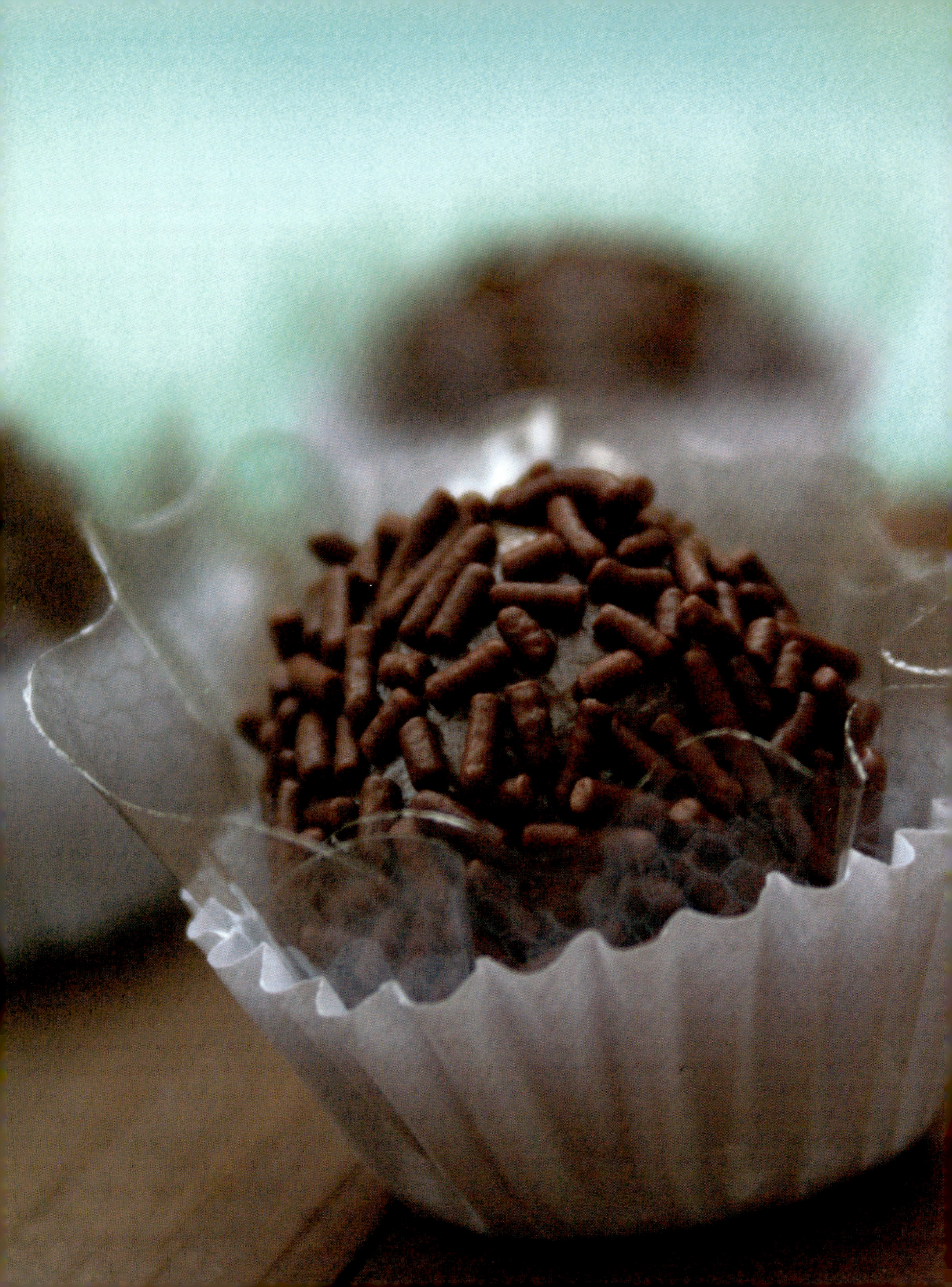

Brigadeiro
The Famous Brazilian Chocolate Bonbon

Brigadeiro is one of the most beloved sweets in Brazil. Easy to make and very popular at birthday parties, kids and adults love it! Creamy in the inside and crunchy on the outside, this bonbon is sometimes called Brazilian truffle and it is a must-try for chocolate lovers.

Yields 20 to 25 bonbons

2 tablespoons unsalted butter
1 can (14 ounces) sweetened condensed milk
3 tablespoons unsweetened cocoa powder
Chocolate sprinkles for topping

In a medium sauce pan set over medium heat, add butter, condensed milk and cocoa powder. Cook, stirring constantly, about 10 to 12 minutes until the mixture thickens and large air bubbles start to form on the surface (you should see quite a bit of the bottom of the pan). Remove from heat and transfer to a plate. Cool to room temperature or refrigerate.

Grease hands with butter or cooking spray. Take 1 teaspoon of mixture and roll into a ball. Roll each ball in chocolate sprinkles and place in small size candy cups. Serve at room temperature, or refrigerate and serve.

Cook's Notes

Certain guidelines must be followed in order to ensure success:

- Stir constantly
- Cook over medium heat
- Make sure the mixture is really thick before removing from heat. Being able to see quite a bit of the bottom of the pan while stirring is the best way to determine when the balls will not fall apart
- Let the mixture cool completely before rolling, or refrigerate for a couple of hours
- Grease hands as much as needed while rolling balls

Brigadeiro also makes a great filling or topping for cakes, brownies and cup cakes.

Cheese Flan with Guava Sauce
(Pudim Romeu e Julieta)

Guava paste and cheese is a classic combination in desserts, especially in the Brazilian state of Minas Gerais. It is so popular, that it has received the name "Romeu e Julieta" (Romeo and Juliette). This combination might sound unusual, but it is extremely successful and it is a hit in this flan recipe.

Serves 12

1 ½ cups sugar
2 cans (14 ounces each) sweetened condensed milk
2 cups whole milk
3 eggs
8 ounces cream cheese
½ cup guava paste, chopped
½ to 1 cup warm water

Pour sugar into a 10-inch mold pan and cook on medium heat directly on stove top for about 10 to 13 minutes, until it melts completely and turns golden brown. Swirl pan so caramel completely covers base and about an inch up sides of the pan. Allow to cool and harden.

Preheat oven to 350 degrees F. Mix sweetened condensed milk, whole milk, eggs, and cream cheese in a large blender. Blend 20 seconds. Strain into a large bowl, removing foam that forms on the surface.

Pour into the caramelized mold pan (caramel must be firm) and cover with aluminum foil.

Place mold pan in a large ovenproof dish filled up with 1 ½ inches of warm water. Carefully transfer to oven and bake 50 to 70 minutes. The flan is ready when a toothpick inserted in center comes out clean.

Remove flan from oven and let cool completely, at least 3 hours. Refrigerate 8 hours or overnight.

To unmold, gently run a small knife around the mold pan. Carefully, flip over to a large plate. Spread guava sauce on top and serve.

Guava Sauce Directions

Add guava paste to a blender or food processor. Slowly add water until desired thickness is achieved. Sauce should have a consistency similar to the caramel.

Cook's Notes

Guava paste can be found in the Latin section of major grocery stores, or at international grocery stores.

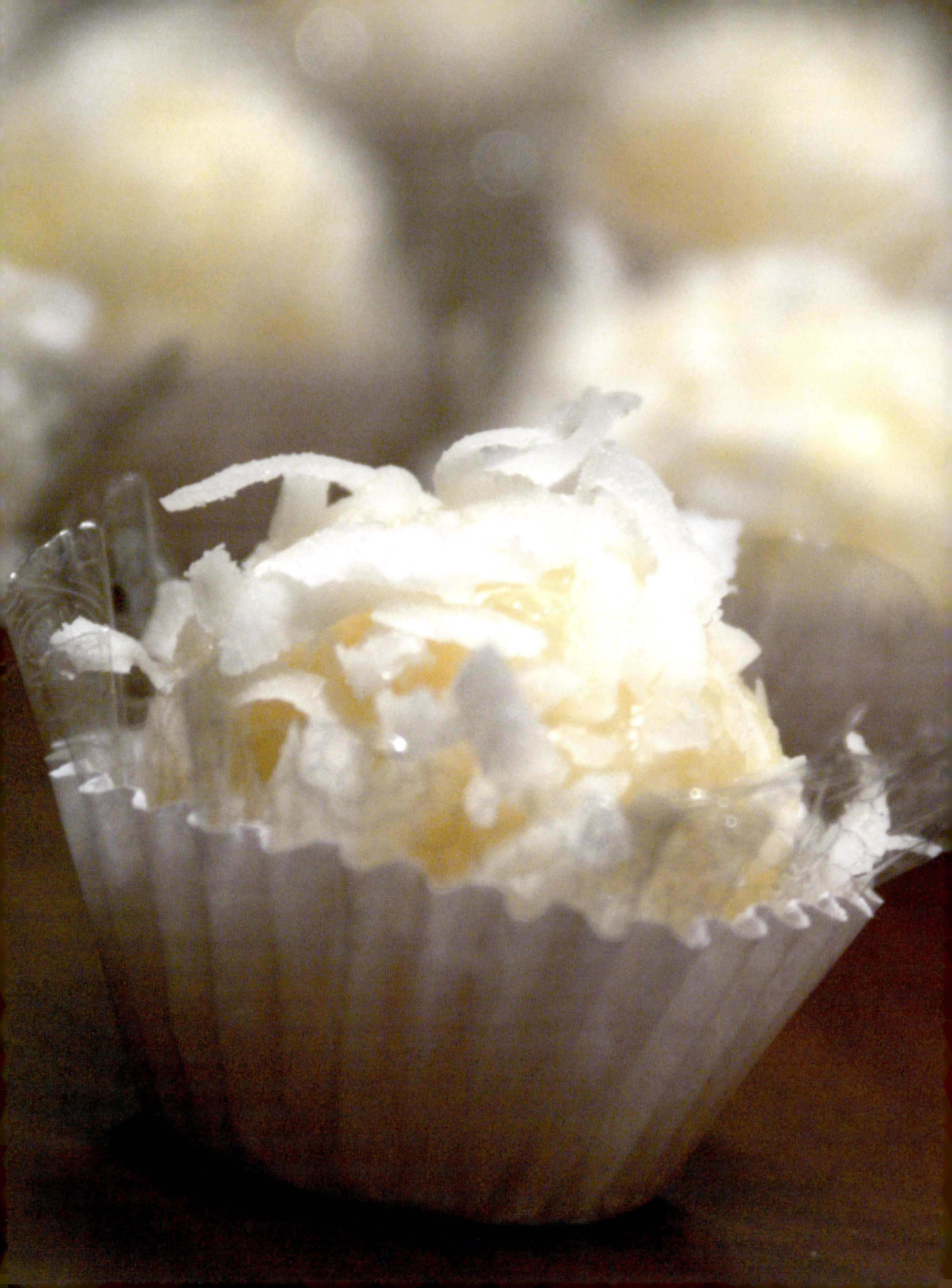

Coconut Balls
(Beijinho de Coco)

Just like Brigadeiros, Coconut Balls are very popular at Brazilian birthday parties pleasing to both kids and adults. Try to use fresh coconut, but if you can't find it, packed dried unsweetened coconut also tastes great. If you love coconut, you will love this!

Yields about 20 to 25 balls

2 tablespoons unsalted butter
1 can (14 ounces) sweetened condensed milk
1 ½ cups unsweetened coconut flakes

In a medium sauce pan set over medium heat, combine butter, sweetened condensed milk and 1 cup coconut flakes. Cook 10 to 12 minutes, stirring constantly, until mixture thickens and large air bubbles start to form on the surface (you will see quite a bit of the bottom of the pan). Remove from heat and transfer to a plate. Let stand, or refrigerate until cool.

Grease hands with butter or cooking spray. Roll 1 teaspoon of the mixture into a ball. Roll ball in remaining coconut flakes and place in small size candy cup. Repeat with each ball. Serve at room temperature or refrigerate until serving.

Cook's Notes

The guidelines for making this recipe successful are similar to the ones for Brigadeiro (page 113):

- Stir constantly
- Cook over medium heat
- Make sure the mixture is thick before removing from heat. Being able to see quite a bit of the bottom of the pan while stirring is the best way to make sure that the balls will not fall apart when rolling them
- Cool mixture completely before rolling, or refrigerate for a couple of hours before
- Grease hands as needed to make the work less messy and the balls look prettier

Fresh coconut flakes taste best. While frozen grated coconut flakes works well for the dough, it can't be frozen for sprinkling the balls. Fresh and frozen coconut flakes are available at international or Latin markets.

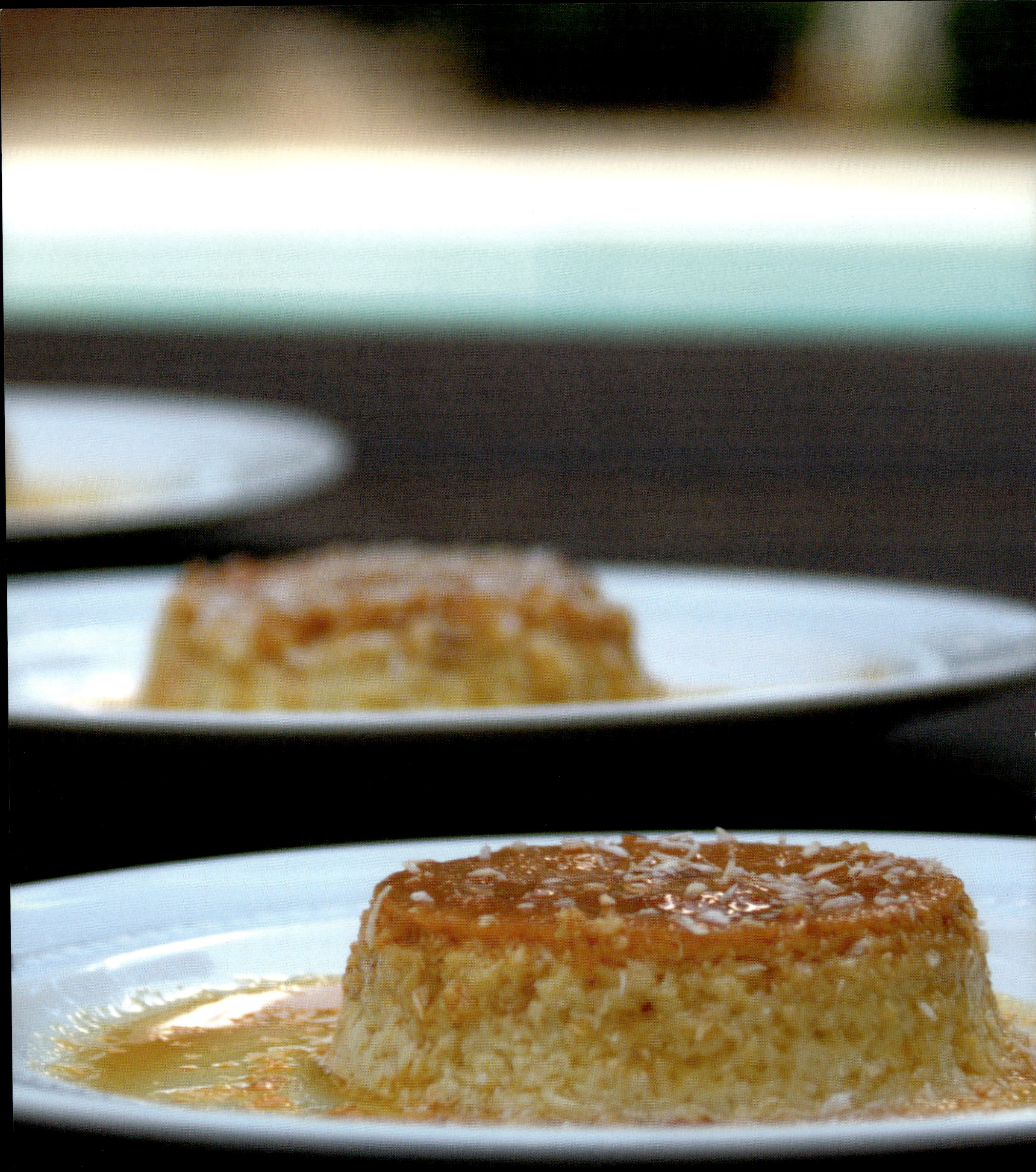

Coconut Flan
(Pudim de Coco)

Coconut Flan is my dad's favorite dessert. In Brazil, my mom makes this flan at least once a month! Less sweet than a regular flan, this Coconut Flan recipe has only five ingredients, and it's delicious!

Serves 10

¼ cup unsweetened coconut flakes
2 cups sugar
1 can (14 ounces) sweetened condensed milk
2 cups unsweetened coconut milk
5 eggs

In a medium skillet, toast coconut over medium high heat, stirring occasionally, until golden brown. Remove from heat and set aside.

Caramel

Pour sugar into medium sauce pan and cook 10 to 13 minutes on medium heat, stirring constantly, until it melts completely and turns golden brown. Divide caramel into 10 individual ovenproof mold dishes, or pour into a 10-inch mold pan. Let cool until it hardens.

Flan

Preheat oven to 350 degrees F. Add sweetened condensed milk, coconut milk and eggs to a blender. Mix one minute at high speed. Divide mix equally into individual ovenproof mold dishes, or pour into mold pan. Cover with foil.

Place pans in a large roasting dish filled with 1 ½ inches of warm water. Transfer to oven and bake for 40 to 70 minutes. The flan is ready when an inserted knife comes out clean. Remove from oven and let cool completely, at least 3 hours. Refrigerate 8 hours.

To unmold, gently run a small knife all around pans. Flip onto individual plates, or a large serving plate. Sprinkle with toasted coconut flakes and serve.

Dulce de Leche and Coconut Layer Cake
(Torta Recheada com Doce de Leite e Coco)

This "white canvas" cake has decadent layers of *dulce de leche* and coconut custard. The meringue that gives it an all-white look is flavored with fresh lime that breaks the richness of the fillings with a slightly tart bite. What I also love about this cake is that it can be decorated to fit any party theme. Check out the pictures of the cute party for my son's third birthday and how easily this cake became a "construction site" cake! It was pretty, fun and delicious!

Serves 20

Cake Ingredients:
2 ½ cups cake flour
1 tablespoon baking powder
Pinch of salt
2 sticks unsalted butter, room temperature
1 ½ cups sugar, plus 8 tablespoons sugar
3 large eggs, separated, at room temperature
2 tablespoons pure vanilla extract
1 cup whole milk, room temperature

Filling Ingredients:
1 tablespoon unsalted butter
2 egg yolks, lightly beaten
1 can (14 ounces) sweetened condensed milk
¾ cup unsweetened coconut flakes, preferably fresh
2 cups *dulce de leche*

Frosting Ingredients:
4 large egg whites
1 ½ cups sugar
¼ cup water
2 tablespoons fresh lime juice

Directions for Cake

Preheat oven to 350 degrees F.

Butter and flour two 9-inch cake pans.

In a medium mixing bowl, whisk flour, baking powder and salt.

In the bowl of a standing electric mixer fitted with the paddle, beat butter with 1 ½ cups of sugar at medium speed until fluffy. Add egg yolks and vanilla and beat until smooth. Slowly add dry ingredients and milk, scraping down sides of bowl as needed, until mixture is smooth.

Add egg whites to a clean mixing bowl. Using a hand electric mixer fitted with clean beaters, beat egg whites 4 minutes at high speed until soft peaks form. Gradually add remaining 8 tablespoons sugar and beat until glossy. Gently fold egg whites into batter, being careful not to over mix.

Scrape batter into prepared pans. Bake in center of oven 40 minutes, until cakes are golden and a toothpick inserted in the center comes out clean.

Transfer cakes to rack and allow to cool slightly. Run tip of knife around edges and invert cakes onto rack to cool completely. Using a serrated knife, split each layer horizontally in half.

Direction for Coconut Custard Filling

In a medium sauce pan over medium heat, add butter, egg yolks, sweetened condensed milk and coconut flakes. Stir constantly until mixture starts boiling slightly. Turn heat to medium-low and keep stirring until the custard thickens slightly. Custard is ready when bottom of pan starts to become visible while stirring and mixture is boiling vigorously, 10 to 12 minutes. Remove from heat and allow to cool completely.

Lime Meringue Frosting

In clean bowl of a standing electric mixer, using clean beaters, beat egg whites at medium-high speed until soft peaks form. In a medium sauce pan, bring sugar and water to a boil over high heat until dissolved. Remove from heat and add lime juice. With mixer at medium speed, carefully drizzle the hot sugar syrup into the egg whites. Turn speed to high and beat until fluffy and slightly warm to touch.

Assemblage

Place a cake layer on a large cake plate and top with 1 cup of *dulce de leche*. Top with a second layer of cake and spread with coconut custard. Top with a third cake layer and spread with remaining cup of *dulce de leche*. Finish with fouth layer of cake. Frost entire cake, swirling decoratively. Let stand at room temperature for at least 2 hours before serving, but preferably overnight.

Homemade Dulce de Leche Directions

It is also possible to make dulce de leche at home: submerge 2 unopened cans of sweetened condensed milk in a large, deep pot of water and bring to a boil. Simmer over moderately low heat for 2 hours, adding water as needed to keep the cans completely submerged. Carefully remove cans and let cool completely before opening.

Cook's Notes

Dulce de leche is South American style caramel and it can be found at international grocery stores, or at large grocery stores (usually next to the sweetened condensed milk shelf).

To balance the richness of the dulce de leche and coconut custard, I used a lime meringue for the topping, which adds a tangy and fresh taste to this decadent cake. The shiny meringue also gives a white canvas look to the cake, making it compatible for any kind of party. The decorations can be added according to the party theme. In this case, I made it for my 3-year-old son's birthday party, so the cake easily became a "construction site" kind of cake once I added stickers and banners. He loved it! My Dulce de Leche and Coconut Layer Cake looks really pretty and it is fairly easy and inexpensive to make.

The layers of dulce de leche and coconut can also be switched to taste. It is possible to make two layers of coconut custard and one layer of dulce de leche; just switch the amount of ingredients accordingly.

CONSTRUCTION
CONSTRUCTION
CONSTRUCTION ZONE
MACHINES WORKING
CONSTRUCTION
3

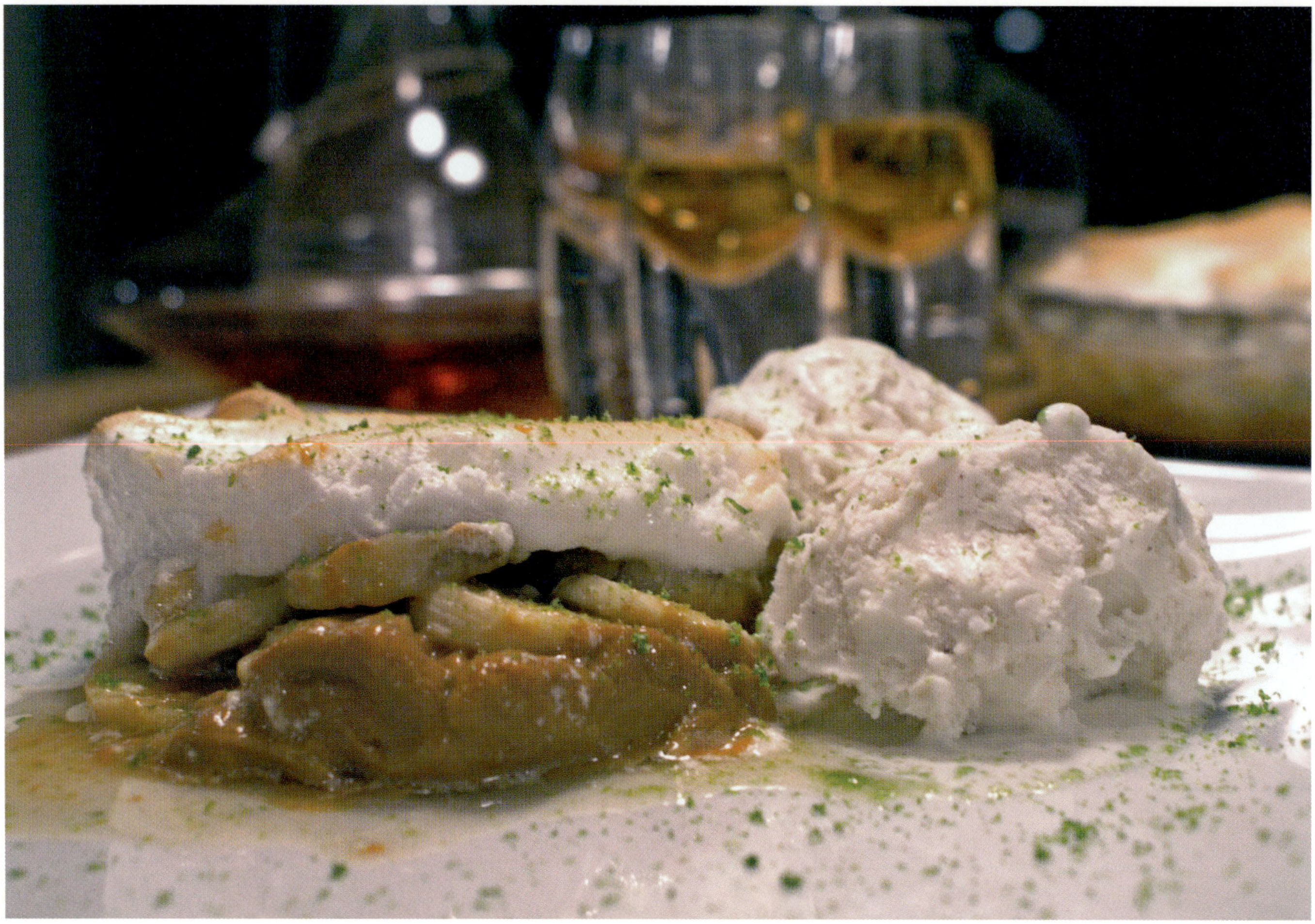

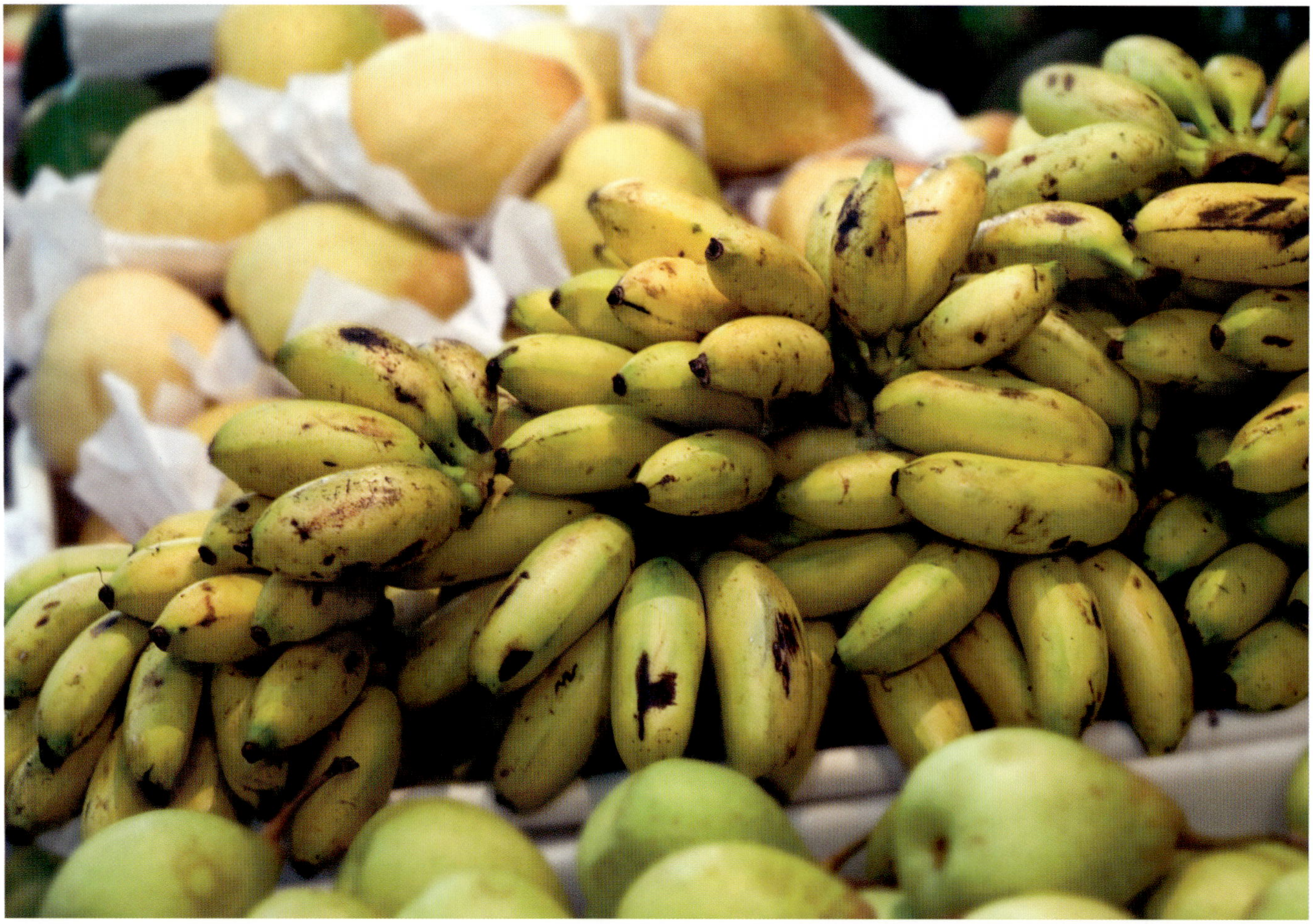

Dulce de Monkey
(Gelado de Doce de Leite e Banana)

I named this recipe *Dulce de Monkey* in honor of my cousin, Marcia, who has a great sense of humor. Marcia is an amazing cook, and she created the original recipe that inspired me to develop this one. I altered the recipe to fit the American palate, making it less sweet. This decadent dessert is even more delicious when served with vanilla ice cream on the side.

Serves 10

8 ounces cream cheese
1 can (14 ounces) *dulce de leche*
5 medium bananas, sliced
6 egg whites
12 tablespoons sugar
Zest of 1 lime or lemon
Vanilla ice cream, for serving

Turn on oven broiler.

In a medium size bowl, mix cream cheese and *dulce de leche* until blended. Spread on the bottom of a 10-inch round ovenproof dish.

Arrange sliced bananas over cream cheese mixture.

Using a hand mixer, beat egg whites 4 to 6 minutes until soft peaks form. Slowly add sugar, one tablespoon at a time, constantly beating until it doubles in size. Gently spread on top of bananas.

Broil until golden on top, 2 minutes.

Refrigerate 4 hours, or overnight. Sprinkle top with lime or lemon zest and serve with a side of vanilla ice cream.

Cook's Notes

Dulce de leche (South American style caramel) can be found in the Latin section of major grocery stores. It is often placed on the shelf next to the condensed milk.

See directions on how to make homemade *dulce de leche* on page 122.

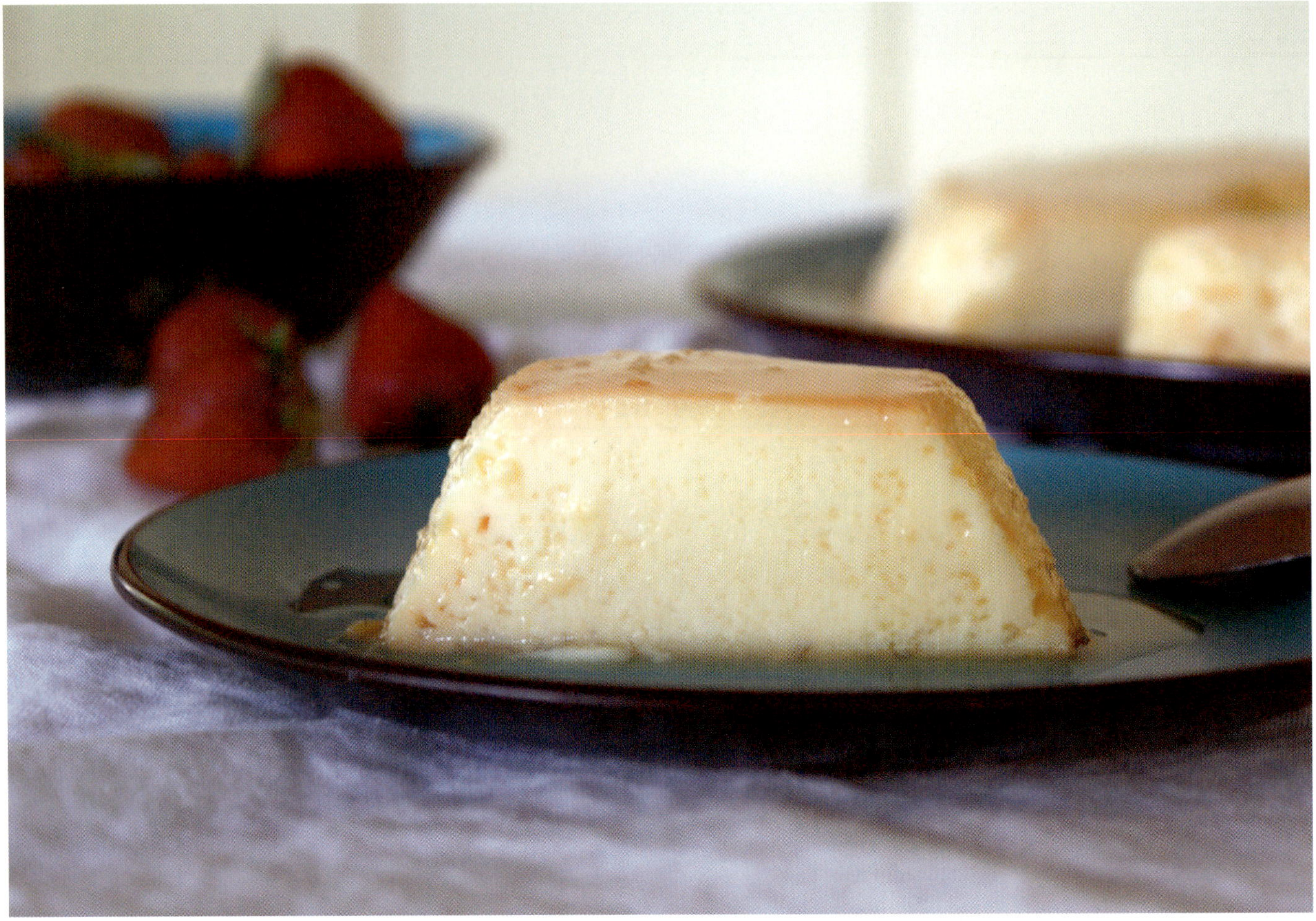

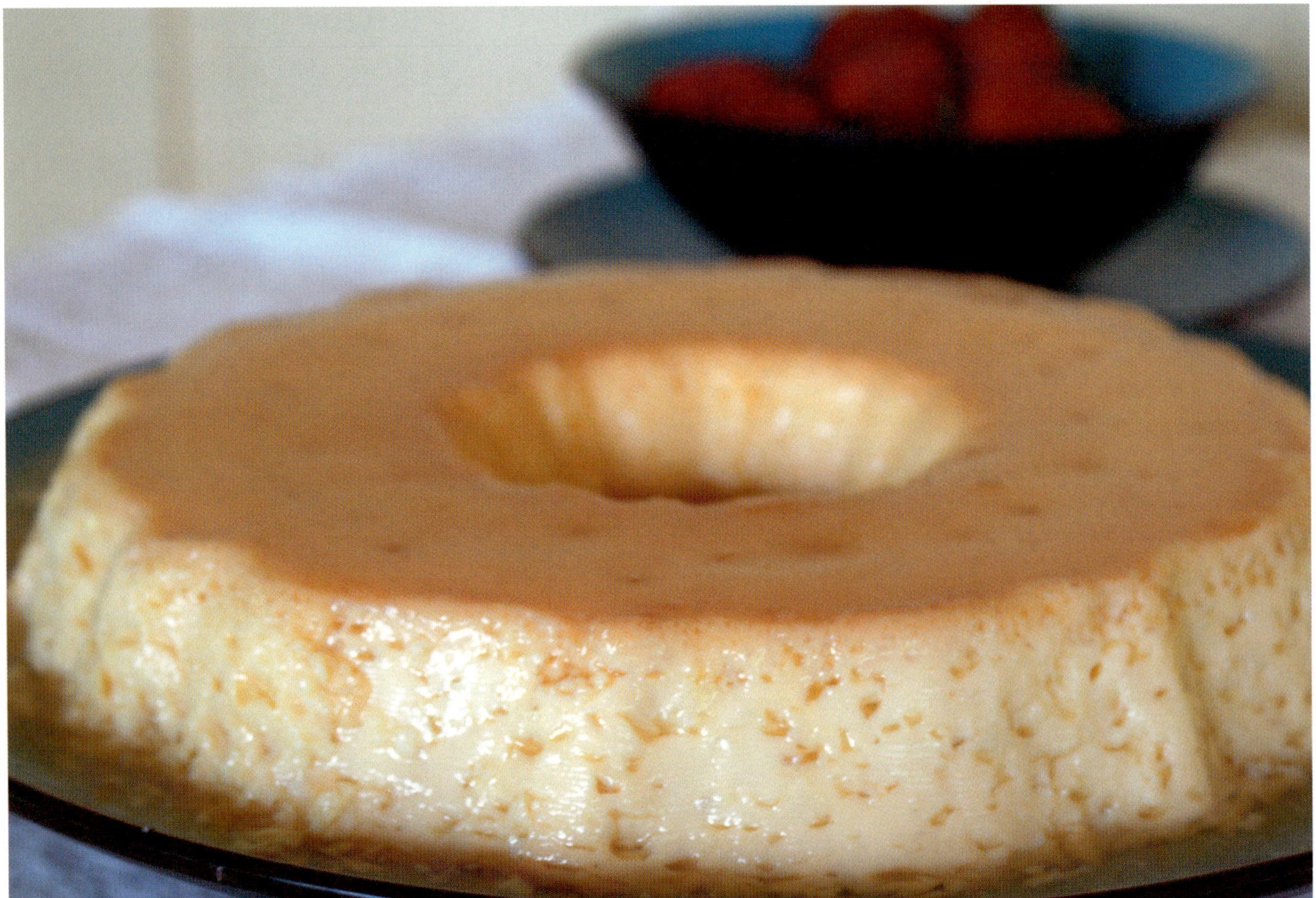

Classic Brazilian Flan
(Pudim de Leite Condensado)

When I see the word flan in a restaurant menu, I always order it. Why? To make sure it is not better than my flan recipe! Creamy, without being overwhelmingly sweet, this is my absolute favorite flan recipe. Make sure you remove the foam that forms on the surface, to achieve a perfectly smooth texture.

Serves 12

2 cups sugar
3 cans (14 ounces each) sweetened condensed milk
3 cups whole milk
5 eggs

Heat large sauce pan to medium and add sugar. Cook 10 to 13 minutes, stirring constantly, until the mixture turns golden brown. Remove from heat and pour caramel into a 10-inch mold pan, swirling caramel to completely cover the base and about 1-inch up the sides. Allow to cool and harden.

Preheat oven to 350 degrees F. Mix sweetened condensed milk, whole milk and eggs in a large blender. Blend for 20 seconds. If the ingredients do not fit all at once, divide them equally into 2 batches. Strain into a large bowl, removing the foam that forms on the surface.

Pour milk mixture into the mold pan (caramel must be hard) and cover with aluminum foil.

Place mold pan in a large ovenproof pan and fill it with warm water, half of pan depth. Carefully transfer to oven and bake 45 to 70 minutes. The flan is ready when you stick a toothpick in it and it comes out clean.

Remove from oven and let cool completely. Refrigerate 8 hours, or overnight.

Gently run a small knife around mold pan. Carefully flip over onto a large plate. Slice and serve, scraping caramel over flan.

Cook's Notes

Baking time may vary depending on the oven. Conducting the knife test after 45 minutes into baking time is the best way to prevent the flan from burning. On the other hand, there are ovens that will need extra baking time of up to 1 hour and 10 minutes. Again, the knife test is the best way to determine when the flan is done.

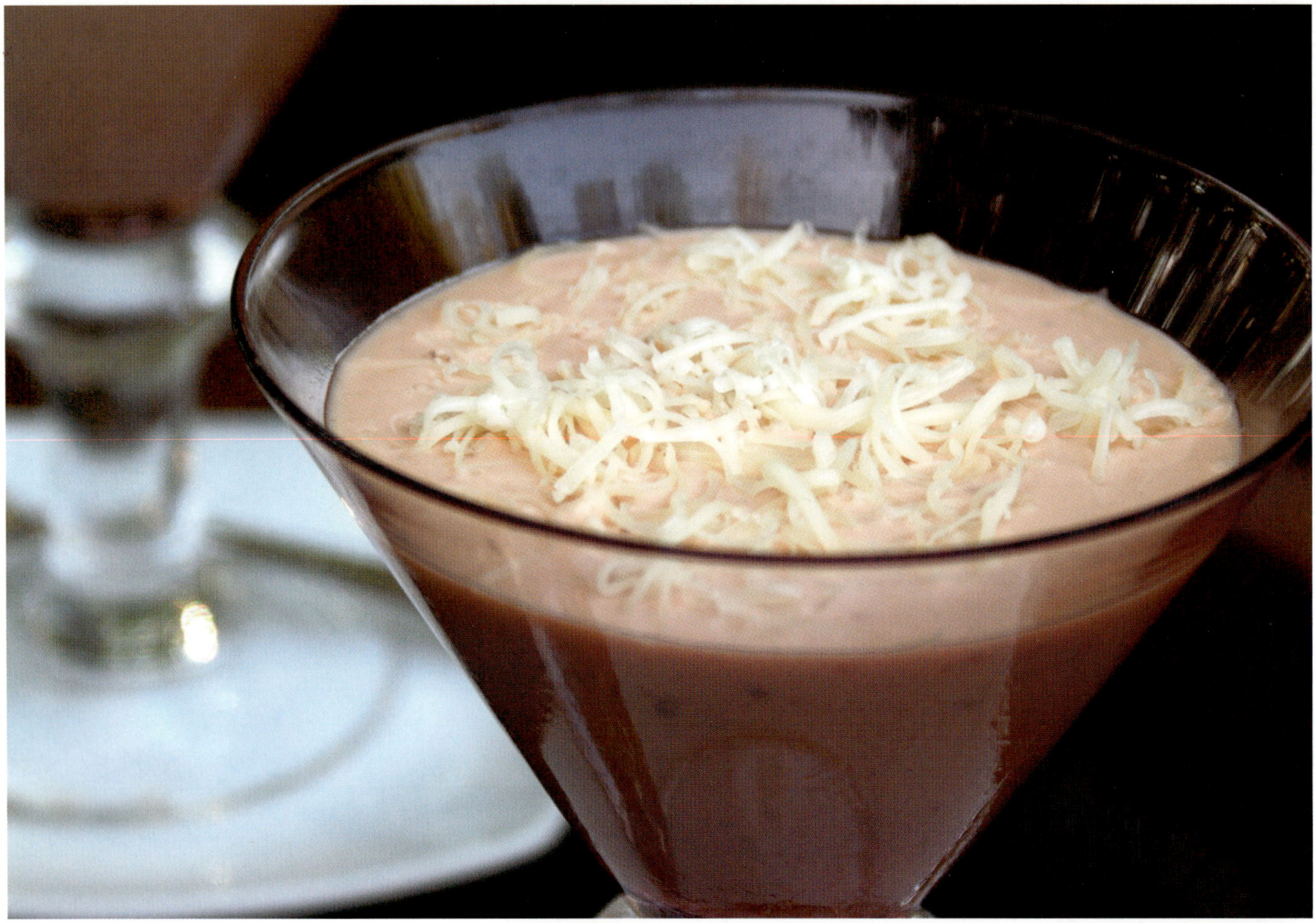

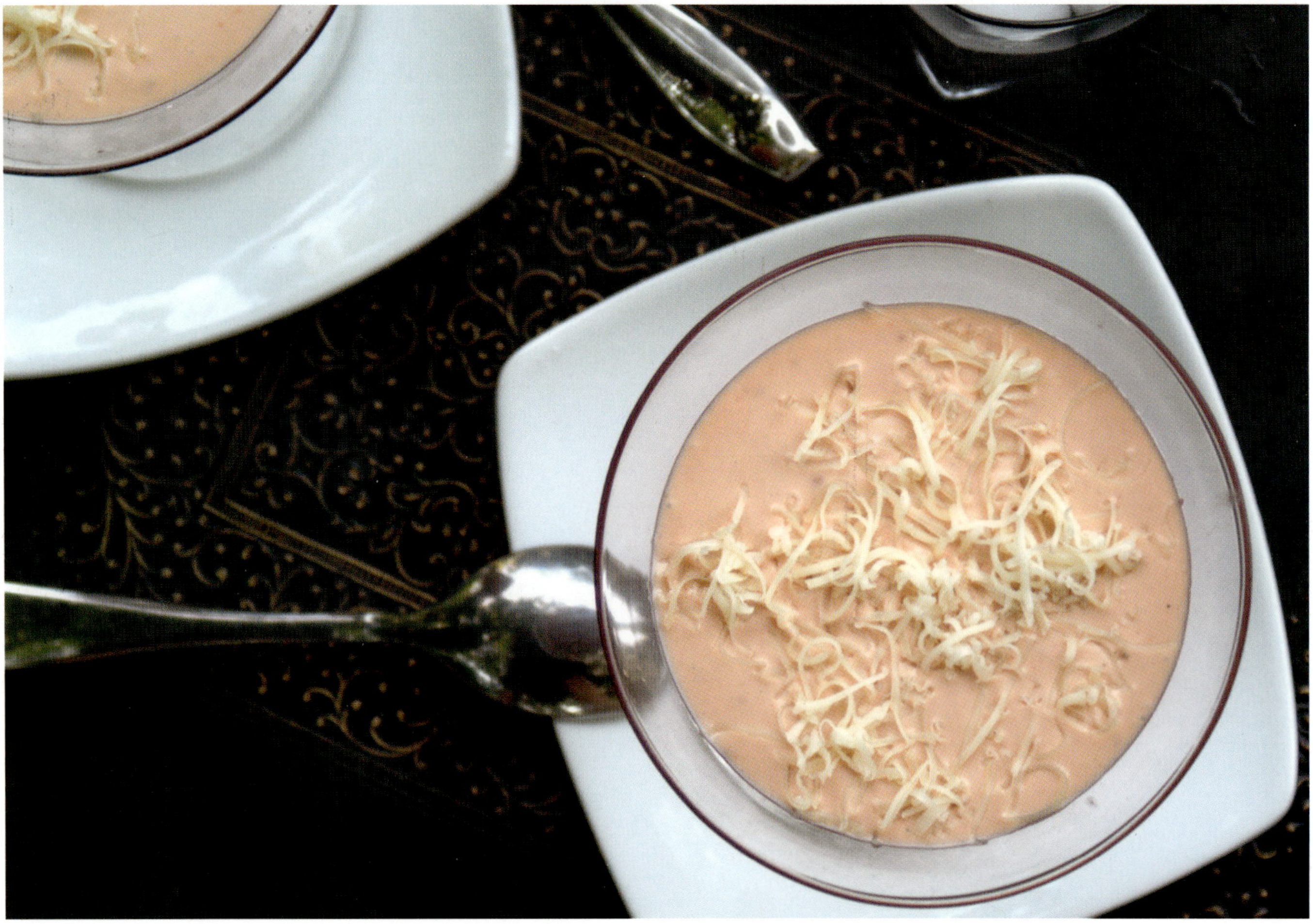

Guava and Cheese Mousse
(Mousse Romeu e Julieta)

Karen, my older sister, makes this recipe all the time and it is delicious! The classic Brazilian combination of guava and cheese appears now in the form of a super easy-to-make mousse. The cheeses break the sweetness of the guava paste, so this mousse tastes balanced, yet decadent and rich.

Serves 8

1 cup guava paste, chopped
1 cup *crème fraîche*
½ can (7 ounces) sweetened condensed milk
8 ounces cream cheese
½ cup shredded Fontina or Gouda cheese, or a mix of both cheeses

Add guava paste, *crème fraîche*, sweetened condensed milk, and cream cheese to a blender. Blend until smooth, 40 to 60 seconds. Pour the mousse into individual dessert cups. Refrigerate 4 hours. Top with cheese before serving.

Cook's Notes

Guava paste may be found in the Latin section of large grocery stores or at international markets. The consistency might vary depending on the brand, so adjust blending time accordingly.

The classic combination of guava and cheese is called "Romeu e Julieta" (Romeo and Juliet) in Brazilian cuisine, because they were "made for each other." It is a delicious and rich pairing!

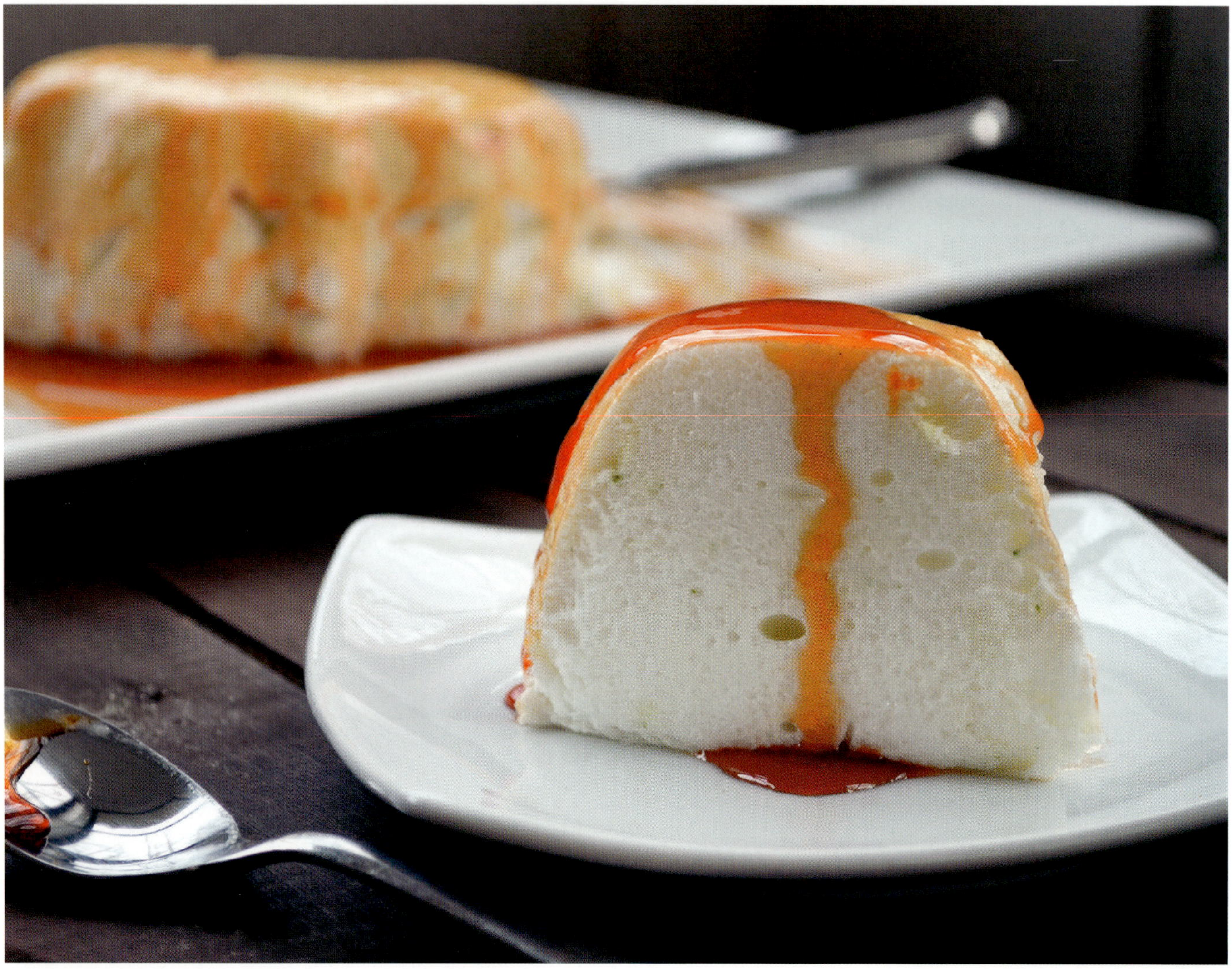

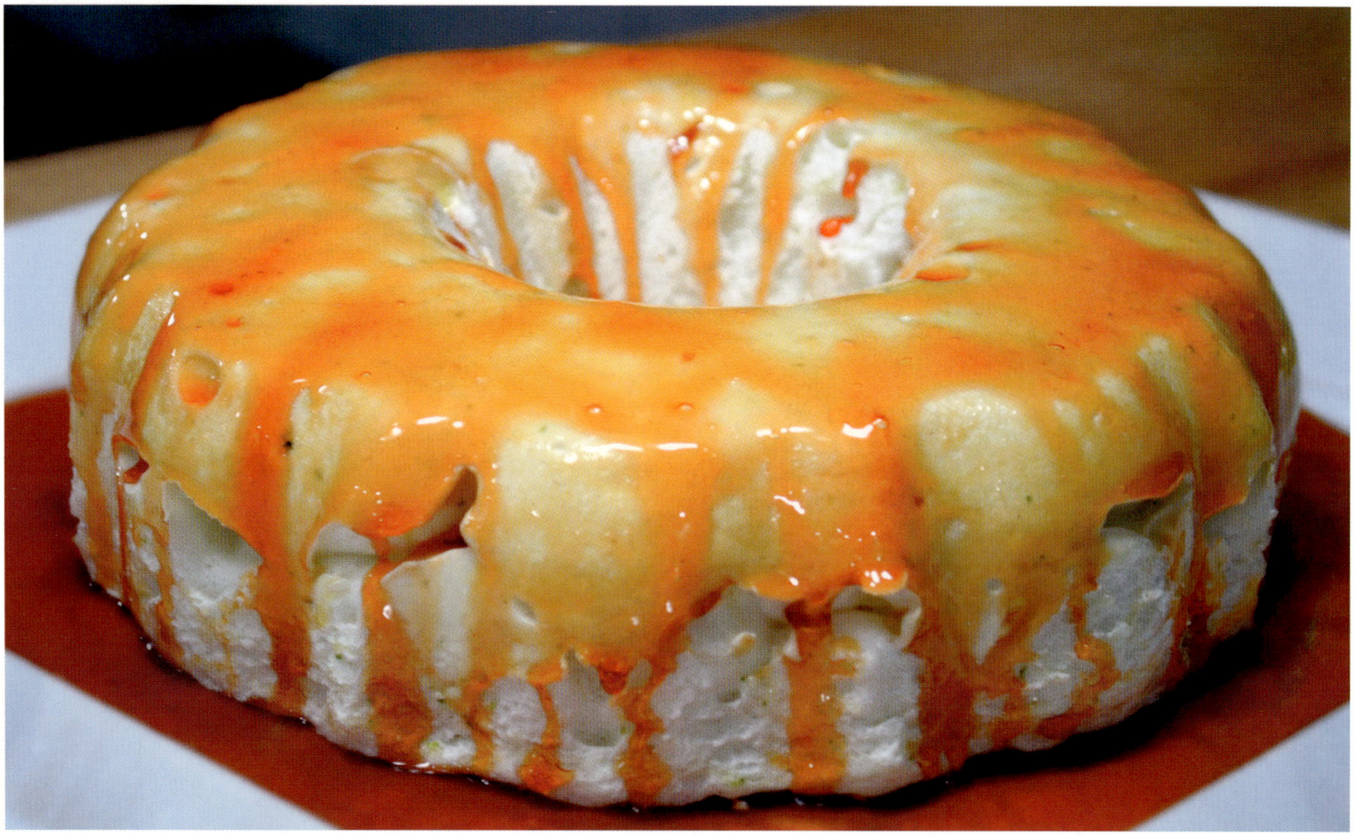

Lime Meringue Flan
(Pudim de Claras)

As a little girl growing up in Brazil, my mom always made this delightful dessert, so it reminds me of my childhood. Sweet, with a hint of lime zest, it is extremely light in texture. The best thing about it is that it only has four everyday ingredients! I promise, you have never tried anything this light before.

Serves 10 to 12

3 ½ cups sugar, divided
10 egg whites
1 pinch salt
Zest of 1 lime

Pour 2 cups sugar into a 10-inch bundt pan. Cook over medium-low heat, directly on the stove top burner, until the sugar melts completely and turns golden brown, 10 to 13 minutes. Swirl the pan allowing the caramel to completely cover the base and about 1-inch up the sides of pan. Set aside to cool and harden.

Preheat oven to 350 degrees F.

In a clean bowl of a standing mixer with the whisk attachment, combine egg whites and salt. Beat 5 minutes on medium-high speed until soft peaks form. Turn speed to medium and slowly add remaining 1 ½ cup sugar; beat until well incorporated, 2 minutes. Turn off mixer and fold in lime zest.

Scoop meringue into bundt pan and cover tightly with aluminium foil. Place bundt pan in a large, ovenproof baking pan half filled with 1 ½ inches of warm water. Carefully transfer to oven. Bake 40 to 60 minutes, or until a toothpick inserted into the center comes out clean.

Remove foil and cool to room temperature. Unmold flan by carefully flipping it over on to a large plate. Scoop caramel over flan. Refrigerate 3 hours or more before serving.

Cook's Notes

You can make the caramel in a medium sauce pan, and then pour into the bundt pan. This is a safer option for beginners, since the bundt pan does not have a handle and it can get really hot during the process.

For this specific flan, the whisked egg whites must be stiff enough to turn the bowl upside-down. Please test slowly!

After scooping the meringue into the bundt pan, gently beat pan against the countertop a few times to avoid air bubbles on the surface. As you beat the pan, it will release air bubbles allowing the flan batter to occupy all available space inside the pan. Do not skip this step, but please be gentle!

Passion Fruit Pie
(Torta Mousse de Maracujá)

Passion Fruit Pie is a popular dessert in Brazil. The word "Mousse" is often added to the title because the texture of the filling is just as light. Sweet, tart, light, fluffy, and crunchy, this pie has it all!

Serves 10

Crust Ingredients:
3 cups Graham crackers, roughly crumbled
6 tablespoons unsalted butter, at room temperature
¼ cup dark brown sugar

Filling Ingredients:
2 cans (14 ounces each) sweetened condensed milk
¾ cup passion fruit pulp
2 tablespoons unflavored gelatin
1/3 cup hot water (not boiling)
3 egg whites

Sauce Ingredients:
¾ cup passion fruit pulp
½ cup sugar
¾ teaspoon unflavored gelatin
1 ½ tablespoon hot water (not boiling)

Crust Directions

Preheat oven to 350 degrees F for 10 minutes.

Add crumbled Graham crackers, butter, and dark brown sugar to a food processor. Pulse 6 to 8 times, until dough is well incorporated. Press dough into a 9-inch pie mold. Using a fork, prick tiny holes on the dough surface, about ½ -inch apart. Transfer to oven and bake until golden brown, 8 to 10 minutes. Remove and let cool.

Filling Directions

Add sweetened condensed milk and passion fruit to a blender. Blend for 10 seconds, until incorporated. Transfer to a large bowl.

In a small bowl, mix gelatin and hot water, whisking vigorously until combined. Add gelatin to passion fruit mix and stir well to combine.

Add egg whites to a clean bowl. Using an eletric mixer, beat egg whites until soft peaks form, 4 minutes. Gently fold egg whites into passion fruit filling, being careful not to over mix. Tip passion fruit filling into pie mold. Cover with plastic wrap and transfer to refrigerator.

Sauce Directions

In a small sauce pan over medium heat, combine passion fruit pulp and sugar. Heat, stirring occasionally, just until sugar melts. Remove from heat and place into a medium bowl.

Mix gelatin and water into a small bowl, whisking it vigorously until combined. Add gelatin to passion fruit sauce and stir well. Cover, and refrigerate for approximately 2 hours, allowing it to thicken. Pour sauce over pie and refrigerate for one more hour. Remove for refrigerator, slice and serve.

Cook's Notes

Frozen passion fruit pulp can serve as a substitute for fresh pulp.

To make fresh passion fruit pulp for this recipe, add the pulp of 5 small passion fruits and 1/4 cup water to a blender. Blend for 10 seconds, strain and use.

In this recipe, I used frozen passion fruit pulp. Frozen passion fruit pulp is available at Latin markets and international grocery stores.

Desserts (Sobremesas)

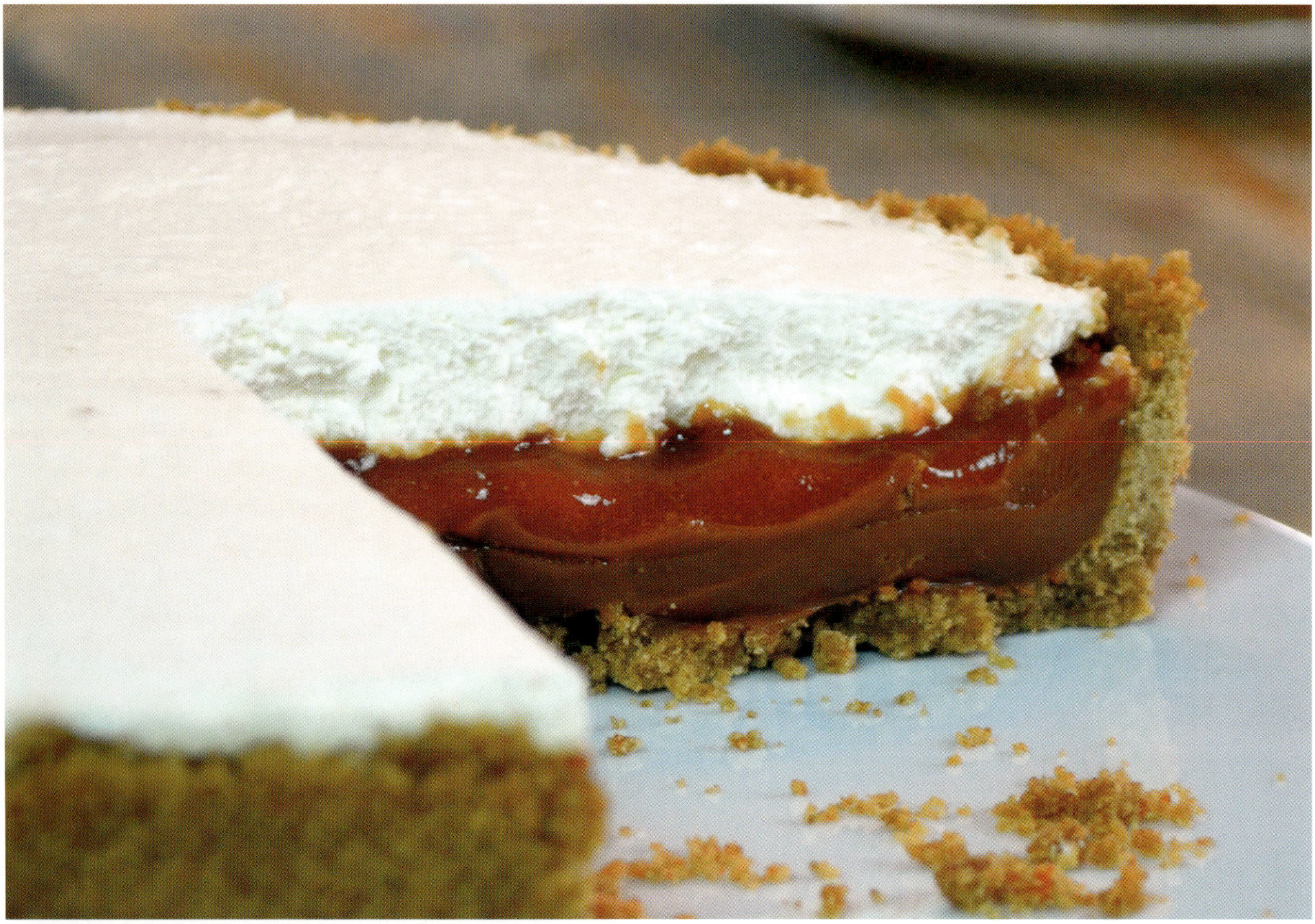

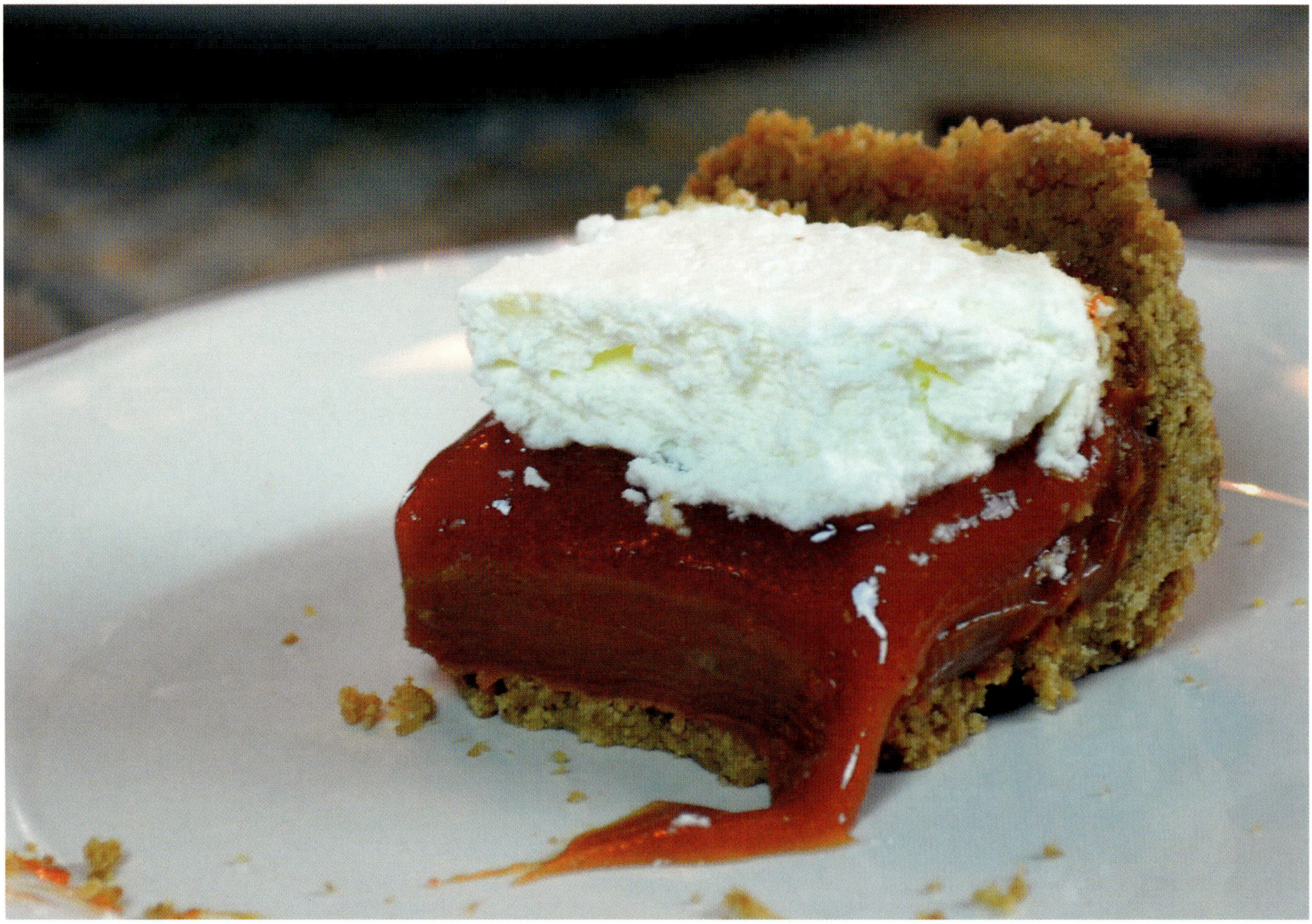

Salted Caramel and Guava Pie
(Torta de Goiabada com Doce de Leite)

South American style caramel is usually known in the US by its name in Spanish: *dulce de leche*. In Portuguese, we call it *doce de leite*. But no matter what it is called, it sure tastes amazing when combined with guava, in a very Brazilian mix of flavors. Sea salt helps to break the sweetness, making this pie a huge hit at parties!

Serves 10

Crust Ingredients:
3 cups Graham crackers, coarsely crushed
6 tablespoons butter, softened
¼ cup light brown sugar

Filling Ingredients:
2 cans (14 ounces each) *dulce de leche*
Sea salt, medium ground
1 cup guava paste, chopped
1 cup warm water
1 ½ cups heavy cream
1 ½ tablespoons powdered sugar

Crust Directions

Preheat oven 350 degrees F.

Place Graham crackers, butter, and brown sugar in a food processor. Process 2 minutes, until blended. Press mixture into a 9-inch pie dish. Bake 7 to 9 minutes, until surface is golden brown. Let cool.

Filling Directions

Spread *dulce de leche* into the pie crust. Sprinkle 2 to 3 pinches of sea salt over *dulce de leche*. Set aside.

Add guava paste to a food processor and pulse with ½ cup water; slowly add remaining water, while pulsing, until desired thickness is reached. For a thicker filling, reduce water to ½ cup. Spread guava sauce over *dulce de leche*.

Place heavy cream and powdered sugar in a medium bowl. Using an electric mixer, beat until firm. Spread cream on top of pie and refrigerate 2 hours before serving.

Cook's Notes

Dulce de leche can be found in the Latin section of the grocery store, or next to the condensed milk.

See directions on how to make homemade *dulce de leche* on page 122.

Guava paste may be found in the Latin section of large grocery stores, or at international grocery stores.

Brazilian Strawberry Shortcake
(Torta Gelada de Morangos)

Brazilians love a good strawberry shortcake! My version has layers of store-bought Angel Food cake (so easy), strawberry gelatine, fresh strawberries, and creamy meringue. But what really makes this dessert so delicious is the home-made custard filling. I have been making this dessert since my college days, and it is delicious!

Serves 10 to 12

3 ounces strawberry gelatin
½ cup hot water (not boiling)
½ cup ice cold water
1 can (14 ounces) sweetened condensed milk
1 cup whole milk
4 egg yolks, lightly beaten
4 egg whites
8 tablespoons sugar
1 can (7.6 ounces) Media Crema (table cream)
¾ of a store-bought Angel Food cake, sliced into ½-inch thick slices (about 15 slices)
2 cups strawberries, stem removed and quartered, plus more for garnish

In a medium bowl, whisk together strawberry gelatin and hot water until dissolved. Stir in ice cold water, cover and transfer to refrigerator. Let chill 1 to 1 ½ hours, or until halfway between liquid and firm. Set aside.

In a medium sauce pan over medium heat, combine sweetened condensed milk with whole milk. Cook, stirring constantly, until mixture begins to boil. Reduce heat to medium-low and slowly add egg yolks, whisking vigorously 3 to 4 minutes until mixture thickens. Remove from heat and cool.

Add egg whites to a clean, medium bowl. Beat egg whites with an electric hand mixer 4 minutes until soft peaks form. Add sugar one tablespoon at a time, beating constantly. Turn off hand mixer and gently fold in table cream. Set aside.

Lay sliced cake on the bottom of a large deep dish (at least 3-inches deep, 10x15). Cake slices should slightly overlap. Pour condensed milk mixture over cake and cover with quartered strawberries. Pour nearly firm gelatin over strawberries. Gently spread egg white mixture over gelatin. Decorate with a few strawberries. Cover and refrigerate at least 3 hours before serving.

Cook's Notes

Media Crema is Latin American style table cream. It can be found in the Latin Section of major grocery stores or at international markets.

Desserts (Sobremesas)

Drinks
(Bebidas)

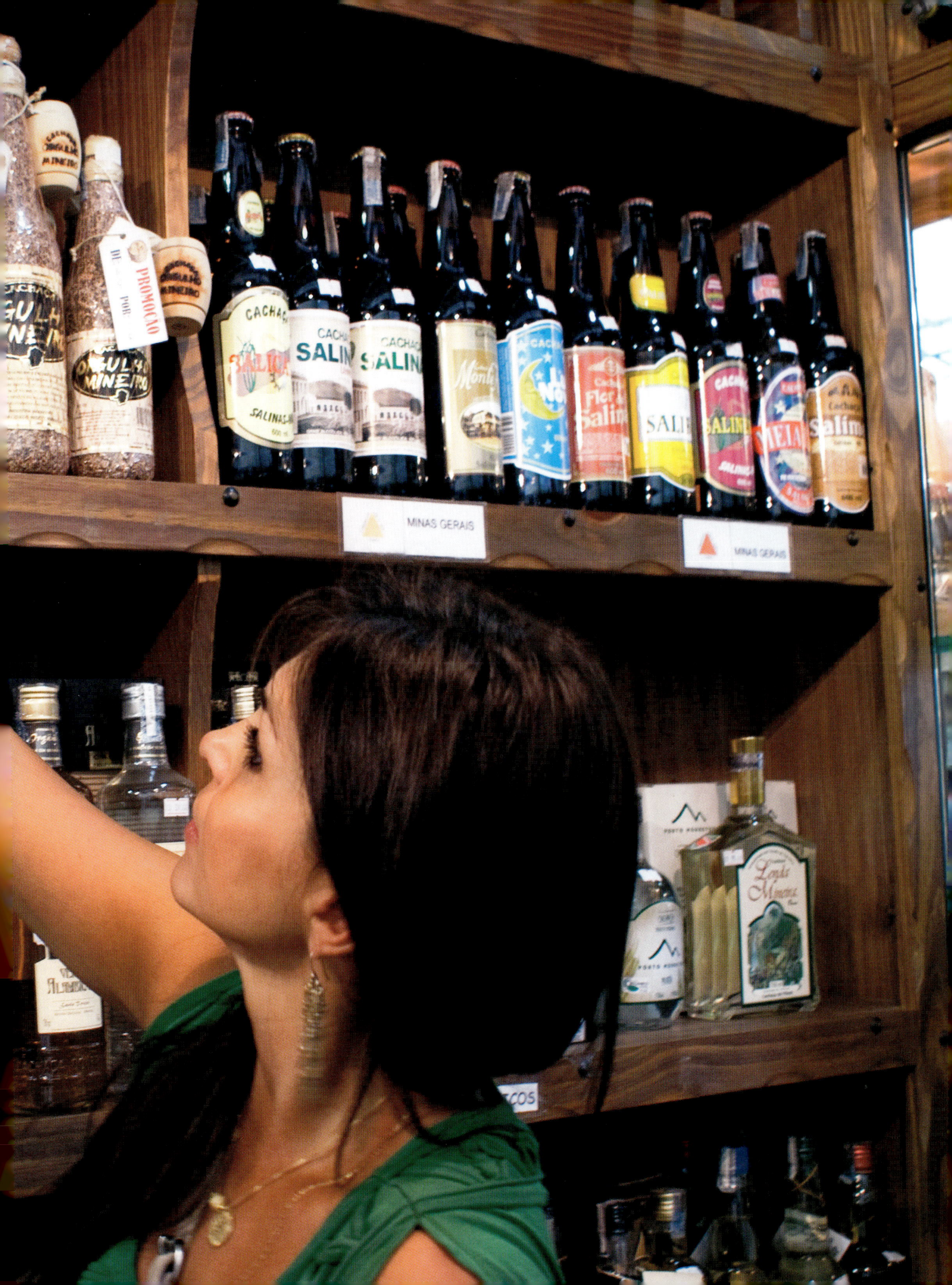
PROMOÇÃO
MINAS GERAIS
MINAS GERAIS

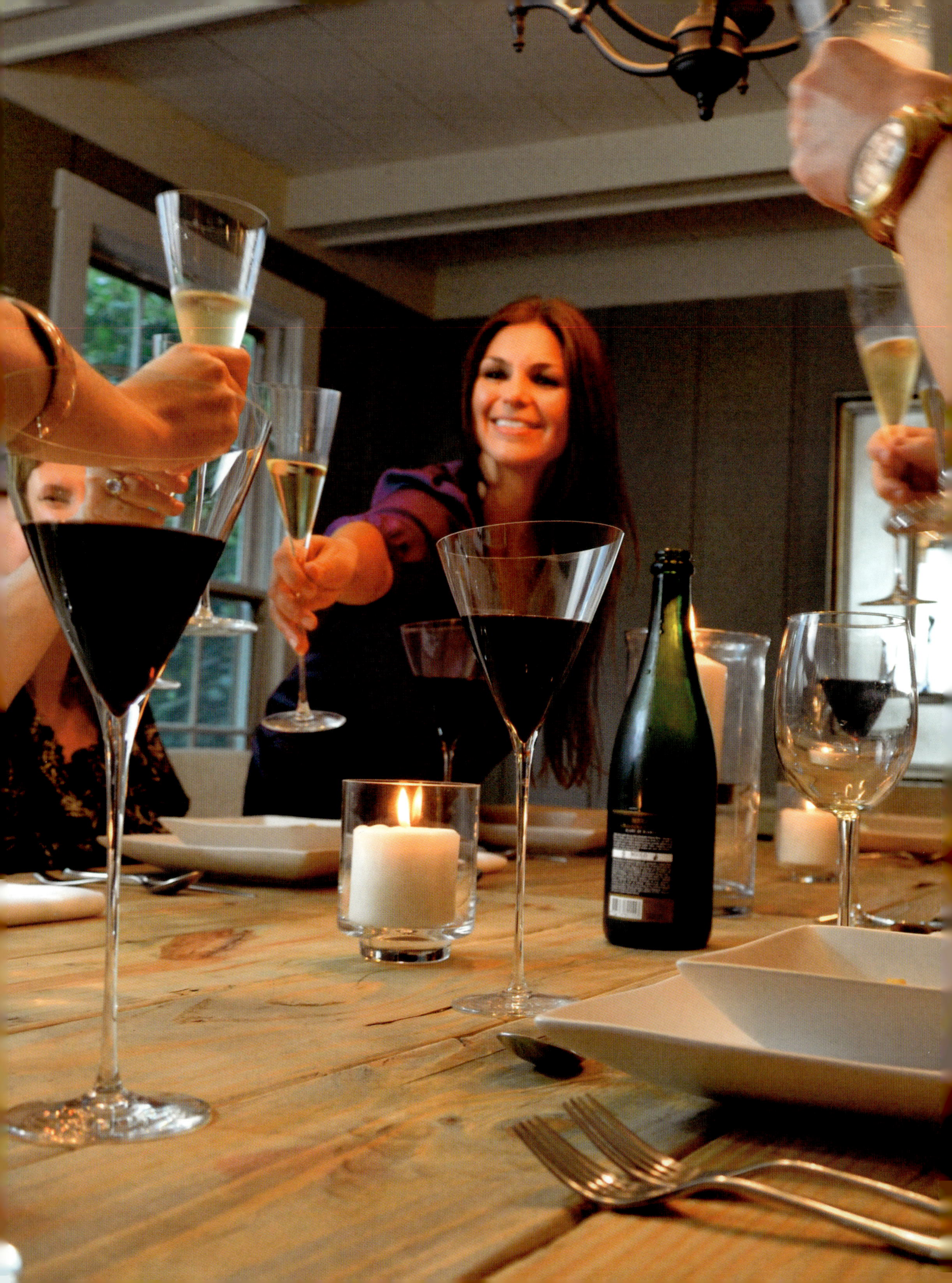

Drinks
(Bebidas)

Caipirinha 142

Passion Fruit Caipirinha (Caipirinha de Maracujá) 144

Pineapple-Mint Caipirinha (Caipirinha de Abacaxi com Hortelã) 146

Caipirinha

Sweet and refreshing, Caipirinha is the most well-known Brazilian drink. The traditional recipe has limes, sugar and cachaça (also known as Brazilian rum). Variations with other fruits like strawberries, kiwi, and cashew fruit are also available, but the popularity of the traditional version is untouched. Be ready, this drink will make you dance!

Serves 1

1 sliced lime (additional for garnishing)
3 tablespoons sugar
1 shot cachaça
¼ cup spring water (optional)
Ice cubes

In a large cup, add lime slices and sugar. Muddle with a pestle until well incorporated.

Stir in cachaça and water. Add ice cubes and serve immediately garnished with lime wedges.

Cook's Notes

Cachaça is a typical Brazilian spirit that can usually be found at large liquor stores. If unavailable, rum or vodka may serve as a substitute. If using rum or vodka to make caipirinha, use brown sugar instead of white sugar.

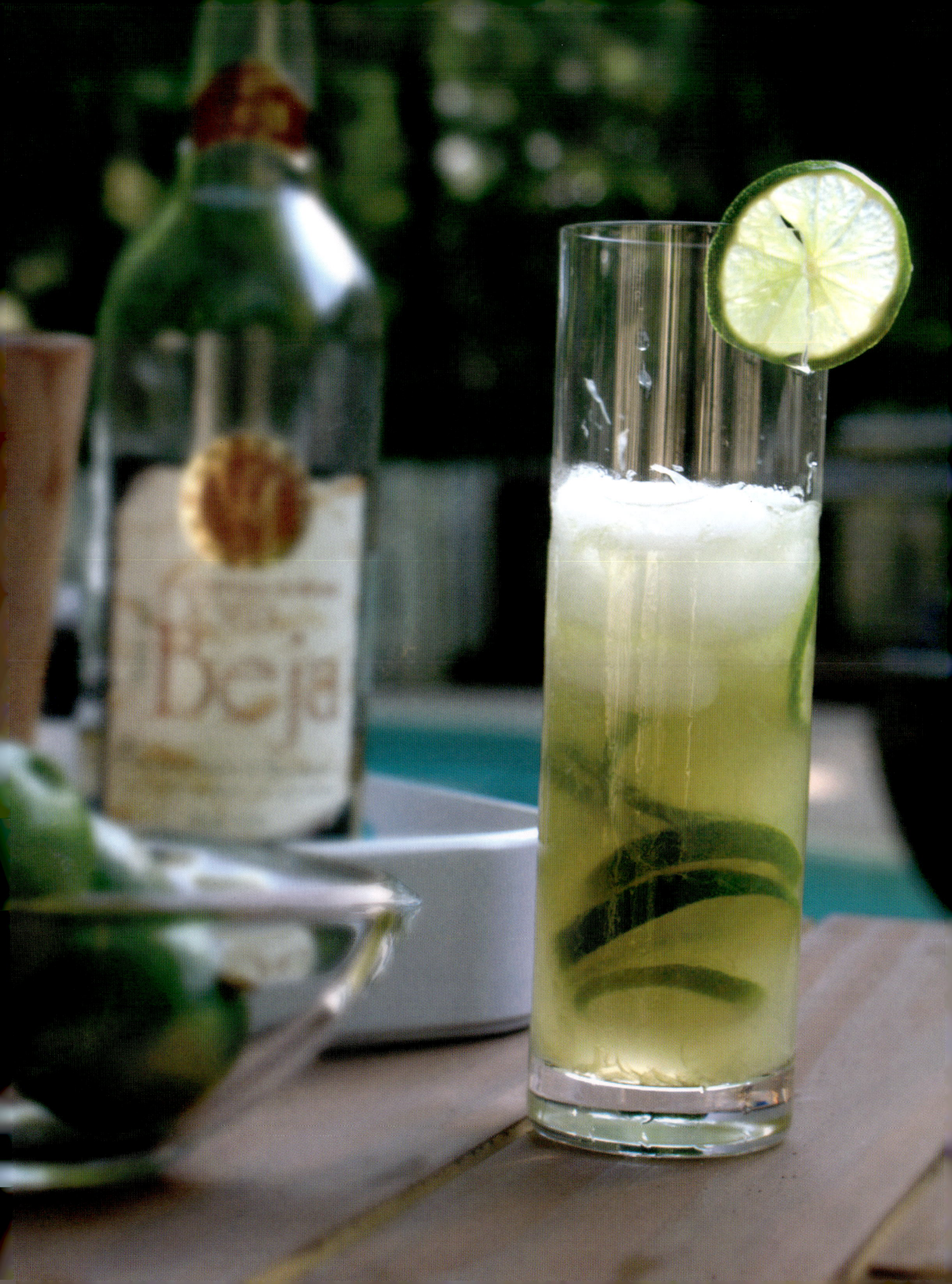

Passion Fruit Caipirinha
(Caipirinha de Maracujá)

The Passion-Fruit Caipirinha is my personal favorite. The combination of fruit, cachaça and sugar is really refreshing, and passion-fruit has the necessary tartness to make a perfectly balanced drink. The seeds are crunchy and add personality to this exotic concoction; but if it they bother you simply strain the drink to enjoy the taste without the seeds.

Serves 1

1 small or ½ large passion fruit
3 tablespoons sugar
1 shot cachaça
1 cup ice cubes

On a working surface, cut passion fruit in half crosswise and scrape the pulp into a glass, preferably a lowball glass. Add sugar and muddle, using a pestle, until sugar and passion fruit are well incorporated. Stir in cachaça and ice. Serve immediately.

Cook's Notes

Adjust passion fruit to taste: add more pulp from an extra passion fruit if you prefer a slightly more tart drink.

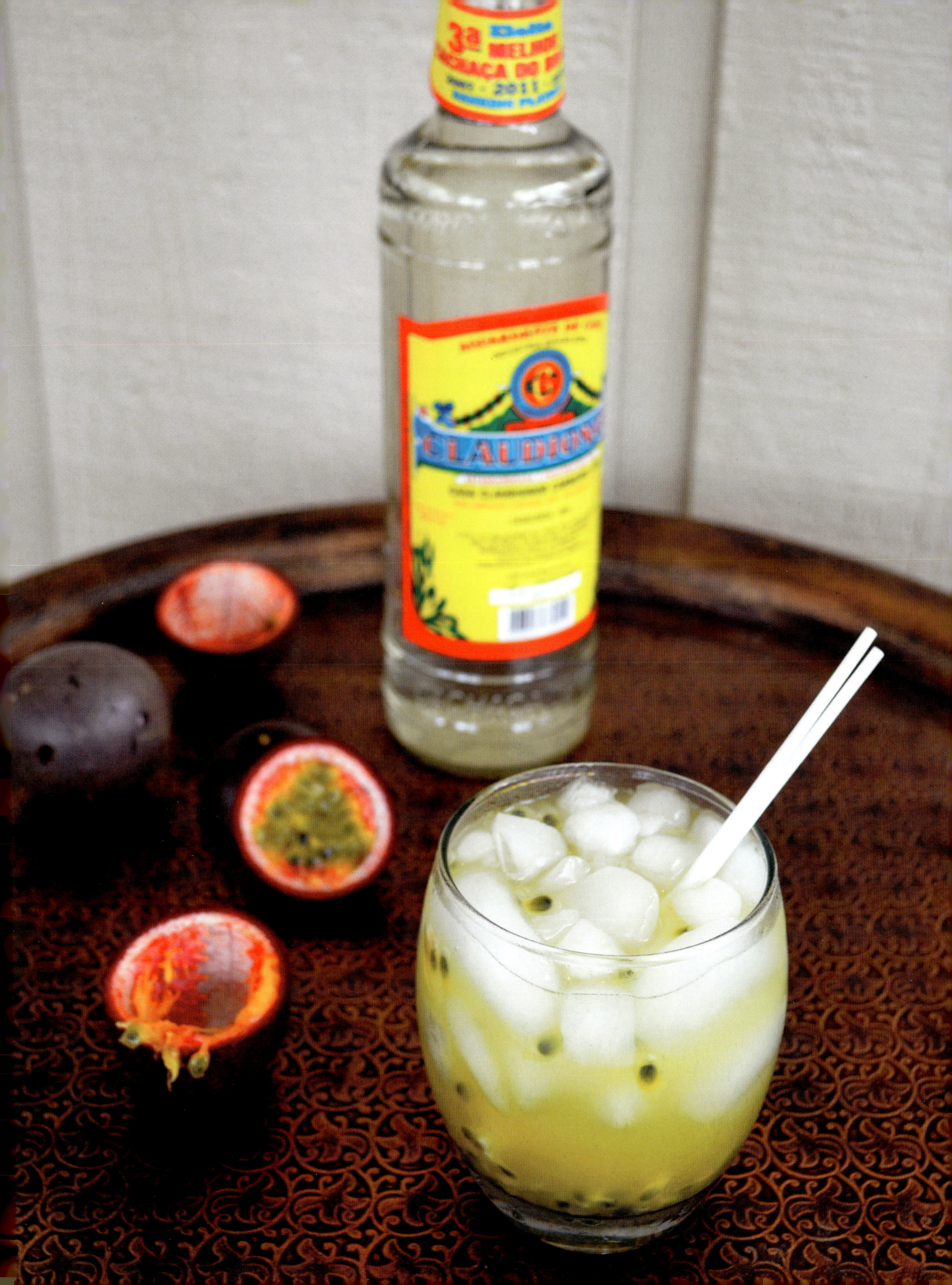
3ª MELHOR
2011

Pineapple-Mint Caipirinha
(Caipirinha de Abacaxi com Hortelã)

Pineapple and mint are a great combination in any drink, and it is no different when mixed with cachaça and sugar. This is another one of my favorite caipirinhas, perfect for the beach, or poolside!

Serves 1

6 mint leaves, torn
2 tablespoons sugar
½ cup diced pineapple
1 shot cachaça
1 cup ice cubes

Place mint and sugar in a glass, preferably a lowball glass. Using a pestle, muddle until a thick paste forms. Add pineapple and muddle until incorporated. Add cachaça and ice cubes and stir. Garnish with mint leaves and serve immediately.

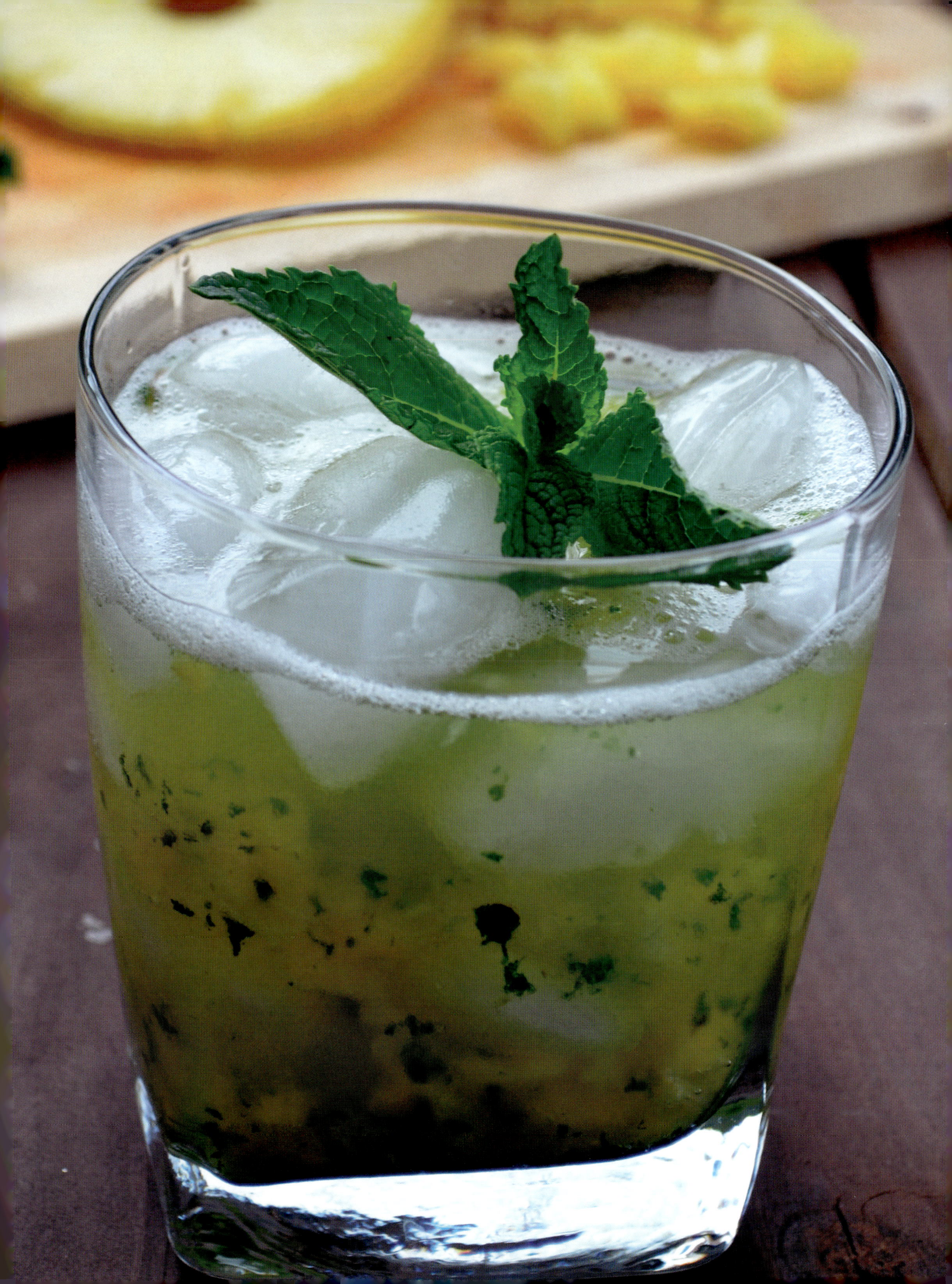

World Inspired Recipes

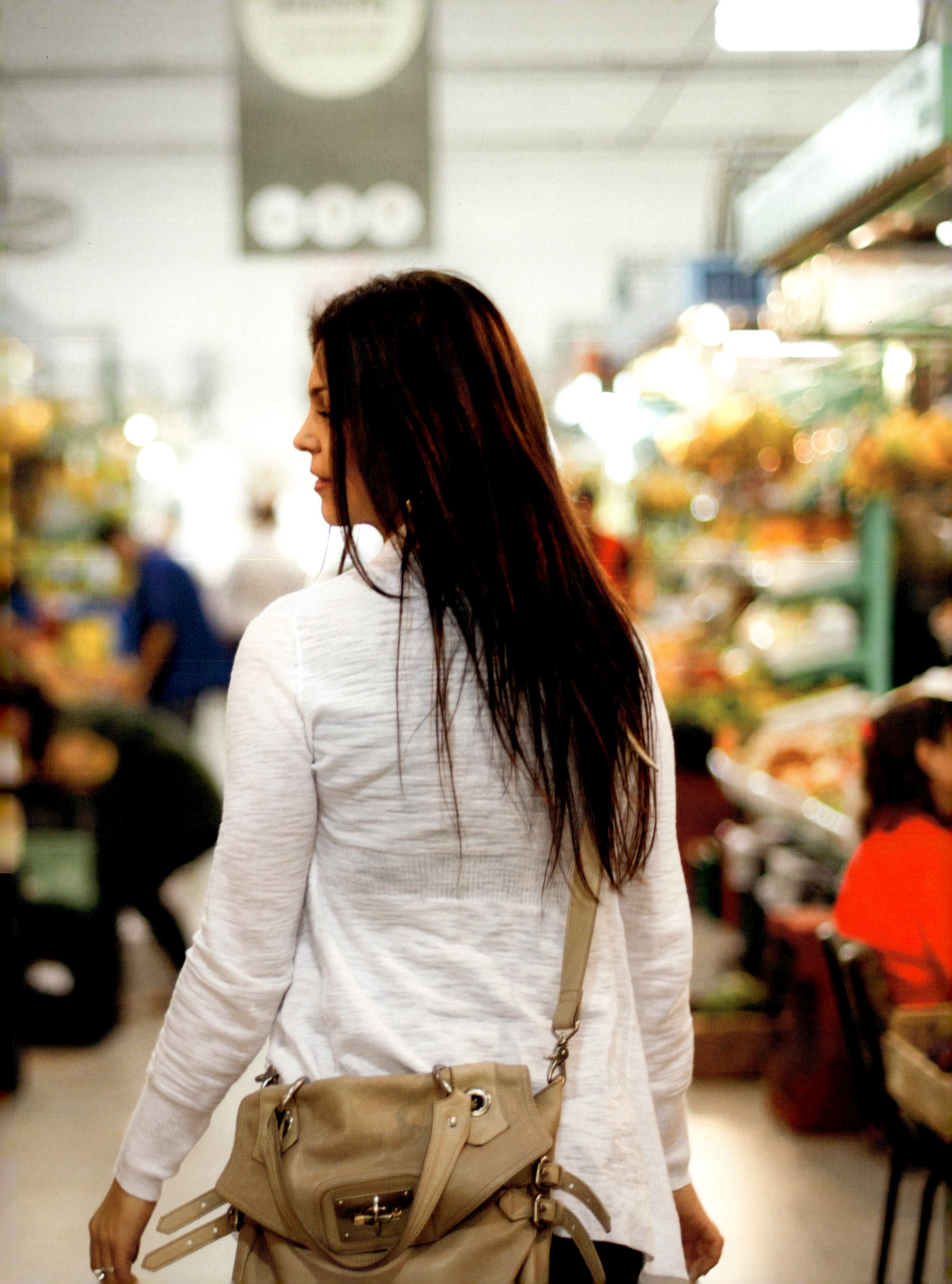

World Inspired Recipes

Fusion 152
Cheesecake with Guava Sauce 150
Chicken Stuffed with Creamy Eggplant Parmigiana 153
Chocolate Cheesecake with Passion Fruit Sauce 154
Fig and Hearts-of-Palm Salad 157
Fish Roulade with Hearts-of-Palm and Mascarpone, over Olive-Apricot Tapenade 158
Goat Cheese Roulade with Roasted Bell Peppers 160
Hamburger with Chimichurri and Provolone 163
Mushroom Stuffed Chicken with Coconut Milk-Lemongrass Sauce 165
Pork Tenderloin with Apricot-Miso Marinade 166
Pumpkin and Coconut Pie 169
Tuna Ceviche with Avocado and Wasabi 171
White Chocolate Flan with Peppermint Caramel Sauce 172

Argentina 176
Chimichurri Sauce 175

Asia 178
Ginger-Basil Shrimp on Toast Cups 177
Pasta Salad with Shrimp and Peanut Butter-Ginger Dressing 179

France 182
Strawberry Aspic 181
Tenderloin with Orange Sauce 183
Tenderloin with Dried Porcini and Fresh Mushrooms 185

Italy 188
Caprese Salad   with Roasted Tomatoes 187
Cheese Ravioli with Chicken Sauce 189
Chicken Marsala with Cream, Garlic and Herbs 191
Eggplant Involtini 193
Mixed Mushrooms Lasagna 195
Penne with Mustard-Marsala Tenderloin 197
Steak Lulu with Gnocchi 199
Asparagus and Shrimp Risotto 200
Four Cheese Risotto 203
Saffron Risotto with Mixed Mushrooms 204
Albondigas Soup 207

Mexico 210
Fish Tacos with Mango-Jalapeno Slaw   209
Watermelon Margarita   211

Middle East 214
Eggplant Antipasto 213
Lamb Stew with Raisins, Pine Nuts and Mint 215

Paraguay 218
Sopa Paraguaya – Paraguayan Corn Bread 216

Spain 220
Smoky Rice with Squid and Shrimp 219

United States 222
Pork Tenderloin with White Wine and Rosemary Marinade 221
Roasted Cauliflower 223
Sausage and Mushrooms Stuffed Bell Peppers 225
Shrimp and Cream Cheese Stuffed Zucchini 227
Stuffed Mushrooms with Sausage, Pine Nuts and Herbs 229
Cynthia's Special White Sauce 231

Uruguay 234
Clericot 233

Cheesecake with Guava Sauce

Brazil meets the United States in this dessert. Guava is one of the most popular fruits in Brazilian cuisine and its sauce complements the rich American cheesecake very well!

Serves 10

2 cups Graham crackers, crumbled
¾ cup butter at room temperature
¼ cup sugar
1 cup (8 ounces) cream cheese
1 cup (8 ounces) ricotta cheese
1 can (14 ounces) sweetened condensed milk

4 egg yolks
¼ cup unsalted roasted cashews, roughly chopped
1 cup frozen guava pulp, defrosted
½ cup sugar
Juice from ½ lime
1 ½ teaspoons unflavored gelatin, dissolved in ¼ cup hot water (not boiling)

Crust

Preheat oven to 325 degrees F. Add Graham crackers, butter and sugar to a food processor. Process until combined, 1 minute. Press into bottom of 9-inch cheesecake pan. Using a fork, prick small holes all over dough. Set aside.

Filling

Add cream cheese, ricotta, sweetened condensed milk and egg yolks to a food processor. Process 40 seconds, until blended. Add cashews and pulse 3 times.

Pour cream cheese mixture over dough and bake in a *bain marie* (water bath) 45 to 60 minutes, until a toothpick inserted in center comes out clean, or an in instant-read thermometer registers 150 degrees F. Remove from oven and allow to cool completely.

Sauce

In a medium sauce pan, add guava pulp and sugar. Cook over medium heat, stirring occasionally, until sugar is dissolved and mixture is warm, but not hot. Remove from heat and gently stir in lime juice and gelatin, until blended. Pour guava sauce over cheesecake. Cover and refrigerate 4 hours.

Cook's Notes

If using a convection oven, preheat oven to 275 degrees F. Bake cheesecake in water bath 25 to 35 minutes.

Bain marie, also known as a water bath, is a large ovenproof pan filled up with 1 ½ inches of warm water. Baking the cheesecake in a *bain marie* prevents cracking.

Frozen guava pulp can be found at the international grocery stores or Latin markets.

It is possible to use guava paste instead of guava pulp in the sauce. Just follow the directions found in my Cheese Flan with Guava Sauce recipe (page 114). The sauce will be a bit richer, but just as delicious!

FUSION

FUSION

Chicken Stuffed with Creamy Eggplant Parmigiana

This is one my husband's favorite meals! He loves when I cook Brazilian food, but we cannot live on Moqueca and Farofa (page 105) every day. So, he loves when I make this Italian-American meal. This is a comforting meal, without being super heavy. The cream cheese adds richness and creaminess, but you can remove it to cut down on calories, if you want. It might lose a bit of its American flair, but the taste remains great!

Serves 4

- ½ cup olive oil
- ½ onion, chopped
- 4 cloves garlic, minced
- ½ eggplant cut into ½-inch cubes
- 1 tablespoon tomato paste
- 2 cups low-sodium chicken stock
- 4 tablespoons Panko (Japanese bread crumbs)
- 2 tablespoons fresh oregano, chopped
- Salt and freshly ground black pepper
- 4 boneless, skinless chicken breasts
- 4 tablespoons cream cheese, divided
- 1 tablespoon tarragon, finely chopped
- 1 tablespoon basil, finely chopped
- 2 tablespoons scallion, finely chopped
- 1 tablespoon aged balsamic vinegar

Heat 2 tablespoons olive oil in a medium skillet over medium-high heat until shimmering. Cook onions, garlic and eggplant 5 minutes, stirring occasionally. Add tomato paste and chicken stock. Reduce heat to medium and simmer 10 to 15 minutes, stirring occasionally, until eggplants are tender and sauce thickens. Transfer to a mixing bowl and let cool 5 minutes. Add Panko and oregano. Season with salt and pepper. Set aside.

Preheat oven to 350 degrees F. Season chicken breasts with salt and pepper. Cut a slit in each chicken breast, forming a pocket. Open chicken pocket and stuff with 2 tablespoons of eggplant mix. Top each with 1 tablespoon cream cheese. Close, securing each pocket with 3 to 4 toothpicks. Transfer stuffed chicken breasts to a greased ovenproof dish. If using a regular oven, bake 35 to 40 minutes, until chicken is fully cooked. If using a convection oven bake 25 to 30 minutes.

In the meantime, place tarragon, basil, scallions and balsamic vinegar in a medium mixing bowl. Slowly add remaining olive oil, whisking vigorously until blended. Add a pinch of salt and pepper.

Place chicken breasts on individual plates, removing toothpicks. Top with 2 tablespoons of herb sauce. Serve immediately.

Chocolate Cheesecake with Passion Fruit Sauce

Chocolate and passion fruit are commonly paired in Brazilian desserts, especially in pies and cakes. So I decided to add a Brazilian touch to an American classic with the result being a decadent dessert, with just enough tartness from the sauce to break the richness of the chocolate cheesecake.

Serves 10

Crust Ingredients:
3 ½ cups Graham crackers, roughly crushed
8 tablespoons butter, softened
¼ cup sugar
1 tablespoon unsweetened cocoa powder

Filling Ingredients:
¾ cup dark chocolate, chopped
¾ cup milk chocolate, chopped
3 eggs, separated
¼ cup fine sugar
3 tablespoons vanilla balsamic vinegar (optional)
12 ounces cream cheese, softened

Sauce Ingredients:
1 cup frozen concentrated passion fruit pulp
4 tablespoons sugar
½ teaspoon unflavored gelatin

Crust

Place Graham crackers, butter, sugar, and cocoa powder in a food processor. Pulse 2 minutes, until it is all incorporated. Press mixture into a 9-inch pie dish. Cover and place in the refrigerator.

Filling

Preheat oven to 325 degrees F.

Place dark and milk chocolate in a microwave-safe bowl and microwave for 30 seconds. Remove and stir. Repeat process, if necessary, until melted. Set aside.

Place egg yolks in a large bowl and whisk in sugar and vanilla balsamic. Slowly add melted chocolate. Add cream cheese and mix until it is all incorporated. Set aside.

Using an electric mixer, beat egg whites until soft peaks form. Gently fold egg whites into the chocolate mixture, until incorporated. Remove pie crust from refrigerator and pour filling over crust.

Bake in a *bain marie* (water bath) 45 minutes to 1 hour, or until a toothpick inserted into center of pie comes out clean.

Sauce

In a medium sauce pan, combine passion fruit pulp and sugar; bring to a light boil and turn off the heat. Dissolve gelatin in 2 tablespoons of warm water and whisk into passion fruit. Transfer to a sealable container and refrigerate 1 to 2 hours, or until sauce starts to thicken, and before sauce hardens.

Pour sauce over pie and refrigerate at least 4 hours before serving. Serve with a side of vanilla ice cream, or home-made whipping cream.

Homemade Passion Fruit Pulp Directions

In an electric blender, mix the pulp of 2 large passion fruits with ½ cup water. Pulse 2 or 3 times until incorporated. Strain and use.

Bain marie, also known as a water bath, is a large ovenproof pan filled up with 1 ½ inches of warm water. Baking the cheesecake in a *bain marie* prevents cracking.

Cook's Notes

Frozen concentrated passion fruit pulp can be found at Latin or international grocery stores. If frozen is unavailable, you can make your own.

FUSION

FUSION

Fig and Hearts-of-Palm Salad

Italy and Brazil are represented in this salad. Hearts-of-Palm and figs are perfectly paired with a reduced balsamic and honey dressing over arugula and shaved Parmesan. Simple to make, this salad will please any guest.

Serves 4

1 cup aged balsamic vinegar
1 tablespoon honey
2 ½ cups packed arugula
2 figs, sliced lengthwise
½ cup hearts-of-palm, sliced
Salt and freshly ground black pepper
Extra virgin olive oil
½ cup shaved Parmesan cheese

Place balsamic vinegar in a small sauce pan and bring to a light boil. Lower heat and simmer 15 to 20 minutes until it is reduced to about ¼ cup. Remove from heat and whisk in honey. Set aside to cool.

Arrange arugula on individual plates and top with figs and hearts-of-palm. Season with salt and pepper. Drizzle with olive oil and the balsamic-honey dressing. Top with shaved Parmesan. Serve immediately.

Fish Roulade with Hearts-of-Palm and Mascarpone, over Olive-Apricot Tapenade

With a touch of Brazil, Italy and Provence, this dish is all over the map, but a trip worth taking. My version of tapenade includes apricots that make it slightly sweeter, so it complements the creamy hearts-of-palm and mascarpone filling in the cod.

Serves 6

4 tablespoons extra virgin olive oil
½ small onion, finely chopped
2 garlic cloves, minced
1 large tomato, peeled, seeded and finely chopped
Salt and freshly ground black pepper
¾ cup canned hearts-of-palm, drained and coarsely chopped
1 tablespoon scallions, finely chopped
1 tablespoon flat-leaf parsley, finely chopped
6 skinless cod fillets, about 5 ounces each
6 tablespoons mascarpone cheese

Heat 2 tablespoons olive oil in a medium skillet over medium-high heat until shimmering. Add onions and cook 3 minutes, stirring occasionally until soft. Add garlic and cook 1 minute until fragrant. Add tomato and cook 2 minutes until soft. Season with salt and pepper. Remove from heat and fold in the hearts-of-palm, scallions, and parsley. Set aside and let cool.

On a work surface, lay each cod fillet between 2 pieces of plastic wrap (double the size of the fillet). Pound out with flat side of a meat mallet, to 1/4-inch thickness. Remove plastic from top and season with salt and pepper. Spread 1 tablespoon of mascarpone cheese on each fillet, followed by 1 ½ tablespoons of hearts-of-palm sauce, pressing sauce down with the back of a spoon. Take ends of plastic wrap and wrap fish into a tight roll. Be sure not to roll plastic into the fish roll. Twist the ends to form a tube and refrigerate for one hour.

Preheat oven to 400 degrees F for 10 minutes. Coat the bottom of a large baking pan with 1 tablespoon of extra virgin olive oil. Unwrap cod fillets and place them on the baking pan, seam side down. Sprinkle with salt and pepper and drizzle remaining olive oil on top. Bake 17 minutes. If using a convection oven, bake 12 minutes. Remove from oven and serve with the Olive-Apricot Tapenade (page 161).

FUSION

Olive-Apricot Tapenade

Yields 1 cup

½ cup Kalamata olives, pitted
½ cup apricots, chopped
1 small garlic clove, crushed
Juice of ½ lime
¼ cup pistachios, shells removed
3 mint leaves
1 teaspoon sugar
Pinch of salt
½ cup extra virgin olive oil

Place olives, apricots, garlic, lime juice, pistachios, mint, sugar and salt in food processor. Pulse until ingredients are blended. Turn on food processor and slowly add olive oil. Refrigerate 3 hours before serving.

Cook's Notes

Olive-Apricot Tapenade may also be used as a dip for bread and crackers.

Goat Cheese Roulade with Roasted Bell Peppers

This recipe reflects modern Australian cuisine, a mix of European techniques with touches of other ethnic traditions. The delicious savory sponge cake is filled with goat cheese, cream cheese, mayonnaise, herbs and roasted bell pepper; topped with cilantro-scallion oil. Perfect served as an hors d'oeuvre, this recipe was passed on to me by a childhood friend who is a phenomenal cook. She now lives in Australia and I hope to visit her soon to have more of her amazing food, and to see Australia, of course!

Serves 6 to 8

Filling Ingredients:
2 red bell peppers
1 cup (8 ounces) cream cheese, at room temperature
1 cup (8 ounces) goat cheese
2 tablespoons fresh dill
2 tablespoons fresh basil, coarsely chopped
1 tablespoon mayonnaise
Salt and freshly ground black pepper
1 tablespoon cilantro, chopped
1 tablespoon scallions, chopped
¼ cup extra-virgin olive oil

Roulade Ingredients:
3 tablespoons unsalted butter
¼ cup all-purpose flour
1 ¾ cups whole milk
6 eggs, separated
½ cup parmesan cheese, finely grated

Turn gas stove to high and place red bell peppers directly over burner (see photo). Roast until peppers turn black and crispy, rotating occasionally with tongs. The surface will look burnt, but the flesh underneath should be perfectly roasted. Once peppers are totally blackened on all sides, remove from heat and set aside for 10 minutes to cool. Remove skin with a clean towel. Do not wash. Cut off stems and remove seeds with the back of a knife. Chop flesh and set aside.

In a food processor, add cream cheese and goat cheese. Process 40 seconds until smooth. Add dill, basil and mayonnaise. Process 30 seconds until blended, scraping down sides if necessary. Season with salt and pepper. Set aside.

In a medium bowl, place cilantro and scallions. Use pestle to mince herbs until incorporated. Slowly add olive oil, whisking until emulsified. Lightly season with salt and pepper. Set aside.

Preheat oven to 350 degrees F. If using a convection oven, preheat to 300 degrees F. Lightly grease a 1-inch deep, 15x10 inch baking tray and line with parchment paper.

In a large saucepan, melt butter over medium-low heat. Add flour and cook 3 minutes, whisking constantly, until mixture is golden brown. Increase heat to medium and add milk, ¼ cup at a time, whisking until combined, 4 to 5 minutes or until mixture is smooth. Remove from heat and whisk in egg yolks, one at a time. Fold in parmesan. Lightly season with salt.

FUSION

Place egg whites in a clean bowl with a pinch of salt. Using an electric mixer, beat egg whites until soft peaks form. Gently mix a quarter of the egg whites into the milk mixture, then gently fold in the remaining egg whites, being careful not to over mix.

Spread roulade mixture evenly into prepared pan and bake 15 to 17 minutes, or until roulade feels springy and firm in the center. If using a convection oven, bake for 10 to 13 minutes, or until firm in the center. Remove from oven.

Slightly overlap 2 sheets of parchment paper on the bench top. Carefully turn roulade over on baking paper and remove pan. Allow to cool 15 minutes. Peel off the paper to prevent it from getting stuck to roulade.

Spread goat cheese mixture evenly over roulade. Sprinkle with chopped roasted bell peppers. Carefully roll up roulade from one of the long sides, using the paper to help shape it into a log. Roll the paper tightly around the roulade to help hold its shape. Carefully transfer to a tray and place in the refrigerator for at least 30 minutes, or overnight. When ready to serve, transfer to a carving plate and carefully remove paper. Cut into ½-inch thick slices and serve with a drizzle of cilantro-scallion oil.

FUSION

Hamburger with Chimichurri and Provolone

This hamburger recipe gets a delicious South American twist: chimichurri sauce. The tangy and flavorful Argentine sauce combined with Provolone and home-made hamburger patties became my husband's favorite burger last summer.

Yields 8 to 10 burgers

1 cup fresh parsley, finely chopped
6 garlic cloves, minced
1 ½ teaspoons smoked paprika
1 tablespoon fresh oregano leaves, finely chopped
¼ cup aged balsamic vinegar
1 cup extra-virgin olive oil

3 pounds ground beef (20% fat)
½ cup seasoned dry Italian bread crumbs
3 eggs
Salt and freshly ground black pepper
8 to 10 slices of Provolone cheese
8 to 10 Kaiser rolls
8 to 10 large lettuce leaves
8 to 10 slices from large tomatoes

Chimichurri

In a medium bowl, add parsley, garlic, smoked paprika, oregano, and balsamic vinegar. Mix until blended.

Slowly add olive oil, whisking constantly. Season with salt and pepper. Cover and transfer to refrigerator. Let sit for at least 3 hours or overnight.

Hamburger

Preheat a charcoal or gas grill.

In a large bowl, carefully mix meat, bread crumbs, eggs, salt and pepper until incorporated. Lightly form hamburger patties and press into shape.

Cook hamburgers 4 minutes then turn and cook 2 minutes longer on the other side. Place a slice of Provolone cheese on each burger and cook for one minute longer, until cheese starts to melt. Remove burgers from grill and cover with aluminum foil.

Grill bread rolls, cut side down, for 1 minute, until toasted. Remove from grill and assemble hamburgers by placing the lettuce on the bottom bun, followed by the the burger, then the tomato. Top with 1 or 2 tablespoons of chimichurri sauce. Serve immediately.

Cook's Notes

This recipe for chimichurri sauce yields about 1 ½ cups. If you have leftovers, use on other grilled steak such as tri-tip and t-bone.

FUSION

Mushroom Stuffed Chicken with Coconut Milk-Lemongrass Sauce

This recipe combines the European technique of rolling the meat around the filling (roulade) with some bold Asian flavors. Covering the chicken with a coconut milk based sauce results in extra moist meat. Serve over jasmine rice.

Serves 8

4 large skinless, boneless chicken breasts
Salt and freshly ground black pepper
2 tablespoons canola oil
1 medium onion, chopped
1 medium yellow or red bell pepper, chopped
1 medium carrot, peeled and chopped
2 garlic cloves, minced
2 cups (16 ounces) baby portabella mushrooms, wiped and sliced

2 tablespoons fresh rosemary, chopped
½ teaspoon chili flakes
½ cup Panko (Japanese breadcrumbs)
2 cups coconut milk
3 tablespoons tomato paste
½ cup low-sodium chicken broth
1 tablespoon lemongrass, chopped
2 tablespoons cilantro, chopped
2 tablespoons scallions, chopped

Use a small carving knife to carefully cut a slit in the chicken breast, starting from the thickest part and working the knife down until you reach the other end of the breast. Be careful not to cut through the meat. You should end up with a chicken pocket. Season with salt and pepper. Set aside.

Heat canola oil in a large skillet over medium-high heat until shimmering. Add onions, bell pepper, and carrot. Cook 5 minutes stirring occasionally until the vegetables are nearly tender. Add garlic, mushrooms, rosemary and chili flakes. Increase to high heat and cook 3 minutes, stirring occasionally, until mushrooms are tender. Season with salt and pepper. Remove from heat and fold in Panko. Set aside and cool completely.

Preheat oven to 350 degrees F. In a blender, mix coconut milk, tomato paste, chicken broth and lemongrass 30 seconds until blended. Set aside.

On a working surface, stuff breasts with ¼ of the mushroom mix. If necessary, use toothpicks to secure stuffing. Transfer stuffed breasts to a lightly greased ovenproof dish and cover with the coconut sauce. If using a regular oven, bake uncovered 65 minutes, or until a thermometer inserted in the thickest part of chicken reads 165 degrees F. If using a convection oven, bake uncovered 45 minutes, or until a thermometer inserted in the thickest part of chicken reads 165 degrees F. Chicken should be fully cooked, but still moist. Remove from oven and transfer to clean working surface. Carve and transfer to individual plates. Drizzle with coconut sauce from pan, and sprinkle with cilantro and scallions. Serve immediately with a side of Jasmine rice.

Pork Tenderloin with Apricot-Miso Marinade

Asian and Italian ingredients are combined in this easy and versatile marinade. Delicious with pork, this marinade works just as well with chicken. If you cannot find pomegranate balsamic, a good quality aged balsamic can serve as a substitute.

Serves 6

4 tablespoons pomegranate balsamic vinegar
4 tablespoons white miso
4 tablespoons apricot jelly
2 teaspoons wasabi
2 tablespoons water
½ cup canola oil
2 ½ pounds pork tenderloin
Salt and freshly ground black pepper

Marinade

In a medium bowl, mix pomegranate balsamic, white miso, apricot jelly, wasabi, and water. Whisk in canola oil until thickened.

Season pork tenderloin with salt and fresh ground pepper. Transfer to sealable plastic bag and cover with marinade. Seal the bag and refrigerate 6 hours, but preferably overnight.

Directions for Grilling

Light a grill to high. Remove pork from plastic bag and transfer to a plate. Cover and let sit 30 minutes.

Spray grill rack with vegetable oil. Sear pork tenderloin for 2 minutes each side. Lower heat to medium and cook 20 to 25 minutes, or until the inside is fully cooked, but still pink.

Transfer to a board and carve into 1 ½ inch slices. Serve immediately.

Directions for Roasting

Preheat oven to 400 degrees F. Heat two tablespoons of canola oil in a large skillet. Sear pork tenderloin 2 minutes per side. Transfer to an ovenproof dish and pour marinade over pork loin. If using a regular oven, bake uncovered 25 to 30 minutes, or until thermometer inserted in thickest part reads 145 degrees F, brushing pork half way through with any marinade drippings. If using convection oven, bake 18 to 20 minutes, or until thermometer reads 145 degrees F. Remove from oven, cover plate with foil and let rest 10 minutes. Carve and serve.

FUSION

FUSION

Pumpkin and Coconut Pie

One of my most popular recipes, this Pumpkin and Coconut Pie was created because I was disappointed with traditional American recipes. Sorry folks, I do mean this respectfully! Come on, nobody has to always like everything, right? So after many years of Thanksgiving disappointments, I had an idea: add coconut to the recipe, just like the delicious traditional Brazilian sweets that combine pumpkin and coconut. Voila! One of my best pies was born.

Serves 12

- 4 cups Graham crackers, roughly crushed
- 8 tablespoons butter, softened
- ½ cup sugar
- 3 cups pumpkin pulp purée from a sugar pumpkin or canned pumpkin purée
- 1 can (14 ounces) sweetened condensed milk, divided
- 1 teaspoon ground ginger
- 1 teaspoon ground cinnamon
- 1 cup grated coconut, preferably fresh

Crust

Add Graham crackers, butter and sugar to a food processor. Process 2 minutes, until blended. Press mixture into a 9-inch pie dish. Set aside.

Preheat oven at 350 degrees F.

Filling

To a food processor, add pumpkin purée, ½ can (7 ounces) sweetened condensed milk, ginger and cinnamon. Process 40 seconds until smooth. Pour mixture into bottom of the pie crust.

Rinse food processor and add remaining sweetened condensed milk and grated coconut. Process 40 seconds until blended. Pour coconut mixture over pumpkin mixture. Transfer to oven and bake 20 to 30 minutes until a toothpick inserted in center comes out clean. Remove from oven and let cool.

Refrigerate two hours before serving or serve at room temperature.

Cook's Notes

To make pumpkin purée from a sugar pumpkin, start with a small-medium sugar pumpkin. Cut off stem. Scrape and discard insides. Cut the pumpkin in half and lay cut side down on a rimmed baking sheet, lined with aluminum foil. Bake at 350 degrees F 1 to 1 ½ hours until fork tender. Remove from oven. Let cool. Scoop out pulp and mash it with a fork or in a food processor.

FUSION

Tuna Ceviche with Avocado and Wasabi

Ceviche is one of my favorite summertime dishes! Easy to prepare and refreshing, my Tuna Ceviche has an Asian flair, due to the wasabi. Sometimes, I like to add ½ cup finely diced peeled cucumber and just a touch of soy sauce to the recipe to make this Latin dish even a little more Asian.

Serves 4

½ pound sushi-grade tuna (sashimi tuna) cut into ¼ inch cubes
½ medium red onion, thinly sliced
½ cup freshly squeezed lime juice
Freshly ground black pepper
2 teaspoons wasabi paste
2 tablespoons olive oil
1 avocado, carefully diced
½ cup fresh cilantro, chopped
Salt
Tortilla chips and/or warm corn tortillas, for serving

Put tuna in a non-reactive glass or ceramic bowl. Add onion and lime juice. Season with pepper. Gently stir and cover with plastic wrap. Refrigerate for 1 to 4 hours, stirring gently with a plastic spatula every 15 minutes.

In a small bowl, mix wasabi paste and olive oil until combined. Set aside.

Just before serving, fold in the avocado, cilantro, and wasabi mixture. Season with salt and stir gently. Serve with tortilla chips or warm corn tortillas.

Cook's Notes

In order to achieve really neat cubes of tuna, place in freezer for about 15 to 20 minutes before cutting and use a very sharp knife.

As a result of marinating the fish in lime juice, its color will change to a really pale pink. This is perfectly fine.

White Chocolate Flan with Peppermint Caramel Sauce

I created this dessert around Christmas time last year because I really wanted to incorporate some traditional flavors from the American holidays into a flan, which happens to be one of my favorite Brazilian desserts! The result is a rich, smooth and amazingly delicious flan, with just a touch of peppermint. For a stronger peppermint flavor, crumble additional crushed candy canes on top.

Serves 12

Ingredients for Caramel Sauce:
2 cups sugar
8 candy canes, finely crushed

Ingredients for Flan:
2 cans (14 ounces each) sweetened condensed milk
2 cups heavy cream
5 eggs
1 tablespoon butter
11 ounces white chocolate chips

Garnish:
2 candy canes, roughly crushed

Caramel Sauce

In a medium sauce pan over medium heat, pour sugar and cook, stirring constantly, 10 to 13 minutes until sugar completely dissolves and mixture turns golden brown. Remove from heat and add crushed candy canes, whisking vigorously until well mixed. Pour caramel into a 10-inch mold pan, swirling caramel to completely cover the base and about 2-inches up the sides. Allow to cool and harden.

Flan

Preheat oven to 375 degrees F. Mix sweetened condensed milk, heavy cream, eggs and butter in a large blender. Blend for 20 seconds. Transfer to a large bowl.

Melt white chocolate in the microwave 2 to 3 minutes, or place white chocolate chips in a small sauce pan over a water-bath on the stove top, and stir until completely melted. Whisk melted chocolate into bowl until incorporated. Using a large spoon, remove the foam that forms on surface and discard.

Pour milk mixture into the mold pan (caramel must be hard) and cover with aluminum foil.

Place mold pan in a large ovenproof pan and fill it with warm water, half pan depth. Carefully transfer to oven and bake 1 hour to 1 hour and 15 minutes. The flan is ready when a toothpick inserted in center comes out clean.

Remove from oven and water filled pan. Let cool for 3 hours. Refrigerate 8 hours or overnight.

Unmolding

Gently run a small knife around mold pan. Carefully flip it over a large plate. Scrape as much caramel as possible and pour over flan. Garnish with crushed candy canes, slice and serve.

Cook's Notes

I used a coffee grinder to finely crush the candy canes that were added to the caramel sauce. It turned the candy canes into a fine powder and it easily incorporated into the caramel while I was whisking, resulting in a perfectly smooth peppermint caramel. Use a blender or food processor, if you don't have a coffee grinder.

To roughly crush the candy canes that garnished the flan, I placed them in a plastic bag and smashed them with a meat mallet.

ARGENTINA

Chimichurri Sauce

Chimichurri is a flavorful sauce, with lots of fresh herbs, garlic and olive oil. Especially delicious over steak, Chimichurri is originally from Argentina, but it is also popular in Uruguay and in the South of Brazil. I became obsessed with this sauce after I went to Argentina in 2011, so when I came back home to the US, I developed my own Chimichurri sauce. My recipe has the additional flavors of aged balsamic vinegar, which gives a touch of sweetness; and smoked paprika, which obviously gives a touch of smokiness. I love it drizzled over any cut of steak, and even over dark meat chicken and salmon; but my favorite cuts to serve with chimichurri are tri-tip and rib-eye.

Yields 1 ½ cups

1 cup fresh parsley, finely chopped
6 garlic cloves, minced
1 ½ teaspoons smoked paprika
1 tablespoon fresh oregano, finely chopped
¼ cup aged balsamic vinegar
1 cup extra-virgin olive oil
Salt and freshly ground black pepper

In a medium bowl, combine parsley, garlic, smoked paprika, oregano, and balsamic vinegar. Mix well.

Slowly add olive oil, whisking constantly. Season with salt and pepper.

Refrigerate for at least 3 hours before serving.

Serve on top of your favorite grilled steak.

ASIA

Ginger-Basil Shrimp on Toast Cups

When you mix shrimp, coconut milk, cashews, shallots, garlic, lime juice chili paste and basil, you know you are creating something delicious! Rich, with a touch of spice and sweetness, this dish will not go unnoticed. Serve in toast cups as an appetizer, or make it a full entrée and serve over rice.

Makes 25 Cups

½ cup cashew nuts, chopped
2 large shallots, chopped
4 garlic cloves, chopped
1 tablespoon chili paste
½ cup fresh basil, chopped
2 tablespoons fresh ginger, peeled and minced
¼ cup fresh lime juice

3 tablespoons sugar
1 can (14 ounces) unsweetened coconut milk
25 large shrimp, shelled and deveined
Salt and freshly ground black pepper
25 slices white sandwich bread, crusts removed
Canola oil, for brushing
Cilantro leaves, for garnish

In a food processor or blender, purée cashews, shallots, garlic, chili paste, basil, ginger, lime juice, sugar and coconut milk until blended. Transfer to a large mixing bowl.

Season shrimp with salt and pepper and add to bowl, turning to coat with the marinade. Cover and refrigerate for at least 4 hours or overnight.

Preheat oven to 300 degrees F. Brush both sides of bread slices with canola oil. Place slices of bread in non-stick muffin pan cups, pressing down so bread slices form to the shape of cups. Bake for 6 to 10 minutes, until the edges are golden brown and the inside is lightly toasted. Remove from oven and let cool.

Preheat oven to 400 degrees F. Transfer shrimp and the marinade to a large ovenproof deep-dish. For a regular oven, bake 18 to 22 minutes, or until shrimp starts to curl. For a convection oven, bake 12 to 17 minutes. Remove from oven and fill each toast cup with 1 shrimp and 2 to 3 tablespoons of sauce. Garnish with cilantro and serve immediately.

Cook's Notes

This hors d'oeuvre may become a main course by simply serving the shrimp and sauce over a bed of jasmine rice. This amount would be enough for 6 to 8 portions.

ASIA

Pasta Salad with Shrimp and Peanut Butter-Ginger Dressing

This salad is a great summer entrée, and if you have an outdoor grill available, the bell peppers and shrimp can be grilled instead of baked or sautéed. If you are not a fan of shrimp, leave it out or replace it with chicken. This salad has enough flavors that stand out even without a protein.

Serves 6

½ cup reduced-sodium soy sauce
½ cup honey
¼ cup rice vinegar
2 tablespoons dark sesame oil
2 tablespoons chili paste
1 ½ tablespoons fresh ginger, minced
1/3 cup peanut butter

½ cup vegetable oil
2 orange bell peppers, cored, seeded and quartered
2 tablespoons extra virgin olive oil, divided
1 pound large shrimp, cleaned and deveined
10 ounces cooked egg noodles
1 ½ cup scallions, finely chopped
3 tablespoons toasted sesame seeds

In a medium bowl, mix soy-sauce, honey, rice vinegar, sesame oil, chili paste, ginger, and peanut butter. Slowly add vegetable oil, constantly whisking until incorporated. If too thick, add 2 tablespoons water. Set aside.

Preheat oven to 350 degrees F. Place bell peppers in a medium baking dish and brush with 1 tablespoon olive oil. Roast 25 to 30 minutes in a regular oven, or 20 minutes in a convection oven. Remove and let cool. Chop and set aside.

In a skillet, heat remaining olive oil over high heat until shimmering. Sauté shrimp 1 ½ to 2 minutes, or until it turns pink and starts to curl. Remove from heat and let cool.

In a large bowl, combine noodles, shrimp, and bell peppers. Fold in dressing and scallions. Top with toasted sesame seeds. Serve immediately or refrigerate up to 4 hours before serving.

Cook's Notes

Red or yellow bell peppers may serve as a substitute for the orange bell peppers.

Egg noodles may be replaced by a different kind of pasta, such as penne or rotini.

FRANCE

Strawberry Aspic

I love the presentation of this old-fashioned French dessert. The strawberry halves look like hearts surrounding the aspic, crowned by more strawberries and mint leaves. I am also a huge fan of the light texture, and slight sweet-tart flavors. The sauce brings it all together, making it perfect!

Serves 4

Aspic
12 ounces strawberry, stemmed
2 packages unflavored gelatin
  (1 scant tablespoon)
1 cup sugar
1 ½ pounds ricotta
3 egg whites
1 tablespoon vanilla extract
8 ounces *crème fraîche*
Fresh mint leaves, for garnishing

Strawberry Sauce
½ cup water
Juice of 1 lime
4 tablespoons sugar
1 tablespoon vanilla extract
¾ cup strawberry, chopped

Cut 4 large strawberries in half. Set aside.

Chop remaining strawberries into small ¼-inch cubes. Set aside.

Dissolve gelatin in ¼ cup hot, not boiling, water. Set aside.

In a medium sauce pan, mix sugar and ¾ cup water. Cook over medium high heat until sugar is totally dissolved. Let cool for 2 minutes, then add dissolved gelatin, whisking gently until mixed. Whisk in ricotta.

Using a hand mixer, beat egg whites 4 to 6 minutes until soft peaks form. Gently fold in vanilla extract, *crème fraîche*, ricotta mixture and chopped strawberries.

Spray a 6-cup mold pan with butter and pour in half of the mixture. Lay halved strawberries around the mold pan. Pour remaining mixture.

Refrigerate at least 8 hours, or overnight. When it is ready to be served, turn aspic over onto a plate. Decorate with fresh strawberries and mint. Serve with strawberry sauce.

Strawberry Sauce

In a medium sauce pan, mix water, lime juice, sugar and vanilla extract. Boil syrup until reduced and thickened. Remove from heat and cool.

Mash strawberries with a fork or potato masher until smooth. Strain to remove seeds. Add sugar syrup and refrigerate a few hours.

FRANCE

Tenderloin with Orange Sauce

I love to think of this recipe as the one that convinced my husband to fall for me. I will never forget his face after taking the first bite of this dish. We had been dating for just about a month, but the flavors on this tenderloin really seduced him!

Serves 8

3 tablespoons butter, divided
2 pounds beef tenderloin, cut into ¼-inch thin strips
¼ cup cognac
Salt and freshly ground black pepper
2 leeks, thinly sliced
1 tablespoon brown sugar
¾ cup freshly squeezed orange juice (about 3 medium oranges)
¼ cup Cointreau
3 tablespoons *crème fraîche*
3 tablespoons flat-leaf parsley, chopped

In a large skillet, heat 2 tablespoons butter on high heat and sauté tenderloin strips for about 2 minutes, or until desired internal meat temperature is reached. Add cognac and season with salt and pepper. Transfer meat and any juices from skillet to a plate and cover tightly with foil.

Add remaining butter to the same skillet and heat until it foams. Add leeks and cook over medium high heat 3 minutes, until soft. Stir together brown sugar, orange juice and Cointreau. Bring to a boil and cook 3 minutes until it starts to thicken. Remove from heat and fold in *crème fraîche* and parsley. Season with more salt and pepper, if needed.

Add tenderloins to sauce and serve immediately with a side of sautéed potatoes and jasmine rice.

Cook's Notes

Cointreau is orange liqueur. Grand Marnier may serve as a substitute.

FRANCE

Tenderloin with Dried Porcini and Fresh Mushrooms

I love to mix dried and fresh mushrooms because I think I get the best of both worlds: the intense flavors of the dried with the interesting texture of the fresh. I love to serve this mushroom sauce with tenderloin, but chicken works well too, and is more budget friendly.

Serves 4

1 cup dried porcini mushrooms
1 cup boiling water
2 tablespoons olive oil
1 small onion, finely sliced
3 rosemary sprigs, leaves finely chopped
¼ cup dry white wine
2 cups white mushrooms, thinly sliced
Salt and freshly ground black pepper
1 cup *crème fraîche*
2 tablespoons unsalted butter
1 pound tenderloin, cut into 1-inch medallions

Place dried porcini mushrooms in a small bowl and cover with hot water. Let sit 10 to 15 minutes. Drain porcini and chop. Reserve water and set aside.

Heat olive oil in a medium skillet over medium-high heat until shimmering. Add onion and rosemary and sauté for 3 minutes. Add chopped dried porcini and cook 2 minutes, stirring constantly. Add white wine and reserved water from the porcini. Cook on high heat, stirring occasionally, until liquid is reduced to about ¼ and appears syrupy. Add white mushrooms and season with salt and pepper. Cook 2 to 3 minutes until mushrooms are tender. Turn off heat and fold in *crème fraîche*. Set aside and cover.

Season tenderloin with salt and pepper. Add butter to a large skillet and set heat to high. Once butter starts to bubble, add tenderloin medallions and cook for about 4 minutes on each side, or until desired meat internal temperature in reached. Turn off heat and add mushroom sauce to the skillet, coating all pieces. Serve immediately.

ITALY

Caprese Salad with Roasted Tomatoes

Caprese salad combines some of my favorite Italian flavors, and this version has a couple of twists to make it slightly sweeter: roasted tomatoes and pomegranate balsamic. To turn this salad into a complete meal, toss with fresh cooked pasta, while still hot. Serve over sliced ciabatta bread, if you wish.

Serves 4

2 cups Campari tomatoes
¼ cup extra-virgin olive oil, divided
8 ounces boconccini
½ cup fresh basil chopped
2 tablespoons pomegranate balsamic vinegar
Salt and freshly ground black pepper

Preheat oven to 350 degrees F.

Place tomatoes on a medium ovenproof shallow pan and drizzle with 3 tablespoons of olive oil, turning to coat well. If using a regular oven, bake tomatoes 15 to 18 minutes or until the surface starts to wrinkle. If using a convection oven, bake 12 to 14 minutes. Remove from oven and transfer to a large bowl.

While tomatoes are still warm, fold in the boconccini and basil. Drizzle with juices from the baking pan. Add pomegranate balsamic, and remaining olive oil. Sprinkle with salt and pepper. Serve immediately.

Cook's Notes

Boconccini is a variety of fresh mozzarella cheese shaped like small balls measuring about an inch in diameter. They are slightly creamier in the inside, compared to regular fresh mozzarella. Small pieces of regular fresh mozzarella may serve as a substitute, if boconccini is unavailable.

Besides pomegranate balsamic vinegar, other varieties that work well with this recipe are strawberry, raspberry, or fig balsamic. Aged balsamic vinegar may also be used.

ITALY

Cheese Ravioli with Chicken Sauce

One of the beauties of Italian cuisine is that, even super easy and achievable recipes turn out great if quality ingredients are used. My Cheese Ravioli with Chicken Sauce is a fine example. Comforting and versatile, this recipe is a great weeknight family meal.

Serves 4

2 tablespoons olive oil
1 pound chicken breast, cut into 1-inch cubes
½ medium onion, chopped
2 tablespoons fresh rosemary, chopped
4 garlic cloves, minced
½ cup dry white wine
1 teaspoon chicken base
½ cup tomato sauce
2 teaspoons smoked paprika
1 teaspoon nutmeg
1 cup heavy cream
Salt and freshly ground black pepper
½ cup cherry tomatoes, cut in half
3 tablespoons fresh basil, chopped
1 package (16 ounces) store-bought, frozen or refrigerated, cheese ravioli

Heat olive oil in a large skillet over medium-high heat until shimmering. Add chicken and sear 2 minutes. Add onions, rosemary, and garlic. Cook 3 minutes, stirring occasionally. Add wine and deglaze the skillet. Add chicken base, tomato sauce, smoked paprika, nutmeg, and heavy cream. Season with salt and pepper. Lower heat to medium and cook 5 to 7 minutes. Turn off heat and fold in cherry tomatoes and basil.

In the meantime, cook ravioli in a large pan of boiling water 4 to 5 minutes. Drain and transfer to a large plate or bowl.

Top with chicken sauce and serve immediately with parmesan cheese on the side.

Cook's Notes

Penne or rigatoni may serve as a substitute for the cheese ravioli.

ITALY

Chicken Marsala with Cream, Garlic and Herbs

I love Chicken Marsala so much! It is one of those sure bets when having groups over. I add heavy cream, garlic and fresh herbs to the classic recipe, making it even more irresistible.

Serves 4

4 medium skinless, boneless chicken breast halves
Salt and freshly ground black pepper
3 tablespoons olive oil
8 ounces Cremini mushrooms, finely sliced
1 medium onion, finely sliced
3 garlic cloves, minced
½ cup low-sodium chicken broth
¾ cup Marsala wine
2 tablespoons fresh basil, chopped
2 tablespoons chives, chopped
2 tablespoons flat-leaf parsley, chopped
½ cup heavy cream

On a working surface, place chicken breast halves between 2 sheets of plastic wrap. Using a meat mallet, pound breasts to an even ½-inch thickness. Season with salt and pepper.

In a large skillet, heat 2 tablespoons olive oil over medium-high heat until shimmering. Add breasts and brown on both sides, turning over once, about 3 minutes per side. Transfer breasts to a platter; cover with foil to keep warm.

Add remaining olive oil to the same skillet. Turn heat to high until oil starts shimmering. Add mushrooms, onion, and garlic and cook 3 minutes, stirring occasionally. Add Marsala wine to deglaze the skillet, stirring well. Add chicken broth and any juices from the chicken platter and stir. Cook for about 3 minutes to reduce. Fold in basil, chives, parsley, and cream. Remove from heat and season with salt and pepper. Add chicken to the sauce.

Serve over a bed of linguini, tossed with olive oil and parmesan.

ITALY

Eggplant Involtini

I am a big fan of Eggplant Involtini because it tastes great and it's a low-carb, gluten-free, highly satisfying meal that the whole family will love.

Serves 8

2 large eggplants
2 tablespoons lemon juice
Salt and freshly ground black pepper
2 tablespoons olive oil
1 medium onion, chopped
2 tablespoons fresh rosemary, finely chopped
1 ½ pounds lean ground beef
2 tablespoons green onions, finely chopped
2 tablespoons flat-leaf parsley, finely chopped
16 slices of Provolone cheese
1 ½ cup store bought marinara sauce
2 cups Cynthia's Special White Sauce (page 233)
2 tablespoons Parmesan cheese

Cut eggplants lengthwise into thin slices. Each eggplant should yield 6 to 8 slices. In a large bowl, mix eggplant slices with lemon juice, salt and pepper. Transfer to a covered microwavable container. Microwave on high 8 to 10 minutes, or until tender. Set aside.

In a large skillet, heat olive oil over medium-high heat and sauté onions 3 minutes. Add rosemary and ground beef. Season with salt and pepper. Cook 10 minutes, stirring occasionally. Remove from heat and fold in green onions and parsley. Set aside.

Preheat oven to 350 degrees F.

Place one slice of Provolone cheese and 1 ½ tablespoons ground beef on eggplant slice and roll. Repeat the process for each slice of eggplant.

In a large ovenproof dish, place ½ cup marinara sauce. In a single layer, place eggplant involtini on top of marinara sauce, keeping rolls very close to one another. Top with remaining marinara sauce and cover with Cynthia's Special White Sauce. Sprinkle Parmesan cheese on top. Bake 15 to 20 minutes, or until sauces are blended and the Provolone cheese has melted. Let stand 5 minutes before serving.

ITALY

Mixed Mushrooms Lasagna

For years I have been making this lasagna recipe for large parties. Because it can be made in advance, it is perfect for big gatherings, allowing the host to mingle with everyone else. This is a vegetarian dish with a meaty and fulfilling texture, thanks to mushrooms and rich-flavored cheeses.

Serves 8

1 pound lasagna noodles
¼ cup olive oil, plus more for coating
1 medium onion, finely chopped
2 garlic cloves, minced
2 ½ pounds mixed mushrooms, wiped and sliced
Salt and freshly ground black pepper
3 cups Cynthia's Special White Sauce (page 233)
2 cups Fontina cheese, shredded
2 cups Gouda cheese, shredded
3 tablespoons Parmesan cheese, shredded

In a large pot of boiling water, cook lasagna noodles 9 to 12 minutes, until *al dente*. Drain and arrange lasagna pieces flat in a single layer on clean, dry towels until ready to use.

To a large skillet over medium-high heat, add olive oil and onions. Cook 3 minutes until soft. Stir in garlic and cook another minute until fragrant. Turn heat to high and add mushrooms to skillet. Cook 2 minutes, stirring occasionally until mushrooms are soft. Season with salt and pepper. Remove from heat and set aside.

Preheat oven to 350 degrees F.

Coat bottom of a large ovenproof lasagna pan with olive oil. Layer 6 to 7 noodles on bottom of pan, overlapping them slightly. Cover with 1/3 sautéed mushrooms and juices that may have accumulated, 1 cup white sauce, 1 cup Fontina cheese, and 1 cup Gouda cheese.

Repeat process.

Finish with a third layer of noodles, the remaining mushrooms and remaining white sauce. Sprinkle with Parmesan cheese. Bake 15 to 20 minutes, or until cheeses have melted. Let sit 10 minutes before serving.

Cook's Notes

Mixed mushrooms for this recipe may include baby portabella, white, shitake, oyster, porcini, etc. The wider the variety, the better and more interesting the flavor.

ITALY

Penne with Mustard-Marsala Tenderloin

Simple and delicious, my Mustard-Marsala Tenderloin sauce goes well with penne, rigatoni, and bow-tie pasta. It is a great weeknight meal that will please the whole family.

Serves 4

2 tablespoons olive oil
1 Vidalia onion, finely sliced
2 garlic cloves, minced
1 tablespoon fresh thyme, minced
8 ounces tenderloin, cut into 1-inch strips
½ cup Marsala wine
¼ cup low-sodium beef broth
2 tablespoons Dijon mustard
2 cups half and half
Salt and freshly ground black pepper
2 tablespoons scallions, finely chopped
2 tablespoons basil, finely chopped
½ cup black olives, coarsely chopped
12 ounces penne pasta

Heat olive oil in a large skillet over medium-high heat until shimmering. Add onions and cook 4 minutes, stirring occasionally, until golden brown. Add garlic, thyme and tenderloin and sear for about 1 minute. Stir in Marsala wine, deglazing the pan. Add beef broth and Dijon mustard. Stir until combined. Add half and half and season with salt and pepper. Cook over medium-high heat 5 minutes, stirring constantly, until sauce starts to thicken. Remove from heat and fold in scallions, basil and olives.

Cook penne pasta in a large pan of boiling water, about 11 minutes. Drain and fold into sauce. Serve immediately with Parmesan cheese on the side.

Cook's Notes

Tenderloin, an expensive cut of meat, may be replaced with t-bone or top-sirloin. If using a cut other than tenderloin, trim all visible fat and cut into ½-inch strips.

ITALY

Steak Lulu with Gnocchi

In this recipe, the gnocchi is submerged into a sauce, loaded with tender steak, red bell peppers and scallions. This versatile steak sauce recipe works well over different pastas and rice; but my husband's favorite is over gnocchi. He loved this dish so much he named it Steak Lulu and asked me to add it to the book. Easy and fulfilling, this is a great meal for a cold evening.

Serves 8

- 2 tablespoons olive oil
- 2 tablespoons butter
- 1 onion, finely chopped
- 1 tablespoon brown sugar
- 1 medium red bell pepper, seeded and finely chopped
- 4 garlic cloves, minced
- 1 ½ pounds tender steak, fat trimmed and cut into 1 ½-inch cubes
- ¼ cup brandy or cognac
- 1 cup dry white wine
- 2 tablespoons tomato paste
- ½ cup low-sodium beef broth
- 1 cup heavy cream
- Salt and freshly ground black pepper
- 1 cup finely sliced scallions
- 16 ounces store-bought frozen gnocchi

In a large skillet, heat olive oil and butter over medium high heat. Add onions and cook about 4 minutes, stirring occasionally, until soft. Stir in brown sugar, bell peppers and garlic. Cook 3 to 4 minutes, stirring occasionally.

Turn heat to high and sear steak 1 minute. Add cognac and deglaze the pan. Reduce heat to medium and add white wine, tomato paste and beef broth. Cook 5 minutes, stirring occasionally. Add heavy cream and cook 2 minutes until it starts to thicken. Season with salt and pepper. Remove from heat and fold in scallions.

Cook gnocchi 3 minutes in a large pan filled with rapid boiling water. Drain and add to steak sauce. Serve immediately with Parmesan cheese on the side.

Cook's Notes

This versatile sauce works well with a variety of pastas including tagliatelle and rigatoni.

Asparagus and Shrimp Risotto

Light and fresh, this Asparagus and Shrimp Risotto is the perfect spring night dinner. To add a citrusy flavor, serve with lemon wedges on the side.

Serves 6

Vegetable Broth Ingredients:
2 carrots
1 onion, quartered
1 leek
1 bouquet garni (3 stalks parsley, 1 sprig thyme and 1 bay leaf tied together in a bundle with a piece of string)
8 cups water

Risotto Ingredients:
2 ½ sticks of butter, divided
2 cups asparagus, cut into ½ - inch slices, dry ends discarded
10 ounces large shrimp, cleaned and deveined
Salt and freshly ground black pepper
1 medium onion, finely chopped
2 cups Arborio rice
½ cup dry white wine
5 cups vegetable broth, preferably home-made
¼ cup scallions, finely chopped

Vegetable Broth Directions

In a large pot, mix ingredients together and bring to a boil. Reduce heat and simmer 45 minutes. Remove from heat and strain.

Risotto Directions

Heat 2 tablespoons of butter in a medium skillet over high heat. Add the asparagus and cook 2 to 3 minutes, stirring occasionally, until tender.

In the same skillet, heat 2 tablespoons butter over high heat and add the shrimp. Cook, stirring occasionally, until it curls and turns pink, 2 minutes. Season with salt and pepper. Remove from heat and set aside.

In a large skillet melt 1 stick of butter (8 tablespoons) at medium high heat. Once it starts to foam add onion and cook 3 minutes, stirring occasionally, until soft. Add rice and stir to coat. Add the wine and stir until it evaporates almost completely. Reduce heat to medium-low and add ½ ladle of vegetable broth, stirring constantly. When the liquid is almost completely evaporated, add another ½ ladle of broth and cook, stirring constantly until liquid is almost completely evaporated. Repeat process until the rice is *al dente*– soft on the outside but somewhat resistant to the bite on the inside. The process should take 22 to 25 minutes. Remove from heat and season with salt and black pepper. Fold in asparagus, shrimp, scallions and remaining butter. Serve immediately.

ITALY

ITALY

Four Cheese Risotto

Some people find the process of cooking risotto tedious as the cook must stand by the stove stirring the rice until it is done. I choose to make it a reason to gather around the stove with friends and sip wine, often enlisting the help of my guests with the stirring. My Four Cheese Risotto is a rich and satisfying dish that can be served as a main course, or as a side for red meat.

Serves 4

3 cups low-sodium beef broth
2 tablespoons olive oil
1 large shallot, minced
1 cup Arborio rice
½ cup dry white wine
Salt and freshly ground black pepper
¼ cup Fontina cheese, shredded
¼ cup Emmental cheese, shredded
¼ cup Parmigiano-Reggiano cheese, freshly grated
¼ cup mascarpone cheese
2 tablespoons chives, finely chopped

In a medium sauce pan, bring beef broth to a light boil. Reduce heat to low and cover with lid.

Heat olive oil in a large skillet over medium-high heat until shimmering. Add shallots and cook 3 minutes until soft, stirring occasionally. Stir in Arborio rice, making sure all the grains are well coated. Cook 1 minute until grains start to swell. Stir in wine and cook until nearly evaporated.

Turn heat to medium-low and add ½ ladle of broth to skillet. Stir constantly until most of the broth has been absorbed by the rice, making sure not to let the rice stick to the skillet. Add another ½ ladle of broth to skillet, stirring constantly. Repeat process until the rice is *al dente*. The whole process should take 20 to 23 minutes.

Remove from heat and lightly season with salt and pepper. Gently fold in Fontina, Emmental, Parmigiano-Reggiano and mascarpone. Place risotto in individual plates and sprinkle with chives. Serve immediately.

Cook's Notes

Vegetable broth may serve as a substitute for beef broth. Refer to Shrimp and Asparagus Risotto (page 202) for homemade vegetable broth.

Saffron Risotto with Mixed Mushrooms

I am not Italian, but I love to make and eat risotto just like a *ragazza italiana*! This recipe was inspired by the traditional Risotto Milanese, a risotto infused with lots of saffron. I added mixed mushrooms, some earthy scented herbs and my Special White Sauce (page 233) to this Italian classic. The result is an extra creamy, perfumed and rich risotto. If you are a vegetarian, use vegetable broth as a substitute for the beef broth.

Serves 4 to 5

1 tablespoon extra virgin olive oil
6 ounces mixed mushrooms (crimini, oyster, shiitake), sliced
1 tablespoon fresh rosemary, minced
1 teaspoon fresh oregano leaves, minced
¼ cup brandy or cognac
Salt and freshly ground black pepper
4 to 5 cups beef broth, preferably homemade

1 teaspoon saffron threads
2 tablespoons unsalted butter
1 small onion, finely chopped
1 ½ cups Arborio rice
1 cup Cynthia's Special White Sauce
¼ cup Parmesan cheese, shredded

In a medium skillet, heat olive oil over high heat until shimmering. Add mushrooms, rosemary and oregano. Sauté about one minute. Add brandy and flame, stirring constantly until flames dye down. Cook two more minutes, until mushrooms are soft. Season with salt and pepper. Remove from heat and set aside.

In a large sauce pan, bring beef broth to a light boil. Reduce heat to low and keep at a low simmer.

Place saffron threads in a small bowl and add ½ ladle of hot beef broth. Set aside for a few minutes to allow ingredients to infuse.

In a large skillet, melt butter over medium high heat. Add onion and cook 2 minutes, stirring constantly. Add rice and stir well until grains are well coated. Reduce heat to medium-low and add saffron threads along with beef broth in which threads were soaking. Season with salt and pepper. Cook, stirring constantly, until liquid is nearly absorbed. Add more beef broth, ½ ladle at a time, stirring constantly until rice is cooked *al dente*. The cooking process should last 21 to 24 minutes and risotto should have a creamy, almost slightly soupy texture when ready.

Remove risotto from heat and fold in mushrooms, white sauce and Parmesan cheese. Divide into individual warm bowls and serve immediately.

Cook's Notes

Cynthia's Special White Sauce recipe (page 233) must be done prior to the risotto, since its cooking time can take up to 1 hour. This sauce will give a wonderful flavor to the risotto and make it extra creamy. If you are in a hurry, substitute with a mixture of ¼ cup butter and ¼ cup mascarpone.

Al dente describes the texture of pasta, rice, or vegetable; and it means it is cooked through but still firm to the bite. In Italian, al dente literally means "to the tooth."

ITALY

MEXICO

Albondigas Soup

When I lived in San Diego, delicious Mexican food was available everywhere. One of my favorite Mexican dishes was Albondigas Soup. Comforting, without being heavy, this soup may be topped with avocado slices, a touch of sour cream, and fresh cilantro.

Serves 8

½ pound sausage, casing removed
1½ pounds fresh ground beef
3 garlic cloves, minced
1 cup cooked rice
1 egg, beaten
1 teaspoon cumin
1 teaspoon coriander
1 teaspoon dried sage
1 tablespoon dried oregano
Salt and freshly ground black pepper

2 tablespoons olive oil
1 large onion, finely chopped
4 carrots, peeled and sliced
2.8 quarts chicken broth
¼ teaspoon cayenne pepper
1 cup elbow pasta, uncooked (optional)
½ cup frozen peas
1 cup scallions, chopped
1 cup cilantro, chopped

To make the meatballs, mix sausage, ground beef, garlic, rice, egg, cumin, coriander, sage, and oregano in a large bowl. Season with salt and pepper. Mix well. Shape about 25 ping-pong size meatballs. Set aside.

In a large pot, heat up the olive oil. Add onions and carrots and cook over medium-high heat for 5 minutes, stirring occasionally until onions are soft. Add chicken broth and season with cayenne pepper. Bring to a boil and add meatballs, one at a time. Add more salt if necessary. Reduce heat to medium and cook about 30 minutes, partially covered. Add pasta an cook for an additional 10 minutes.

Add frozen peas and cook 3 minutes. Remove from heat and fold in scallions and cilantro. Serve immediately with a side of corn tortillas.

Cook's Notes

The elbow pasta is optional and is not traditionally part of this recipe.

MEXICO

Fish Tacos with Mango-Jalapeno Slaw

There is no other food that reminds me more of the amazing years I spent in San Diego than fish tacos. I used to go "fish taco hopping" from restaurant to restaurant with my husband in search of San Diego's best fish taco. The result of our taste tests is this flavorful recipe. Enjoy!

Yields 10 to 12 Tacos

Ingredients for Mango-Jalapeno Slaw:
1 large, ripe mango, peeled and diced
½ medium red onion, diced
2 cups red cabbage, shredded
2 jalapenos, seeded and minced
1 cup cilantro, chopped
½ cup mint leaves, finely chopped
Juice of 2 limes
Juice of 2 medium oranges
3 tablespoons brown sugar

Ingredients for Fish and Tortillas:
2 pounds skinless cod, cut into 1 to 1 ½-inches wide x 4-inches long fillets
Salt and freshly ground black pepper
3 tablespoons olive oil
10 to 12 corn tortillas, warmed

Directions for Mango-Jalapeno Slaw

Add mango, red onion, red cabbage, jalapenos, cilantro, mint, lime juice, orange juice and brown sugar to a medium mixing bowl. Gently stir to combine. Serve immediately, or refrigerate until serving.

Directions for Fish

Place fish fillets on a large working surface and season with salt and pepper.

In a large non-stick skillet over medium-high heat, place olive oil until shimmering. Working in batches, fry cod fillets, 2 to 2 ½ minutes per side, until they flake easily. Transfer to a plate lined with paper towels.

Top each warm tortilla with one fish fillet and 2 to 3 tablespoons of Mango-Jalapeno Slaw. Serve immediately.

MEXICO

Watermelon Margarita

Spicy, sweet and refreshing, my Watermelon Margarita Martini brings back the amazing memories of my wedding weekend in Playa del Carmen, Mexico. I am a fan of spicy drinks, so I prefer to use cayenne pepper around the rim. If you think cayenne pepper is too spicy, chili powder will add a touch of heat without being overwhelming.

Serves 1

¾ cup watermelon, chopped
1 teaspoon sugar
1 shot tequila
¼ shot Cointreau
1 cup ice cubes
1 lime wedge
Salt for the rim
Cayenne pepper or chili powder, for the rim

In a shaker, muddle watermelon and sugar. Add tequila, Cointreau and ice. Shake vigorously for a few seconds.

Wet the outside rim of a martini glass with the lime wedge. Fill a small saucer with some salt and chili powder or cayenne pepper. Dab rim into the mix while slowly turning glass so the outer edge is covered. Strain watermelon margarita into the glass and serve immediately.

MIDDLE EAST

Eggplant Antipasto

This eggplant antipasto is one of my mom's most popular recipes. She usually serves it with a Middle Eastern spread of pita bread, quibe (kibbeh), and tabbouleh. Inspired by the traditional eggplant spread called Baba Ghanoush, this dip may be served on top of grilled meat or lamb, or just as an appetizer with breads and toasts.

Yields about 5 cups

¾ cup extra-virgin olive oil
1 large onion, chopped
6 garlic cloves, minced
1 red bell pepper, cored and finely chopped
1 green bell pepper, cored and finely chopped
2 large eggplants, cut into 1-inch cubes
1 cup raisins
1 cup walnuts, roughly chopped
¾ cups low-sodium soy sauce
Salt and freshly ground black pepper
½ cup scallions, finely chopped
½ cup parsley, finely chopped

In a large skillet, heat olive oil until shimmering. Add onion, garlic, red bell pepper, green bell pepper and eggplant. Cook 10 minutes over medium-high heat, stirring occasionally, until vegetables are soft.

Add raisins, walnuts and soy sauce. Cook 10 minutes, or until ingredients are blended. Add salt and pepper to taste. Fold in scallions and parsley.

Serve at room temperature, or slightly chilled, with a side of mixed breads and warm pita bread.

Cook's Notes

This Eggplant Antipasto freezes well. In fact, after a few days in the refrigerator this recipe tastes even better.

This is a great antipasto for big parties, since it can be made ahead and served at room temperature.

MIDDLE EAST

Lamb Stew with Raisins, Pine Nuts and Mint

The trick to enhancing the flavors in this dish over the stove top is to marinate the lamb overnight. Serve this flavorful lamb with plain warm couscous and pita bread.

Serves 6 to 8

1 cup dry white wine
½ cup honey
4 garlic cloves, minced
2 pounds lamb meat, fat trimmed, cut into 2-inch cubes
Salt and freshly ground black pepper
½ cup cracked wheat (medium) bulgur
¼ cup pine nuts
3 tablespoons extra virgin olive oil
½ medium onion, chopped
1 tablespoon rosemary, minced
3 medium tomatoes, chopped
½ cup raisins
2 tablespoons mint, finely chopped
2 tablespoons basil, finely chopped

In a medium mixing bowl, combine white wine, honey and garlic. Place lamb in a large sealable container and season with salt and pepper. Top with wine mixture. Refrigerate overnight.

The next day, place cracked wheat in a bowl and cover with hot water. Let soak 20 minutes. Drain and set aside.

In a medium skillet, sauté pine nuts 3 minutes until lightly toasted. Set aside.

Remove lamb from refrigerator. Strain and save marinade.

Heat olive oil in a large sauce pan over medium-high heat. Add onion and rosemary; cook 4 minutes, stirring occasionally. Stir in lamb; cook for 2 minutes. Add marinade and tomatoes. Reduce heat to medium and cook, stirring occasionally, for 10 to 12 minutes, or until lamb is cooked. Remove from heat and fold in cracked wheat, pine nuts, raisins, mint and basil. Test for salt and pepper. Serve immediately.

Sopa Paraguaya – Paraguayan Corn Bread

Paraguayan corn bread, a staple in Paraguay, is a creamy and flavorful savory side dish. It is also popular in the Brazilian region of Mato Grosso do Sul, where my father used to own a cattle ranch. This recipe reminds me of the fun days I spent there as a child. Traditionally served with beef stew in Paraguay, I like to serve it as an appetizer by topping the grilled slices of bread with fresh tomato and cilantro salsa.

Serves 12

6 tablespoons butter
2 medium onions, finely chopped
2 cups whole milk
2 cups cornmeal
2 ½ cups mozzarella cheese, roughly grated
Salt and freshly ground black pepper
3 eggs, separated

Directions

Preheat oven to 375 degrees F. If using a convection oven, preheat oven to 300 degrees F. Grease a loaf pan with 1 tablespoon butter. Set aside.

In a large sauce pan, melt 2 tablespoons butter over low heat and add onions. Cook 10 minutes, stirring occasionally, until onions are soft. Stir in milk and allow to heat without boiling. Slowly add cornmeal, ¼ cup at a time, stirring constantly until smooth (mixture should become really thick, but smooth). Remove from heat and stir in cheese, remaining butter, and egg yolks. Season with salt and pepper.

Place egg whites in a clean bowl. Using an electric mixer, beat egg whites 3 to 4 minutes, until soft peaks form. Gently fold egg whites into cornmeal mixture, until incorporated, being careful not to over mix.

Pour mixture into prepared loaf pan. If using a regular oven, bake 35 to 40 minutes, or until a toothpick inserted in the center comes out clean. If using a convection oven, bake 25 to 30 minutes.

Remove from oven and flip over onto a carving board. Allow to cool for a few minutes. Slice and serve.

Cook's Notes

For a quick and delicious twist, turn gas grill to high and grill slices of corn bread on both sides, 1 ½ minutes per side. Top with fresh salsa and serve immediately.

PARAGUAY

SPAIN

Smoky Rice with Squid and Shrimp

My Smoky Rice recipe was inspired by the traditional Paella, a fairly time consuming dish that might contain different kinds of meats like rabbit, chicken, sausage, and many varieties of seafood. I wanted to develop a quicker and easier recipe, so I use only two kinds of fast cooking seafood, shrimp and squid. The rice is well flavored with saffron, vegetable broth, clam broth, garlic and smoky paprika, so the deep flavors of traditional paella are still there. Serve with lime wedges on the side for an added taste of citrus.

Serves 4

¼ cup extra-virgin olive oil
½ pound large shrimp, shelled and deveined
Salt and freshly ground black pepper
1 cup Arborio rice
1 tablespoon tomato paste
1 ½ tablespoon smoked paprika
3 garlic cloves, minced
1 small pinch of saffron, crumbed
2 cups clam broth
2 cups low-sodium vegetable broth
½ pound baby squid, bodies cut into ¼-inch rings
1 tablespoon flat-leaf parsley for garnish
2 limes, cut into wedges, for serving

In a large, deep skillet, heat olive oil until shimmering. Season shrimp with salt and pepper and add to skillet. Cook over high heat without stirring or moving skillet, about 2 minutes or until one side is lightly browned. Transfer shrimp to a plate.

Add rice to skillet and stir 2 minutes until opaque. Stir in tomato paste, paprika, garlic and saffron. Stir 1 minute, until rice is toasted and sizzling. Stir clam broth and vegetable broth and bring to a boil over high heat. Boil about 10 minutes until rice is still a little crunchy and half of the broth is absorbed. Lower heat and simmer about 8 minutes until rice is nearly tender and liquid is soupy but slightly reduced. Stir in squid. Lay the shrimp on top, cooked side up. Cover and simmer two minutes, or until squid and shrimp are cooked through and rice is tender. Garnish with parsley and serve immediately with lime wedges on the side.

UNITED STATES

Pork Tenderloin with White Wine and Rosemary Marinade

There is no way to go wrong with this pork tenderloin recipe. The secret is to allow the meat to marinate for several hours, or overnight, in the refrigerator. This is one of our favorite summertime meals.

Serves 6 to 8

½ cup white wine
2 tablespoons Dijon mustard
2 tablespoons honey
2 tablespoons rosemary, chopped
½ red onion, finely chopped
1 teaspoon smoked paprika
Salt and freshly ground black pepper
2 pounds pork tenderloin

In a medium bowl, combine white wine, mustard, honey, rosemary, red onion and smoked paprika. Season tenderloin with salt and pepper and transfer to a sealable plastic bag.

Carefully pour marinade into bag. Remove as much air as possible from inside bag. Transfer to refrigerator and let marinate for at least 6 hours, or overnight.

Preheat grill on high for 20 minutes. Sear pork tenderloin for 1 to 2 minutes on all four sides. Reduce heat to low and cook 15 to 20 minutes, or until a thermometer inserted in the thickest part of the meat reads 140 degrees F. Transfer to a plate and cover loosely with foil. Let stand 10 minutes. Transfer tenderloin to a carving board and cut into ½-inch slices. Serve immediately.

UNITED STATES

Roasted Cauliflower

My husband wants to lick the plate when he eats this dish. It goes great with any meat, especially roasted chicken and light flavored fish such as tilapia.

Serves 8

1 large cauliflower, trimmed and cut into small, even sections
6 tablespoons olive oil
Salt and freshly ground black pepper
1 cup Cynthia's Special White Sauce (page 233)
Bread crumbs, for topping

Preheat oven to 400 degrees. Toss cauliflower with 4 tablespoons of olive oil and season with salt and pepper. Arrange cauliflower in a single layer on large baking dish and roast for 25 to 35 minutes, stirring and turning occasionally.

Pour white sauce over roasted cauliflower and sprinkle with bread crumbs. Serve immediately.

Cook's Notes

Cauliflower is done when it reaches a golden brown color, but personal preference and oven temperature differences are what determine the baking time. The best way to check for tenderness is to carefully slice a small section of one of the florets and try it.

UNITED STATES

Sausage and Mushrooms Stuffed Bell Peppers

I like to call this recipe "crazy good" just because it is that delicious! Sweet Italian sausage, pine nuts, mushrooms, and herbs are the perfect filling for the bell peppers. Use different colors of bell peppers for a fun presentation.

Serves 8

¼ cup milk
2 tablespoons Panko (Japanese breadcrumbs)
1 egg
2 tablespoons Parmegiano-Reggiano cheese, grated
2 tablespoons pine nuts, toasted
2 tablespoons red onions, chopped
6 ounces (3/4 cup) white mushrooms, wiped and chopped
16 ounces sweet Italian sausage, casing removed
2 tablespoons fresh basil, chopped
2 tablespoons scallions, chopped
2 tablespoons parsley, chopped
Salt and freshly ground black pepper
4 large bell peppers, halved lengthwise and cored, stems left intact
¼ cup olive oil
1 cup canned tomato sauce
1 cup low-sodium chicken broth

In a large bowl, add milk, Panko, egg, cheese, pine nuts, red onions, mushrooms and sausage. Season lightly with salt and pepper. Fold in basil, scallions and parsley.

Using lightly moistened hands, divide the mixture among the pepper halves and lightly pack.

In a large skillet, heat olive oil until shimmering. Add the stuffed peppers, filling side down, and cook about 4 minutes over high heat until well-browned. Turn bell peppers and cook about 4 minutes longer until skins are browned and blistered. Add tomato sauce and chicken broth to the skillet. Cover and simmer over medium heat 8 to 10 minutes until the sausage filling is cooked through, and the peppers are tender. Transfer to plates and serve immediately.

Cook's Notes

Make ahead and refrigerate overnight. This dish tastes great the next day.

UNITED STATES

Shrimp and Cream Cheese Stuffed Zucchini

Creamy and decadent, this stuffed zucchini recipe is definitely worth its calories. This hours-d'oeuvre can be assembled a day ahead and baked fresh when your guests arrive.

Serves 6

2 tablespoons olive oil, plus more for brushing
1 large Vidalia onion, finely chopped
1 red bell pepper, finely chopped
½ fennel bulb, finely chopped
2 garlic cloves, minced
4 plum tomatoes, finely chopped
½ teaspoon crushed red pepper
Salt and freshly ground black pepper
12 ounces medium shrimp, shelled and deveined, finely chopped
2 tablespoons parsley, finely chopped
2 tablespoons dill, finely chopped
6 zucchinis halved lengthwise
6 ounces cream cheese

Preheat oven to 400 degrees F.

In a skillet, heat olive oil. Add onion, bell pepper, fennel and garlic. Cook over moderately high heat 7 minutes, stirring constantly, until tender. Add tomatoes and crushed red pepper. Cook 6 minutes until thickened. Season with salt and pepper. Remove from heat. Let cool slightly. Stir in shrimp, parsley and dill. Set aside.

Using a spoon, scoop out the flesh of the zucchini, leaving ¼ inch shell all around. Brush with olive oil. Season shells with salt and pepper and stuff with shrimp filling. Transfer to a greased baking pan. If using a regular oven, bake 28 to 32 minutes, until the filling is cooked through and the zucchinis are tender. If using a convection oven, bake 20 to 24 minutes.

Preheat broiler and position rack 6 inches from the heat. Top each zucchini with 1 tablespoon cream cheese and broil 3 to 5 minutes, until the cream cheese is golden brown and starts to melt. Remove from oven and serve immediately.

UNITED STATES

Stuffed Mushrooms with Sausage, Pine Nuts and Herbs

Served hot or warm, this is one of my go-to appetizers for large gatherings. My stuffed mushrooms are always a crowd pleaser!

Makes 24 units

1 pound mild Italian sausage, casing removed
3 tablespoons pine nuts
2 tablespoons Panko bread crumbs
2 garlic cloves, minced
1 tablespoon grated parmesan
1 egg, beaten
3 tablespoons milk
2 tablespoons scallions, chopped
2 tablespoons flat-leaf parsley, chopped
2 tablespoons fresh basil, chopped
Salt and pepper
¼ cup olive oil
24 white mushrooms (about 1 ½ pounds) stemmed

Preheat the oven to 375 degrees F.

In a medium mixing bowl stir together the sausage, pine nuts, Panko bread crumbs, garlic, parmesan, egg, milk, scallions, parsley, basil, salt and pepper until everything is well incorporated.

Drizzle a large baking sheet with about 1 tablespoon olive oil, to coat. Spoon filling into mushroom cavities and arrange on baking sheet, cavity side up. Drizzle remaining oil over the filling of each mushroom. Bake about 30-35 minutes until sausage is cooked through and the mushrooms are tender. Serve immediately.

UNITED STATES

Cynthia's Special White Sauce

This is my classic, delicious, gluten-free white sauce recipe. I usually make it in large batches to store in the refrigerator. When a dish calls for béchamel, I substitute with my own white sauce. It takes longer to cook than a béchamel, but the wait is worth it! It is perfect over vegetables such as cauliflower, potatoes, and asparagus; and over dishes like lasagna, sautéed chicken, and baked fish. Try adding scallions and parsley. It is a simple, versatile recipe with just 5 ingredients, but the secret to developing the flavors is slow-cooking the half-and-half until the desired thickness is achieved.

Yields 1 ½ to 2 cups

2 tablespoons olive oil
½ medium onion, finely chopped
3 large garlic gloves, minced
4 cups half and half
Salt and freshly ground black pepper
1 teaspoon freshly ground nutmeg

Heat olive oil and sauté onions in a large sauce pan over medium-high heat 4 minutes until soft. Add garlic and cook an additional minute. Add half and half and bring to a boil. Turn heat down to medium-low and simmer stirring occasionally for 45 to 60 minutes, or until sauce has reached the desired thickness. Season with salt, pepper, and nutmeg. Serve immediately or store in refrigerator.

Cook's Notes

This sauce is versatile and may be kept in the refrigerator for up to 2 weeks. As it takes longer than most white sauces to cook, I recommend making a double batch to use for other recipes. Adjust cooking time accordingly; if doubling ingredients, it could take up to 1 ½ hours.

Recipes Using Cynthia's Special White Sauce

Chicken and Asparagus Mini-Pies - page 24
Eggplant Involtini - page 195
Mixed Mushroom Lasagna - page 197
Roasted Cauliflower - page 225
Saffron Risotto with Mixed Mushrooms - page 206

URUGUAY

Clericot

When I visited Punta del Leste, Uruguay, I noticed a lot of people in bars and restaurants ordering this large jars of white wine mixed with fruits. It did not take us long to join the crowd and ordering our own. Delicious and refreshing, Clericot is traditionally prepared with white wine, but I prefer to use sparkling wine because of the bubbles. Use a dry white or brut sparkling wine, and add sugar to taste.

Serves 6

1 small apple, diced with skin on
1 orange, peeled and sliced
2 small peaches, peeled and diced
1/3 pineapple, peeled and diced
5 strawberries, quartered
5 cherries, seeded and quartered (optional)
5 tablespoons sugar
1 bottle dry sparkling white wine

Add apple, orange, peaches, pineapple, strawberries, and cherries to a large pitcher. Mix in sugar and enough sparkling wine to cover fruit. Cover and refrigerate 2 hours.

Remove from refrigerator and pour over remaining sparkling wine. Add 3 to 4 cups of ice. Serve immediately.

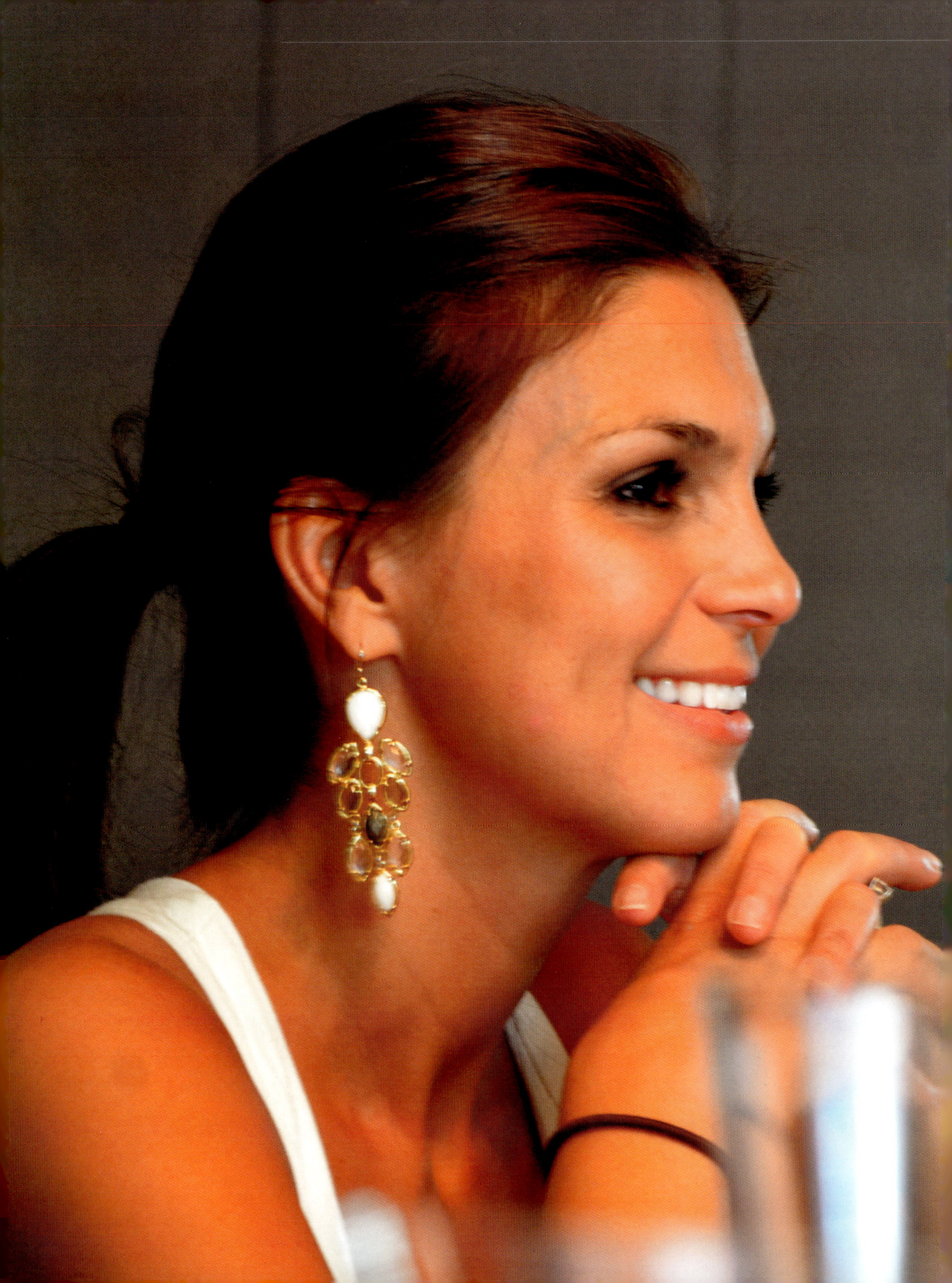

Acknowledgements

The finalization of this project has been a dream come true to me, and it would not had been possible without the help of some amazing people.

For the beautiful graphic work in this book, I thank an artist, businessman, designer, web and media developer, recipe critic, foodie, father, and husband: Steve Presser. I praise his continuous love, dedication, and support. He is the one who made me believe in this project and pushed me forward to complete it. A huge thank you for saying that I could do anything, especially during those times that I was extremely tired and ready to give up. Without him, this book would never have happened.

English is not my first language. That does not stop me from writing all of my recipes and posting most of them on my website without being edited. My passion for cooking and sharing my recipes is too strong to be intimidated by inevitable English mistakes. When writing a cookbook, the rules are not the same. This time my recipes had to be written perfectly. I would like to say a huge thank you to Helen Presser, an experienced librarian who has reviewed several books before. She spent countless hours correcting long recipes, and was an extremely important part of finalizing the book. Helen Presser also happens to be my mother-in-law and grandmother to my son.

For her creative vision on the cover shots, and some other photos taken in the Brazilian market in Curitiba, Brazil, I thank the talented photographer, Carol Sábio. She is not only a great photographer but also a very sweet person. Working with Carol was so much fun!

For some of the photos of family and friends taken at my house, I would like to thank Kelly Gayer. His creative talent is always appreciated.

I am a self-taught cook, but I would not be the kind of cook that I am today if I had not grown up eating delicious homemade meals. To my mom, Anadir Ferreira, thank you for feeding me "real" food every day. The simplicity of her meals awakened my palate and made me love food ever since I was young. Thank you for contributing the Eggplant Antipasto and Chicken Pot Pie recipes, and for teaching me how to make the best flan in the world!

Some other amazing home cooks allowed me to share a few of their delicious recipes in this cookbook. A huge thank you to my sister Karen Ferreira for the rich Guava and Cheese Mousse recipe; to my cousin Marcia Toledo Cordova for the decadent Dulce de Monkey recipe; to Leila Soares (Comadre Leila) for the delicious Salpicão recipe; to my friend Geo Ribas for her unique Goat Cheese Roulade; to an extraordinary cook that I haven't met yet, Dorah Guimarães, for the festive Pork Tenderloin with Dried Apricots-Gouda-Mascarpone Filling recipe.

To every friend and family member who has joined me at my dinner table and complimented my food, I am thankful for their kind, encouraging words. Cooking for them was my real-life cooking school.

To my son, Sebastian, I am thankful to him for being the little food critic that he is, and occasionally asking me to cook bland food just for him. The day will come when he realizes what he is missing! And on that day, I will still be cooking up a storm in my kitchen, and teaching him about real flavor.

Recipe Index

Appetizers
Chicken and Asparagus Mini-Pies (Empadinhas de Frango com Aspargo) 24
Cod Croquettes (Bolinho de Bacalhau Fresco) 27
Eggplant Antipasto 213
Ginger-Basil Shrimp on Toast Cups 177
Goat Cheese Roulade with Roasted Bell Peppers 160
Pastel 33
Pastel with Meat and Cheese Filling (Pastelzinho de Carne com Queijo) 35
Shrimp and Cream Cheese Stuffed Zucchini 227
Shrimp and Yuca Bowl (Escondidinho de Camarão) 39
Stuffed Mushrooms with Sausage, Pine Nuts and Herbs 229
Tuna Ceviche with Avocado and Wasabi 171

Salads
Brazilian Style Chicken Salad (Salpicão) 37
Caprese Salad with Roasted Tomatoes 187
Fig and Hearts-of-Palm Salad 157
Hearts-of-Palm, Mushrooms, and Fresh Mozzarella Salad (Salada Verde com Palmito, Cogumelos e Queijo Branco) 31
Pasta Salad with Shrimp and Peanut Butter-Ginger Dressing 179

Soups
Albondigas Soup 207
Creamy Hearts-of-Palm Soup (Creme de Palmito) 29
White Chili (Creme de Feijão Branco) 42

Breads and Savory Pies
Brazilian Cheese Bread (Pão-de-Queijo) 21
Chicken Pot Pie, Brazilian Style (Empadão de Frango) 94
Shrimp and Hearts-of-Palm Pie (Empadão de Camarão e Palmito) 72
Sopa Paraguaya – Paraguayan Corn Bread 216
Traditional Brazilian Cheese Bread from Minas (Pão-de-Queijo Mineiro) 23

Pasta and Grains
Asparagus and Shrimp Risotto 200
Cheese Ravioli with Chicken Sauce 189
Four Cheese Risotto 203
Mixed Mushrooms Lasagna 195
Penne with Mustard-Marsala Tenderloin 197
Saffron Risotto with Mixed Mushrooms 204
Smoky Rice with Squid and Shrimp 219
Steak Lulu with Gnocchi 199

Meat
Brazilian Style Stroganoff (Estrogonofe) 79
Eggplant Involtini 193
Hamburger with Chimichurri and Provolone 163
Lamb Roulade with Tomatoes and Gouda, Mint Pesto, and Farofa (Carneiro Recheado com Tomate e Queijo, ao Molho de Menta e Farofa) 80
Lamb Stew with Raisins, Pine Nuts and Mint 215
Pork Tenderloin with Apricot-Miso Marinade 166
Pork Tenderloin with Dried Apricots, Gouda, and Mascarpone (Lombo Recheado com Damascos Secos, Queijo Gouda e Mascarpone) 82
Pork Tenderloin with White Wine and Rosemary Marinade 221
Sausage and Mushrooms Stuffed Bell Peppers 225
Tenderloin with Orange Sauce 183
Tenderloin with Dried Porcini and Fresh Mushrooms 185

Chicken
Brazilian Chicken Stew (Chicken Bobó) 88
Chicken Fricassee (Fricassé de Frango) 90
Chicken in a Pumpkin with Coconut Milk (Frango na Abóbora com Leite de Coco) 93
Chicken Marsala with Cream, Garlic and Herbs 191
Chicken Stuffed with Creamy Eggplant Parmigiana 153
Mushroom Stuffed Chicken with Coconut Milk-Lemongrass Sauce 165

Seafood
Black-Eyed Pea Fritters (Acarajé) 52
Fish Casserole (Peixada) 57
Fish Moqueca (Moqueca de Peixe) 59
Fish Roulade with Hearts-of-Palm and Mascarpone, over Olive-Apricot Tapenade 158
Fish Tacos with Mango-Jalapeno Slaw 209
Layered Shrimp with Toast and Savory Meringue (Camarão à Marta Rocha) 62
Pumpkin with Shrimp (Camarão na Moranga) 65
Salmon with Coconut Milk and Cashews (Salmão ao Leite de Coco e Castanhas de Caju) 66
Salmon with Mango Sauce and Coconut Rice (Salmão ao Molho de Manga com Arroz de Coco) 68
Salmon with Passion Fruit Sauce (Salmão ao Molho de Maracujá) 71
Shrimp Bobó (Bobó de Camarão) 50
Shrimp Moqueca (Moqueca de Camarão) 61
Coconut Milk and Dried Shrimp Stew (Vatapá) 54

Sides
Black Beans (Feijão Preto) 101
Cashew Rice Pilaf (Arroz de Castanha de Caju) 83
Coconut Rice (Arroz de Coco) 68
Farofa 105
Rice (Arroz Branco) 103
Roasted Cauliflower 223
Yuca Purée (Purê de Mandioca) 67

Sauces
Chimichurri Sauce 175
Cynthia's Special White Sauce 231

Desserts
Avocado and Candied Cashews Pie (Torta de Abacate com Castanhas de Caju) 110
Brazilian Strawberry Shortcake (Torta Gelada de Morangos) 134
Brigadeiro - The Famous Brazilian Chocolate Bonbon 113
Cheese Flan with Guava Sauce (Pudim Romeu e Julieta) 114
Cheesecake with Guava Sauce 150
Chocolate Cheesecake with Passion Fruit Sauce 154
Classic Brazilian Flan (Pudim de Leite Condensado) 127
Coconut Balls (Beijinho de Coco) 117
Coconut Flan (Pudim de Coco) 119
Dulce de Leche and Coconut Layer Cake (Torta Recheada com Doce de Leite e Coco) 120
Dulce de Monkey (Gelado de Doce de Leite e Banana) 125
Guava and Cheese Mousse (Mousse Romeu e Julieta) 129
Lime Meringue Flan (Pudim de Claras) 131
Passion Fruit Pie (Torta Mousse de Maracujá) 132
Pumpkin and Coconut Pie 169
Salted Caramel and Guava Pie (Torta de Goiabada com Doce de Leite) 133
Strawberry Aspic 181
White Chocolate Flan with Peppermint Caramel Sauce 172

Drinks
Caipirinha 142
Clericot 233
Passion Fruit Caipirinha (Caipirinha de Maracujá) 144
Pineapple-Mint Caipirinha (Caipirinha de Abacaxi com Hortelã) 146
Watermelon Margarita 211